Brothels, Depravity,
and Abandoned Women

Brothels, Depravity, and Abandoned Women

Illegal Sex in Antebellum
New Orleans

Judith Kelleher Schafer

Louisiana State University Press
Baton Rouge

Published by Louisiana State University Press
Copyright © 2009 by Louisiana State University Press
All rights reserved
Manufactured in the United States of America
First printing

Designer: Tammi L. deGeneres
Typefaces: Bembo & Gotham
Printer and binder: Thomson-Shore, Inc.

Chapter 7 first appeared, in somewhat different form, as "The Murder of a 'Lewd and Abandoned Woman': *State v. Abraham Parker*," *American Journal of Legal History* 44 (2000): 19–39, and
is reprinted by permission.

Library of Congress Cataloging-in-Publication Data
Schafer, Judith Kelleher, 1942–
  Brothels, depravity, and abandoned women : illegal sex in antebellum New Orleans / Judith
Kelleher Schafer.
    p. cm.
  Includes bibliographical references and index.
  ISBN 978-0-8071-3397-2 (cloth : alk. paper) 1. Prostitution—Louisiana—New Orleans—
History. 2. Brothels—Louisiana—New Orleans—History. 3. Sex-oriented businesses—Lou-
isiana—New Orleans—History. 4. Sex customs—Louisiana—New Orleans—History. 5.
Women—Louisiana—New Orleans—Social conditions. 6. New Orleans (La.)—Social condi-
tions. I. Title.
  HQ146.N6S33 2009
  364.15'34097633509034—dc22
                                        2008031983

The paper in this book meets the guidelines for permanence and durability of the Committee on
Production Guidelines for Book Longevity of the Council on Library Resources.♾

For Tim, once more,
and for Ashley and Gregory

There is a house in New Orleans
They call the Rising Sun
And it's been the ruin of many a poor girl
And God, I know I'm one

Oh, Mother, tell your children
Not to do what I have done
Spend your lives in sin and misery
In the house of the Rising Sun

—FOLK SONG

God-dammit . . . my guns are ivory-handled. Nobody but a pimp for a cheap New Orleans whorehouse would carry one with pearl grips.

—GENERAL GEORGE S. PATTON JR.,
IN FRED AYER JR., *Before the Colors Fade* (1964)

I realize that it comes as an enormous revelation to the American public that there might have been prostitutes in New Orleans. I mean, who knew?

—SENATOR PATRICK LEAHY, D-VT.,
New Orleans Times-Picayune, 8 JUNE 2002

Have you ever been to a restaurant in New Orleans? One out of three women is for sale.

—TUCKER CARLSON, *New Orleans Times-Picayune,* 13 JULY 2007

CONTENTS

Illustrations follow page 59.

Acknowledgments

Be warned that writing books involves endless hard work.
—ECCLESIASTES 12:12

Anyone who has written a book knows the truth of this Old Testament adage. I am extremely fortunate to have had the strong support and encouragement of my family, friends, and colleagues while writing this book. And I am blessed that many of those people fall into more than one of those categories.

My colleagues in the History Department at Tulane University have provided support and friendship since 2005, when I joined the department. I am also grateful to the dean of the Tulane Law School, Larry Ponoroff, for his and other deans' support throughout the twenty-one years that I have taught at the law school. My former colleagues at the Murphy Institute, Rick Teichgraeber, Ruth Carter, and Jon Riley, continue as friends, if no longer colleagues.

Irene Wainwright and (now retired) Wayne Everard, archivists of the New Orleans Public Library, tirelessly retrieved cases for me without complaint. Without their help in finding many of the materials upon which this book is based, it would never have seen the light of day. Archivists Marie Windell (also now retired) and Florence Jumonville cheerfully helped me retrieve the case records of the Supreme Court of Louisiana, which are housed at the University of New Orleans. Wilbur Meneray, Kevin Fontenot, and Leon Miller assisted in finding some of the illustrations for this book in Tulane's Howard Tilton Library's Special Collections, and they kindly allowed me to use them without charge. Sally Stassi of the Historic New Orleans

Collection also spent a great deal of time helping me find interesting drawings of the "scarlet sisterhood" in antebellum New Orleans. All these archivists were extremely generous with their time and expertise.

The late Bennett H. Wall, friend, mentor, and drinking companion, encouraged me at the inception of this project. Although he should not be blamed for the book's shortcomings, Ben, more than anyone else, taught me about the profession of history and, especially, how to write. I have his picture in my office on a shelf behind me, where he can look over my shoulder as I work at my computer. I miss him every day.

Special thanks to Paul Finkelman, friend and colleague. Paul's amazing ability to organize conferences and shepherd publications has resulted in my having many more publications than I would otherwise. He has greatly enhanced my career, and I owe him a large debt of gratitude. I am especially grateful to him for inviting me to participate in the working group on the law of slavery at the Gilder Lehrman Center for the Study of Slavery, Resistance, and Abolition at Yale University. It has been an energizing intellectual experience.

Heartfelt thanks to my friends and fellow members of the Juniper Society of New Orleans: David Combe, James Gill, Henri Schindler, and Tommy Tucker. Although we were scattered by Katrina, we have fearlessly reassembled to drink gin on the first Thursday of each month. Their support and affection mean a great deal to me.

Others who deserve thanks for assorted reasons include the members of TUFF (Tulane University Fishing Fanatics), Victoria Allison, Warren Billings, Jim Boyden, Emily Clark, Catherine Clinton, Ray Diamond, Terry Fitzmorris, Herman Freudenberger, Ginger Gould, Perry Jamieson, Bob Kerachuk, Alecia Long, the late Frank Monachino, who taught me to love the opera, Kent Newmyer, Vernon Palmer, Larry Powell, Jonathan Prichett, Sylvia Rodrigue, Randy Sparks, the late Glenda Stevens, John Suttles, and Helen Ulrich. None of these good people should be blamed for any errors in this book. I am fully capable of making mistakes without their help. I am also grateful for the support and encouragement of Alisa Plant of LSU Press. Alisa morphed from copy editor of my last book to acquisitions editor for this one, and it has been a real pleasure to work with her. Many thanks to Larry Reilly, associate editor of the *American Journal of Legal History*, for permission to reprint "The Murder of a 'Lewd and Abandoned Woman': *State v. Abraham Parker*," in vol. 44 (2000): 19–39.

I continue to enjoy and appreciate the affection and support of my dear friends Fr. Terry Davis, Edward F. Haas Jr., and Margaret S. Kessels, as well

as of longstanding friends Suzanne and William Hammel, Kay and Paul La-
peyre, Marky and Uwe Pontius, and Suzanne and Ted Reveley.

Of course, it is my family that anchors me in good times and bad. This
includes my dear brother, Cody A. Kelleher; my uncle, Louis Rabouin; my
beloved children, Ashley E. Schafer and T. Gregory Schafer; and Greg's
wife, Elizabeth, who joined our family in 1997. And there is a new Schafer
since the publication of my last book: Andrew Gregory Schafer, a new generation of native New Orleanians, born 25 March 2005, to Liz and Greg. He
is a great joy to me. Finally, my most profound gratitude and affection go to
my main man for forty-five years, Timothy G. Schafer, the love of my life.
He made all of my dreams come true. This book is for him again, for all the
reasons he knows best.

Brothels, Depravity,
and Abandoned Women

INTRODUCTION

The "oldest profession" was hardly new to New Orleans in the era just before the Civil War. From the earliest days of French colonial New Orleans—a primitive, mosquito-infested, and disease-ridden enclave precariously situated in a giant, graceful curve of the mighty Mississippi River—the city offered few attractions to entice people, especially respectable women, to become its residents. When a priest suggested to one of the first governors of Louisiana that he send away all disreputable women to raise the moral tone of the colony, the governor responded, "If I send away all the loose females, there will be no women left here at all, and this would not suit the views of the King or the inclinations of the people." To help build the population of the colony, the king of France, Louis XIV, simply emptied La Salpêtrière prison. In February 1721, eighty-eight former convicts, including a large number of prostitutes, disembarked in New Orleans. These women would become the founding mothers of the city. A nun belonging to the Ursuline order, which established a convent in New Orleans in 1727, wrote a letter complaining about the number of prostitutes in the Crescent City. "As for the girls of bad conduct, although they are closely observed here and punished severely by putting them on a wooden horse and whipped by all the soldiers of the regiment that guards our city, there are more than enough to fill a refuge." She ruefully observed: "For not only debauchery, but dishonesty and all other vices reign here more than elsewhere." Other, more respectable women would arrive soon. In the same year that the Ursulines established their convent, the famous "casket girls" (because they carried small chests of clothing) came to marry the men of the colony. Apparently all found husbands quickly, since a French official noted, "This merchandise was soon disposed of." One historian has remarked on the incredible fecundity of the casket girls and the tragic infertility of the prostitutes, as almost all of Louisiana's most important families of French descent trace their origin to the former while none claim to have descended from the latter.[1]

As one writer observed, however, New Orleans did not attain its full status of "spectacular wickedness" until it fell under American rule. The city had grown into a bustling metropolis by the 1850s. This decade saw a construction boom in the city, during which many of the recognizable landmark buildings of the Crescent City emerged: the Customs House, the Pontalba apartments, Gallier Hall (called Municipal Hall), the grand St. Charles Hotel (recently torn down), and a complete renovation of the St. Louis Cathedral, including a new, taller steeple. The population of New Orleans swelled from 102,193 in 1840 to 168,675 in 1860 as thousands of immigrants from many countries, especially Ireland and what would become Germany, poured into the city each year. Between 1841 and 1850, a total of 188,000 immigrants came to New Orleans; between 1851 and 1860, another 254,000 arrived. Frederick Law Olmsted, a visitor to the city in the 1850s, commented on the diverse origins of the city's population and the resulting "variety in the tastes, habits, manners, and moral codes" of the inhabitants. Another visitor, Benjamin Latrobe, described the "gabble of tongues" he heard in the city, which he compared to "the residence of a million or two frogs."[2]

New Orleans has long had a reputation for being a wicked and vice-ridden city. One antebellum observer commented that the city resembled "a perfect Sodom." This anonymous commentator described in an indignant tone how New Orleanians desecrated the Sabbath by holding bullfights and cockfights on that day as well as scheduling Sunday planning meetings attended by the mayor, other city officials, and prominent citizens in order to plan a series of masked balls. This writer, outraged by such a display of indifference to the Sabbath and the waste of time by public officials, expressed amazement that city leaders granted licenses for what the commentator called "masked brothel balls. . . . The assemblage of prostitutes and lewd women at these [ball] rooms, is without exception . . . the most wanton, debasing and licentious exhibition of human passion ever witnessed. There are three of these Ball Rooms . . . open every night and filled to overflowing. The excessive drinking and carousing . . . enables the girls to induce men . . . to accompany them home." On Christmas Eve 1855, the *New Orleans Daily Picayune* noted that the Fifth District Court of New Orleans had issued an injunction to shut down the Globe Ballroom. The police officer arrested "quite a number of colored folks, both male and female, bond and free. . . . These balls, where white and colored people indiscriminately mix and mingle . . . stand foremost among our city's curses . . . it is high time that such a degrading public amalgamation should be prohibited." In an article entitled "Terpsichore in the Old Third," the *Picayune* described these balls as "again in full blast, and blasting indeed are they to the prospects of all who attend." The reporter noted that the men at these balls were "sailors who happen to be sots, professional pickpockets, blacklegs [card sharks] and boys on the road to ruin," while the women represented "the frailest of the frail and the vilest of the vile." He noted that the Stadt Amsterdam and the Lion's Den, two notorious dance halls/brothels, would flourish "with the price of blood, the coffers will be fattened." The anonymous commentator noted the "immense" number of drinking houses in the city as a contributing factor to the high crime and vice rate. On Christmas Day, the *Picayune* reported that sixty African Americans faced Recorder Clement Ramos after their arrest in the Globe Ballroom: Ramos fined those who were free people of color ten dollars; the slaves, five dollars. If they could not pay, the reporter observed, the slaves could satisfy their fine by accepting a whipping by the sheriff. Apparently city officials descended on and closed ballrooms with some frequency. Henry Kmen noted the city's ballrooms' reputation for being places frequented by public women. He stated that in 1840 the city council closed a ballroom because "the numerous females attending . . . are principally or altogether women of the town."[3]

Phil Johnson has speculated that by the 1850s New Orleans had become "the prostitution capital of all America." This writer estimated that the income generated by the sex market ranked second only to that of the port of New Orleans in dollar value. Indeed, a contemporary observer stated that prostitutes worked in at least three-fifths of all houses in a large part of the city. This writer characterized the number of brothels in New Orleans as "immense" and observed: "It is not unusual to see the windows and doors of every house as far as the eyes can recognize them, filled with these girls." An 1849 Orleans Parish grand jury complained of "the many violations of decency that are permitted too frequently . . . by those lewd and abandoned creatures to occupy those suitable residences for men of business in the most central part of our city." The situation had not improved by 1855, when another Orleans Parish grand jury observed: "Lewd and abandoned women have invaded almost every street in the city . . . with proper efforts on the part of the police, we might soon no longer be shocked with the revolting spectacle that has too long disgraced our city." But petitions by citizens complaining of women of "bad reputation," who "exhibited themselves at the doors and windows of their homes," fell on deaf ears. The underfunded and understaffed police struggled to prevent crime and keep the peace, but the force was so inadequate that whole sections of town were left without police coverage. Even when police attempted to do their duty, local citizens sometimes thwarted them. In 1850 the *Picayune* reported that authorities arrested one James Allen for "trying to snatch lewd women away from police" in a raid on a Gallatin Street brothel. As that decade wore on, city officials pulled money from the police department and lowered the salaries of other city employees (including judges) to invest in new transportation ventures, especially railroads. This shift of city funds meant that the police earned low salaries and therefore proved more susceptible to bribes. Policemen made forty-five dollars a month before 1855 and only fifty dollars from 1855 to 1862, a little more than unskilled male manual laborers. As a result of poor wages, low morale, and the inadequate number of patrols, the city earned the reputation of being one of the most violent, vice-ridden, and dangerous cities in the country.[4]

A near epidemic of sexually transmitted diseases must have existed in antebellum New Orleans. Each day, local newspapers carried large front-page advertisements by several physicians claiming that they had a sure cure for these "private diseases." For example, Dr. James's notice ran in the *Louisiana Courier* daily from 1851 to 1860. His dispensary, located on Customhouse Street (conveniently near several brothels), dispensed medicines that the doctor claimed "permanently eradicated" such diseases as syphilis, gonorrhea, and gleet (a urethral discharge). Dr. James promised a cure for gonorrhea in twenty-four hours "or no pay." He also promised to help people "who have privately and improperly injured themselves in that secret and solitary habit which ruins the body and mind, unfitting them for either business or society." He listed the effects of such practices on the body as "weakness of Back and Limbs, Pain in the Head, Dimness of Vision." Dr. James further stated that the effects of the "solitary habit" on the mind are "Confusion of ideas, Depression of Spirits, Evil Forebodings, Aversion to society, Self Distrust, Love of Solitude, Timidity, etc." Another physician, Dr. Watson, claimed he could cure "all those complaints that are called venereal." Watson, whose office was also located on Customhouse Street, claimed that hundreds of New Orleanians could supply proof of his cures, but he stated that he could not use testimonials to prove his claims, as "these are matters that require the nicest secrecy." Under the headline "Secret Diseases—Glad Tidings," Dr. Hunter claimed to be "well known in the United States for the cure of Venereal Diseases." He further stated, "The superiority of the Hunterian system of curing, over the ordinary treatment, [is] that the poison is thoroughly taken out of the blood, cutting off all possibility of a return." Dr. Mullen advertised that his cure of sexually transmitted diseases—a cure that did not use mercury—"has the approval of the most distinguished surgeons of Paris, London, and New York." He claimed that every patient who had sought his services left completely cured. He also advertised that he could reverse impotence brought about by overindulgence in sexual relations or by "self pollution" (masturbation). Dr. L. C. Thompson claimed in his advertisement that he could cure all "Syphilitic Diseases" with a medicine invented by Dr. Leroy of Paris, providing relief for people who suffer from this "loathsome affliction."[5]

Antebellum New Orleans was a city plagued not only with disease but also with violent crime. On Christmas Day 1852, the *Picayune* reported that the Orleans Parish grand jury complained that the police promoted rather than obstructed the commission of crimes. "Rogues go 'unwhipped of justice' because their offences are undiscovered, or if known, winked at." An 1855 editorial stated: "There is probably no other city in the Union in which the existing laws are so grossly neglected as they are in New Orleans. Our police officers seem to think their *individual emolument* is the sole object . . . and that the *public good is a matter of no moment*" (italics in original). In 1856 more than fifteen hundred criminal cases awaited trial in the First District Court of New Orleans, which served as the city's criminal court. The clogged docket meant that by the time the court heard a case, the witnesses often had left town, and the court would have no choice but to abandon the prosecution of the case and release the accused. In 1849 alone, police made an astonishing 25,706 arrests, including those for maiming, murder, and arson as well as lesser crimes such as assault and battery, larceny, pickpocketing, swindling, and harboring runaway slaves. This number represents almost one-quarter of the entire New Orleans population. An 1860 editorial in the *Picayune* railed against the frequency of murder in the city—a crime so often committed, the editorial observed, that it threatened the police themselves, two of whom had been killed and one seriously wounded in the past week. In a Christmas Day editorial in 1859, the *Daily True Delta* charged that "murder seems to have become one of the daily recurring topics of the reporters of the city papers; the record of one deed of blood has hardly dried when another recital of crime follows it, each chapter a brutal and bloody continuation of the preceding." Between 1859 and 1861, the Orleans Parish coroner held inquests over the bodies of 132 murder victims, about one a week. And according to one writer, a full two-thirds of the homicides committed in the vice-ridden areas of the city went unreported.[6]

Chronically too few in number and poorly paid, the New Orleans police struggled, often unsuccessfully, to suppress crime. Newspaper editorials constantly complained of the inadequate number of policemen on the beat. In 1855 the *Picayune* expressed amazement in a front-page editorial that a person could walk "at night two miles through the most thickly populated portions of New Orleans without encountering a single watchman, and more especially that this can be done night after night at different hours." The New Orleans police sometimes resorted to extortion. In 1857 a Second District policeman came before the mayor, charged with collecting sixty dollars from a woman suspected of "keeping a disorderly house." The woman claimed that she paid the policeman the money "in order to save herself from the consequences of prosecution." In one instance a customer of a brothel fatally stabbed a policeman who had broken down the door of the house. The *Picayune* reported that the incident had happened "in a house of bad repute on Gravier street. It is said that he [the policeman] had been in the habit of visiting the house, and being refused admittance on the night in question, he broke open the door . . . and was dangerously stabbed . . . in the left breast" by a man in the house. Sometimes policemen demanded sex from public women. In 1852, a watchman of the Second District, Charles O'Donnell, went to the brothel of Ann Spriggins on Gallatin Street and, "after insulting and assaulting her, threatened to pull down her house, then shut up and finally arrested her, should she stand in the doorway after dark, unless she consented to certain propositions made by him." One of the witnesses, a police officer, indicated that the officer who arrested her often slept in the house. The attorney for Spriggins argued that a man who would "kiss and tell" could not be considered credible. The recorder agreed and discharged Spriggins. However, he warned her to "leave her present neighborhood and reform her mode of life." He also lectured the policeman on the "impropriety of setting such an example for the citizens." Two years later the *Picayune* reported a "terrific row" on Gallatin Street that originated in the California House, "a notorious den kept by one Johnson." The disturbance involved gunshots and the throwing of brickbats. Police arrested two of the leaders, Archy Murphy and David Kinney, who each had to post a thousand-dollar bond to appear before the First District Court for assaulting the police. The reporter observed: "It is time that Gallatin street was cleaned out by the police. It is filled with low groggeries and is the resort of the worst and most abandoned of both sexes. Thieves, murderers, prostitutes and drunkards congregate there . . . a policeman named Phillips, who appears to be connected in some way with the gang, endeavored to prevent the arrest of the rowdies, and has been suspended." In one remarkable case, a policeman actually helped a man accused of murder to escape the city. Peter Johnson, alias "Dutch Pete," owned the infamous California House on Gallatin Street. In 1857 he fatally stabbed James Dacey in his establishment, after which Johnson mysteriously disappeared from the city. Strange rumors circulated about the city that a policeman had assisted his escape, and subsequent events confirmed the rumor. An intercepted letter, addressed to Johnson in Havana under an assumed name, fell into the hands of the person whose name Dutch Pete had assumed. When he read the letter, he realized that a New Orleans police officer had written the letter to an escaped murderer. In the letter the officer took credit for putting the investigating officer "on the wrong scent," allowing Johnson to make good his escape. The letter writer also bragged how he had disposed of Johnson's property and his "mistress or woman." He warned Johnson not to return to New Orleans for at least a year, as "testimony concerning his guilt was given in a most emphatic manner before the Coroner's jury, which had brought in a verdict against him." The policeman told Johnson that he believed that "with proper industry, and the application of the proper means, the witnesses might all be got to clear out." The person who had received the letter mailed it to the office of the *Picayune,* and the editor turned it over to the chief of police. Dutch Pete returned to New Orleans eight months later. Police arrested him, but the officer who had written him in Havana had obviously done his work well. Six witnesses present on the night of the murder testified that they had not seen the incident and did not know who had stabbed Dacey. No more information about the outcome exists, but it was this kind of intriguing story that induced me to fully explore these records.[7]

This book is one that I never planned to write. It is a book that I found, quite accidentally, on the way to looking for something else. In my research for my last book, *Becoming Free, Remaining Free: Manumission and Enslavement in New Orleans, 1846–1862,* I kept finding cases from the First District Court of New Orleans that shed light on vice, sex, and prostitution in New Orleans. The original manuscript records of the First District Court of New Orleans are housed in the City Archives, located at the New Orleans Public Library. These trial transcripts provide the main primary source for this study. Incredibly rich and varied, these trial court transcripts have never been systematically used by scholars to study vice, crime, or prostitution in New Orleans during the antebellum period. These records reveal extensive details concerning attitudes about sex, sex across the color line, and the operation of prostitution in the Crescent City before the Civil War. They also demonstrate the gritty day-to-day workings of the local courts. Of course, as these were trial courts and not appellate courts, they did not generate case reports. No indexes exist by subject, and cases can be retrieved only by docket number. To find individual cases, one must examine each page of the voluminous minute books, the clerk of court's daily record of every case that came before the court on each day, and note the docket numbers of the desired cases. Cases before 1855 are on microfilm, but those between 1855 and 1862 must be examined in the original. In most instances these were still tied up in the red tape (now faded to brown) with which the clerk of court bound them 150 years ago. By necessity, I have confined myself to heterosexual women prostitutes in this study, since not a shred of concrete evidence exists in these records of male prostitution, or even of lesbianism or homosexuality, although surely both existed. There is not one case on the docket of the First District Court of New Orleans, the criminal court, of a prosecution for homosexual sex or even for "crime against nature" or sodomy. Nor did the newspapers ever report that one of the city's recorders ruled on such activity. In 1857, the *Picayune* referred to the arrest of "eight or ten other male and female specimens of the lewd and abandoned type." Whether those arrested consisted of public women and their male associates or actual male prostitutes cannot be ascertained. A set of crime statistics published by the *Picayune* in 1854 reported one case of sodomy, but there is no indication as to whether the charge involved an act with an animal, oral sex, or sex between homosexuals.[8]

Laws against the "detestable crime" of sodomy were in place as early as the Spanish period, when conviction for this crime could result in execution, subsequent burning of the body, and forfeiture of the person's property to the Spanish treasury. The second section of the Crimes Act of 1805, the only criminal code of American Louisiana until the twentieth century, provided that anyone convicted of the "detestable and abominable crime against nature, committed with man or beast, shall suffer imprisonment at hard labor for life." It is surprising that no evidence exists that the authorities enforced these laws during the 1840s and 1850s or, indeed, that they were broken.[9]

Convictions for brothel keeping and prostitutes fighting with each other and robbing their customers, however, appear repeatedly in the antebellum newspapers and in the court records. I first discovered the cases involving people charged with "keeping a disorderly brothel." Since the records of the First District Court have recently become available to scholars, I decided to dig further and look at every case in which the prosecutor charged a woman with larceny or assault and battery between 1846, when the First District

Court began to operate, and 1862, when the court closed after the city surrendered to Union forces in the Civil War. In all, I examined more than two thousand trial transcripts. This search proved quite fruitful, as many of these assault and battery and larceny cases involved prostitutes. I also examined every case in which a woman brought a writ of habeas corpus before the court. The phrase *habeas corpus* literally means "you have the body of [name]." It is a writ directed to a sheriff or jailor that instructs the official to produce the person in court so that a judge may decide if he or she is being illegally held. It serves as a protection from having a person thrown into prison without a charge and kept there indefinitely. A writ of habeas corpus forced the presiding judge to either charge the person with a crime or release him or her. Many cases that invoked the writ of habeas corpus turned out to be public women contesting their imprisonment because they had been charged with vagrancy or some other trumped-up charge designed to get them off the streets.

The second important primary source proved to be the city newspapers, especially the *New Orleans Daily Picayune*. I read the morning and evening editions of every day's paper from March 1846, when the First District Court opened, to April 1862. The *Picayune* embellished the criminal court records with gossipy details and also gave daily reports of the recorder's courts, whose records have not survived. The newspaper provided daily reports of arrests, fines, and sentences given to prostitutes by the city's recorders. These officials served as committing magistrates and, as such, provided the first hearing for all crimes and offenses committed, from murders to misdemeanors. Recorders sent more serious cases to the First District Court for trial. For lesser offenses, they could order confinement in the workhouse, impose a monetary fine, or order a whipping (for slaves only).

The city's newspapers gave detailed descriptions of the appearance and workings of the First District Court of New Orleans and the four recorder's courts in the city. The Presbytere, located across from the Place d'Armes (now Jackson Square), housed not only the criminal court but all the other district courts, one of the city's four recorder's courts, the Supreme Court of Louisiana, and the conveyance, mortgage, and court records of the city from its founding onward. Newspaper editorials and grand jury reports characterize this extremely overcrowded building as "not only unsafe, but as dangerous in the highest degree." Observing that the building contained more than 100,000 land titles and that once in each generation title to every piece of property in the city passed through these courts, an Orleans Parish grand jury recommended the construction of a new "fire-proof" building large enough to accommodate the courts and their records. Another Orleans Parish grand jury stated that the courthouse might be destroyed by fire at any minute. The building had caught fire twice before, but firefighters had extinguished the blazes. A newspaper reporter described the courtroom of the First District Court as being too small, "furnished with mean, dilapidated and rickety furniture. . . .The windows opening on the court present broken panes of glass, through which the wind this morning, whistled most unpleasantly." On at least two instances in November 1858, the unheated court adjourned when the judge deemed it too cold to conduct business. The building also proved smelly, humid, and hot in the summer. One reporter described the sights and stench of the court: "There were over 100 prisoners in the dock, and the lobby was crowded to its utmost capacity by their numerous friends, without counting the habitués, court-room loafers, ready-to-bail-you spectators, observers of human nature and such fry. Let us imagine the combined essence of bad whiskey, worse gin, garlic, onions, cigars, chewing and smoking tobacco, issuing from 500 mouths and nostrils, and add to this the perspiration of many individuals, more or less unwashed, evaporating from their greasy garments." Another newspaper reported the "extreme disorder" of the courtroom, noting that its furniture presented a "most wretched character." The judge did not even have a proper chair upon which to sit, only a "common bench." Another writer commented that "no changes, or piece-meal patching, can make the venerable building a fit theater for the administration of law and justice in New Orleans." However, this author noted, the chances of getting a new courthouse "appear to be as remote as ever."[10]

Recorder's courts, which met six days each week, fared no better in decor or atmosphere. One reporter complained that the recorder's courtroom of the First District had not been swept for weeks, as the court owned no broom for this purpose. The usual practice, that of using an alleged runaway slave unclaimed by his or her master to clean the courtrooms, no longer worked, since the owner of the slave supposed to sweep the courtroom had retrieved him. Another reporter noted that the First District recorder's courtroom "is filthy enough to generate disease." In 1852 the *Picayune* reported that the clerk of the First District Recorder's Court had a twelve-inch-long baby alligator in his desk. After several complaints of excessive heat, the city finally paid for ice for Recorder Gerard Stith's court in mid-July. Often as many as a hundred unfortunate people faced the recorder in each of the city's four recorder's courts each morning. The great majority of the charges consisted of accusations of drunkenness, fighting, vagrancy, or being "dangerous and suspicious" or "lewd and abandoned," as the court termed public women. "Here we have the lewd, abandoned creature, gazing with bold looks on the court; she feels no shame, long ago she has given up all the feelings of her sex—she has forgotten—and here she stands, the picture of effrontery and low vice." Cases involving larceny, assault and battery, disturbing the peace, and harboring runaway slaves also filled the docket of the recorder's courts each day. Often the descriptions of recorder's courts found in the newspapers made fun of the people unlucky enough to be hauled before these tribunals. One newspaper called the Second District's recorder's court "Genois Varieties," a reference to the recorder, Joseph Genois, and the vaudeville-like atmosphere of his court. One reporter described the court as containing so many accused and so many spectators that they "annoy the court, and officers in the discharge of their duties, and the crowd usually make such a chattering and noise that it is frequently almost impossible to hear the important testimony of witnesses."[11]

From the newspapers and court cases the names of individual public women emerged, which led to finding cases in which they faced charges for other crimes and misdemeanors, such as assault and battery, larceny, robbery, vagrancy, being drunk and disorderly, insulting white people (only for prostitutes who were free women of color), and harboring slaves. I also found cases in which public women stiffed landlords on several months' rent and then skipped town. One case involved a group of public women attacking their landlord, a notorious slave trader, Theophilius Freeman, smashing his possessions, and vandalizing his house when he attempted to collect the rent. Finally, I used census data and tax records to ascertain ownership of brothels and to identify groups of prostitutes listed as living together. The 1850 and 1860 census records proved less useful than the court records and the newspapers. The census of 1850 did not usually list the occupations of women. The census of 1860 is in places impossible to read because the census taker used very light ink or pencil. The few prostitutes found in the census of 1860 gave their occupations as "servants." Public women probably did not wish to tell the census taker their real occupation. Both censuses revealed that a large majority of sex sellers came to New Orleans from Ireland. Of course, there were exceptions. A number of Louisiana-born free women of color worked as public women, and not infrequently slave owners forced their slave women into prostitution and then collected their fees. In one case a slave woman, the property of a wealthy white tobacco merchant, ran a brothel for white prostitutes, collected a fee from them for each assignation, and turned the money over to her master.[12]

Extensive research indicated that, unlike New York in the antebellum period, and unlike St. Louis after the Civil War, few women owned their own houses of prostitution in antebellum New Orleans. Most rented their houses from prominent white businessmen and professional men who could make far more money renting to a brothel than to a respectable family. These large real estate owners understandably resisted reform and efforts to eradicate prostitution. Their interests required a city policy that kept real estate taxes low, which would maximize their rental revenue, and only half-hearted efforts to eradicate the sex trade. Evidence exists that more women than men managed brothels for the male landlords and that more women faced arrest on the charge of keeping a brothel. Arrest records from December 1853 to June 1854 show that thirty-six women but no men faced charges of keeping a brothel. Merchants also supported prostitution, as they depended on public women to boost sales in the apparel and accessories needed to attract their customers. The police proved unable to suppress prostitution; some took bribes, and others actually served as guards for the brothels. But the sex trade's highest profits went into the pockets of the wealthiest land owners and merchants, many of whom were judges, physicians, merchants, attorneys, and city officials. As for the women, many lived short, violent lives in which they were subject to brutality from their customers and sometimes from each other. In 1852 the *Picayune* described conditions on Girod Street, an area filled with brothels: "Rows of low tenements may be seen there leaning against one another as if for support . . . the fronts of all are shattered and broken, and a few crazy creaking steps lead to each door. There is a red curtain in every window, and drunkenness and vice seem to peep through patched panes . . . each of these rickety sheds brings to its owner a monthly payment of $25 or $30. . . . They are generally kept by women."[13]

John McDonogh, a wealthy merchant and plantation owner, personified the real estate tycoons who rented to brothels. McDonogh became infamous for renting houses to prostitutes in respectable neighborhoods. When surrounding property owners sold their homes rather than live near a noisy and disreputable brothel, McDonogh purchased those houses at a fraction of their value. He then evicted the brothel and sold the properties at a considerable profit. McDonogh also refused to maintain his property and became a millionaire slum landlord. Known throughout New Orleans as a cheapskate, he steadfastly refused to support increases in the taxes on real estate, even when they would have been used for railroad construction or other civic improvements.[14]

Why would women become prostitutes in antebellum New Orleans? Overwhelming evidence indicates that in most cases women had few other choices and limited opportunities to support themselves. The male-dominated society of the antebellum period closed the professions and higher education to them. Marriage offered a more honorable alternative, but some women preferred the independence of the single life to marriage, which could be unexciting and usually involved physically demanding housekeeping chores. Many young women struck out on their own to find "respectable" jobs, only to find the wages to be below subsistence. In the 1850s many working women received wages as low as one dollar a week. Little surprise that some women saw prostitution as a solution to the miseries of their lives and a means of financial survival. As one historian has noted, becoming a woman of the town was at once a social and economic choice—a means of supporting oneself and a way of bargaining with men at a time when few other strategies existed for economic subsistence. Sudden changes in a woman's life could also force her to become a public woman. Widowhood, single-motherhood, divorce, and desertion moved women into prostitution as a relatively easy way to support themselves. As one woman tellingly stated: "No work, no money, no home." [15]

Sometimes women and girls became influenced by prostitutes who told them that they led "an easy, merry life." In addition, one writer noted that local pimps, disguised as city officials, met the immigrant boats from Ireland and encouraged the more attractive women to come home with them. As a result, pretty Irish women not infrequently spent their first night in the United States in a brothel. For example, on 27 June 1852 the *Picayune* reported that a young woman went to the Second District police station and made an affidavit "respecting a series of deceptions and atrocities practiced upon her." She had arrived on an immigrant ship on 18 April. A man went on board the ship soon after its arrival and told her that he had a position for her in a "respectable house." She followed him to a dwelling on Madison Street, kept by a Mrs. Barmer. After a few days, she discovered that the house was one of "bad repute," and she told Mrs. Barmer that she wanted to leave, that "she was an honest woman." Mrs. Barmer told her that she could not leave, that she had the right to force her to stay, and she demanded six dollars a week for rent and fifty cents for washing. When the woman complained, Barmer "abused her and beat her" and then locked her in a room with a man who "did violence to her." Following this incident, Barmer repeatedly locked her in rooms with other men. After a few weeks, the woman became ill and went to Charity Hospital. After her release, she returned to Barmer's house to retrieve her clothes and some money she had left there. Barmer refused her admittance, and the young woman went to the police. Barmer, upon being questioned by the recorder, stated that the young woman had been taken to her house by a man who said he would marry her and that she had never worked for her or been beaten or abused by her. The case never went to trial, and one can only imagine the future of this young girl, alone and "ruined" in New Orleans. White female immigrants were in some instances the victims of sexual assault by black men even before they disembarked. In another instance, a ship carrying a large number of Irish and German immigrants caused a riot when rumors spread that the free African American crew members had taken "the most unpardonable liberties with the female immigrants during the passage." After they had been "ruined," probably many drifted into prostitution after they disembarked. Newly arriving immigrants constituted a large group of women to be exploited. In one month in 1851, 2,731 immigrants disembarked in New Orleans. Irish comprised 877 of this number, Germans 522, and from France and other European countries 788.[16]

A New York physician, William W. Sanger, wrote the first comprehensive study of prostitution in the antebellum period. Sanger based his 1858 work on a questionnaire that he administered to 2,000 public women in New York. In response to the question of why they had become prostitutes, 513 of these women cited "inclination" as their motive, while another 525 claimed "destitution" as the cause. The third largest number said that they had been "seduced and abandoned" and had become public women after the seduction and abandonment. Other causes, in descending order, consisted of "drink and the desire to drink," bad treatment by parents or husbands, viewing prostitution "as an easy life," "bad company," persuasion by other public women, being "too idle to work," "violated," "seduced on board immigrant ships," and "seduced in emigrant boarding houses." Sanger concluded that 6,000 prostitutes lived in New York, that the majority of them were fifteen to twenty-five years old, and that five-eighths of them were foreign-born. He also found that public women lived an average of only four years after becoming prostitutes and that fully half of them suffered from sexually transmitted diseases. He also concluded that not enough opportunities for employment in respectable callings existed for women in New York and what employment existed produced inadequate wages. Sanger noted that almost half of the public women he studied began their work careers as domestic servants. Being a servant was often a backbreaking and boring job, and many turned to prostitution because of their desire for a change, a life that seemed exciting, and a chance for a higher income. He also found that prostitution ventures consumed $4 million of capital in New York and that the annual expenditure on public women averaged more than $7 million.

Although no comprehensive contemporary study exists of public women in New Orleans during this same period, overwhelming evidence indicates that Sanger's conclusions about the characteristics of prostitution and motives for becoming a public woman held true for the Crescent City.[17]

In New Orleans, slaves and free women of color monopolized domestic service, closing another door for unskilled immigrant women in their attempts to find work. Respectable jobs for women usually required harder work, longer hours, and lower wages than selling sex did, and some turned to prostitution for more manageable and profitable work hours. As one prostitute stated, "I don't mind being a whore. I just mind not being able to *not* be a whore. The work that's available to me is so limited, so limited, that I'm actually . . . grateful to work in the sex industry. That's not right." [18]

In 1860 the *Picayune* reported on a case in which a woman dressed as a man came before the First District Recorder's court. The accused related her name as Minna Brown, shocking the spectators who had assumed that she was a man. According to the reporter, she was "smiling, blushing, and spitting tobacco juice." In her defense, she stated that "she could not get along as a woman, making small wages and not getting paid half the time, and being strong and healthy, she had shipped as a deckhand on a steamboat" for the past six months. She claimed to be a "good fellow" and stated that she preferred to remain a man. The recorder fined her ten dollars for dressing as a man, but her words show clearly the difficulties women faced in trying to support themselves. Another woman, Mary Coulter, attempted to commit suicide by jumping into the Mississippi River. A police officer rescued her, and when asked why she had tried to end her life, she expressed anger that he had interfered with her intention to kill herself. She said "she had long struggled against her troubles, had worked hard and tried every other means to make a living, but all had been disappointment to her, want, sorrow and ill-treatment—life was a burthen, [*sic*] and she was determined to get rid of it. . . . What will become of this frail creature? . . . Her history is probably that of a hundred others." Some women turned to prostitution after being deserted by a husband or lover. A Mexican woman named Catherine Domingo came to New Orleans with her lover after the Mexican War, and he promptly abandoned her. The *Picayune* reported her as "young and pretty, and the usual consequences followed her abandonment. . . . The Mexican girl is no longer a stranger. She has acquaintances, but they are of the lowest and vilest class. She has learned sufficient of the language to swear in a manner unknown to any but the most degraded of her sex . . . and the simple, credulous Aztec girl is now a confirmed and drunken harlot." The following year, the *Picayune* noted that Catherine House, alias Domingo, "was found in a lumber yard on St. Joseph street, in suspicious proximity to a negro [*sic*], and who is also charged with being an incorrigible vagrant, was sent down for sixty days." Four years later, New Orleans police arrested Domingo, along with another public woman, Jane Boyle, for "stealing Pierre Fortier's watch and chain, under very mysterious circumstances, and also with being drunken vagrants." Recorder Henry M. Summers sent them to the workhouse for three months. In 1854 Domingo faced charges of stealing seven dollars from a Mrs. Kurns and also of throwing a chair at a police corporal in the police office. The *Picayune* described her as "curst as Petruchio's Kate." Public women sometimes enticed other women into the profession. The *Picayune* reported that one "miserable old wretch," Mary Miller, alias Mother Miller, and two other women, Mary Banks, alias the One-Eyed Dragon, and Ellen O'Keefe, alias the Pet of the Workhouse, decoyed Mary O'Donnell into an "infamous den" on the corner of Girod and St. Mary streets. The newspaper noted that Mary O'Donnell had only recently immigrated to New Orleans before being decoyed by the "fiend" Mary Miller. The court discharged O'Donnell, sent the other three women to the workhouse, and in addition fined Miller twenty-five dollars. While prostitution corrupted many poor women and girls, it did provide a way for them to make more money than they would have earned in traditional women's occupations, and prostitutes usually were more financially secure than were housewives.[19]

Prostitution constituted a survival strategy for many women. Arguably it was not the worst form of exploitation that a nineteenth-century woman could face. Although it was a perilous and degrading occupation that generated disgust from "respectable" society, many public women regarded their profession as a better alternative to other survival strategies they might have chosen. Given nineteenth-century society's restrictions on women, many faced a series of demoralizing choices. They could enter into marriage for economic security, they could work for near-starvation wages, or they could enter the sex trade. Most choices women faced involved some sort of trade-off.[20]

1

SELLING SEX AND THE LAW

In the antebellum period, most American states did not consider selling sex a criminal act. However, the states often used vagrancy laws or other charges—such as disorderly conduct, indecent exposure, obscene language, drunkenness, and lewd behavior—to punish public women for practicing their profession. State law and city ordinances punished those who managed brothels under the general rubric of nuisance laws. The states did not criminalize selling sex in the United States until the Progressive Era. Accordingly, selling one's body for sex did not constitute a distinct criminal act in antebellum New Orleans. A city ordinance of 1817 noted that any woman or girl "notoriously abandoned to lewdness" who committed scandal or disturbance of the peace could incur a fine of twenty-five dollars for each offense or, if she could not pay the fine, a confinement of one month in prison. Thus the ordinance did not prohibit prostitution as long as no scandal or disturbance occurred. An 1818 Louisiana law made it a criminal offense to keep "any disorderly inn, tavern, ale-place, tippling house, gaming house or brothel," an offense punishable by either a fine or imprisonment at the discretion of the court. A Louisiana statute of 1855 reiterated the 1818 act. The city of New Orleans prohibited individuals by ordinance from renting rooms to or "harbor[ing]" a woman or girl "notoriously abandoned to lewdness" if she caused a nuisance in the neighborhood. The penalty for this offense consisted of a fifteen-dollar fine for each twenty-four hours that a person provided lodgings for such women.[1]

An 1845 city ordinance forbade "lewd women" to enter cabarets or coffeehouses; nor could they have a drink in one of these establishments. Violation of this ordinance resulted in a twenty-five-dollar fine or a month in the workhouse for those who could not pay the fine. This ordinance required the police to apprehend any women in violation of this ordinance and bring them before one of the city's recorder's courts. [2]

According to another city ordinance, passed in 1846, people who violated nuisance laws and public decency were subject to a fine of $50. In August 1850 brothel owner Harry Wilson appeared before Justice of the Peace Alexander Derbes to answer to a charge of "keeping a disorderly brothel on Gallatin street" in violation of the 1846 ordinance. Derbes fined Wilson fifty dollars, and Wilson appealed to the Supreme Court of Louisiana. His attorney, Henry Train, argued that the city did not have the right to pass such an ordinance and therefore it was unconstitutional; he also asserted that the ordinance could not be legal because the same offense constituted a criminal act under state law. The supreme court rejected this reasoning, affirmed Justice Derbes's ruling, and ordered Wilson to pay the fine. This ruling would allow New Orleans city officials the discretion to prosecute brothels that the city deemed "disorderly" while allowing others to continue their business. In order to get a city official to proclaim a brothel "disorderly," people had to present proof that the inmates of the brothel had frequently disturbed their sleep or disrupted their businesses. [3]

Under general nuisance laws, police arrested public women on many occasions. Often prostitutes found themselves facing recorders for being "drunk, lewd and abandoned" or for drinking in a barroom. For example, in 1854 the *New Orleans Daily Picayune* reported that "Harriet Kennedy, Mary Smith, Johanna Wright, Catherine Kane, and Helena Cotibo, four [*sic*] lewd and abandoned women, were arrested on Phillippa street last night, for being drunk, disturbing the peace and halloing [*sic*] murder. These women created more noise and disturbance than fifty men could possibly have done." The recorder sentenced two of the women to a fine of ten dollars or twenty days in the workhouse and the other three to a fine of five dollars or ten days' imprisonment. Few women would have chosen going to the workhouse if they could pay the fine. One grand jury report indicated that the workhouse buildings were "insufficient and in bad condition" and noted that "women are seated on the damp floor of their cells, there being no benches or even bunks, they all sleep on the floor." In the same report, the grand jury noted that "requisitions for food and materials for steady work were not furnished, disorder and insubordination results." In 1853 the *Picayune,* under the headline "Rowdy Women," reported that three other women, "Mary Branay, Mary Nolan and Mary O'Brien (what a pity that the name of Mary should be so disgraced!) were yesterday fined $10 each by Recorder Winter, for being found drinking at a grog shop, and for not having that chastity of character and manner that become true women." The recorder sent them to the workhouse for sixty days. The newspaper also noted the arrests of "two vagrant white women [who] were fined $3 for being caught coming out of a drinking shop in Phillippa street," a street known for its large number of brothels.[4]

Often police arrested public women under the city's general "Nuisance and Offenses" ordinance, an 1856 consolidation of a number of acts prohibiting certain kinds of behavior. Police arrested both women and men for indecent exposure. Section 24 of this act prescribed arrest and a fine for anyone who "shall strip naked for bathing, or show himself naked, or in any indecent apparel, or bathe in the daylight in the Mississippi River." For example, under the headline of "Another Venus," the *Picayune* reported with a decidedly mixed metaphor that Mary Connor "was arrested on Montegut street, last night, for exhibiting herself to the gaze of the astonished residents of that quiet street in a costume similar to that of Eve in Paradise, before she thought of the fig leaf." Another woman, Catherine Sheehan, had to face the recorder for being drunk and "indecently exposing her person." Police brought thirteen women "of bad reputation" before the recorder in 1852 for "making an indecent exposure of themselves at the doors and windows of their residences." The recorder sent them to the workhouse for thirty days. A neighbor's complaint sent Suzanne, a free woman of color, before the recorder for "keeping a house at the corner of Royal and St. Peter street, which is contrary to the ordinances made and provided for public decency. The females who live with Suzanne are said to expose themselves on the balcony in a little too much of that simple attire known as the 'Georgia costume.'" The *Picayune* defined a "Georgia uniform" as nothing but "a shirt collar and spurs," a slang expression for partial or total nudity.[5]

Not surprisingly, all the arrests for indecent exposure occurred in the warmer months of the year, and the *Picayune* delighted in describing the offenders as "prowling about" in various stages of nudity. Police arrested Mary Foster in June 1854 for "being drunk, disturbing the peace, using obscene language and indecently exposing her person." The recorder ordered her to serve sixty days in the workhouse. In July 1854 a neighbor complained that five "ladies of easy virtue . . . are in the habit of prowling about the streets in attire which, however comfortable in this hot weather, can hardly be termed decent." The *Picayune* reported another group of women residing on Burgundy Street as "being lewd and abandoned and prowling about the sidewalks in indecent attire." In August 1854, another neighbor stated that a Mrs. Dixon could be seen "prowling about in indecent attire, and in some instances, when the nights were very warm, dispensing with all attire and exhibiting her fair proportions to vulgar gaze." The following month the *Picayune* reported that "a nocturnal Venus," Emeline Kiezer, walked down Gravier Street in the nude. In July 1857 the newspaper reported that "four females of Perdido street were arrested for rudely and nudely making model artist exhibitions of themselves, to the great scandal of the neighborhood." The following month, Recorder Gerard Stith sentenced Eliza Hughes for "being drunk and exposing her person." Police arrested three women in separate incidents for public nudity in October 1857. In an article entitled "A Sad Wicked World," the *Picayune* reported that police took a nameless female to the watch house "in a state of almost entire nudity, followed by a crowd which, regardless of the rain, seemed determined to get a glimpse of this humiliating spectacle. Five year ago the woman in question was one of the fairest in the city, but recently she added the sin of intemperance to her other failings." Apparently she had been involved in a fight with another woman in the course of which "all her clothes were stripped off with the exception of a portion of one undergarment." The next day, police arrested Ann Brown for "being drunk, lewd, abandoned and almost naked on the public streets." Recorder Stith ordered her to pay twenty dollars or go to the workhouse for two months. She managed to bargain him down to a fine of ten dollars. Two weeks later one Mrs. Helsinger faced arrest for indecent exposure for "raising her dress to an immoderate height when crossing from street to street." In September 1855 police arrested Mary O'Neil for "making a beastly spectacle of herself by running through the streets as a model artiste. Mary ought to be ashamed of herself." That same month, the *Picayune* noted that Mary Sheridan, "uncovered except over her shoulders," received a ten-dollar fine or fifteen days in the parish prison. One couple, John Legendre, alias Sunday Sam, and Maria Hellman, faced a charge of together "violating the rules of public decency." In 1854 the *Picayune* reported that James Campbell and Bridget McGraw "saw fit to expose their persons to the public gaze with the free and easy manner of dress very acceptable in the Fejee [*sic*] Islands but not at all suitable to the rules of decency which govern this community." The couple each received a fine of ten dollars and a "stern lecture."[6]

Officials also arrested men who indecently exposed themselves. In August 1854, police arrested two men charged with "bathing in contravention to the ordinances, indecently exposing their persons." In January 1858, the *Picayune* reported one John Murphy as having taken an "air bath on the public streets. . . . The full dress of a Georgia major would be decent compared with the primitive garment worn by Murphy." The recorder sentenced him to six months at hard labor in the workhouse. Police arrested several other men in the 1850s for indecent exposure. Sentences varied from five to twenty-five dollars to a month in the workhouse.[7]

An 1806 act of the Louisiana territorial legislature had made it illegal to use obscene language under penalty of a twenty-dollar fine. An ordinance of the city of New Orleans in 1856 prohibited "indecent or vulgar language" in any public place, including streets, cemeteries, public squares, and levees. City officials occasionally used laws against obscene language to get public women off the streets. For example, in 1859 the *Picayune* reported that "Mary Smith, a lewd and abandoned woman, who indulges in obscene language in the streets, without regard to the chaste care of the more virtuous of her sex, will pay ten dollars fine or go to the Workhouse." In 1856, Recorder J. L. Fabre fined a woman named "New York Mary" five dollars "for a too free use of her tongue." Two women faced Recorder Gerard Stith on the same day in 1857 for using bad language. Mary Spencer, "who called Mary Wright, of Carondelet street, some of the worst names in the vocabulary of Billingsgate [a London market famous for fish and foul language], had to pay a fine of $15 or go to prison for twenty days." Sarah Cook, "for uttering words unfit for ears polite . . . was politely requested to pay a fine of $20, and the request was made in so pressing a manner that she found it impossible to refuse." Ellen Lewis, who had already paid a fine of ten dollars for "improprieties of conduct," faced the recorder again, this time for using obscene language. The recorder fined her fifty dollars and required her to post a peace bond of five hundred dollars. In 1861 the *Picayune* reported that "Mary Ann Williams, Bridget Nicholson, Bridget Galagher, Helen Wilson, four *traviate* of Conti street, were arrested for insulting Harry Pardo and wounding his feelings with their obscene language." The two Bridgets went to the parish prison, and the other two posted peace bonds. Adelaide Balfour and Kate Wilson, "two of the hooped frailties of Perdido street," faced Recorder Stith for "obscenity in word and deed." Eliza Sickles, "a frail specimen of humanity," when charged with being drunk and using obscene language, went to the workhouse for sixty days. Police arrested a few men for obscene language, but the authorities used these charges mostly against public women as a way of getting them off the streets, at least temporarily. The fines paid by these women can be seen as something akin to a tax on sin.[8]

New Orleans recorders also punished people—both men and women—

for dressing as members of the opposite sex, under the general nuisance laws that forbade improper conduct. Six men faced charges for dressing as women in the 1850s. In 1851, Paul Small created quite a sensation by dressing in a "Bloomer" costume and parading through the streets. The *Picayune* observed that he has "unsexed himself" by "promenading in the streets in women's apparel." Police caught Alexander F. Marchi wearing women's clothes in 1853. The *Picayune* reported that "the charge does not specify what the man attempted while wearing the female toggery, but the mere fact of assuming that costume is contrary to the ordinances." The same month, the authorities arrested Patrick McCarty for being disguised in women's clothes "for some bad purpose." The following year Joseph Henry faced Recorder Peter Seuzeneau for wearing women's clothing. He attempted to run to avoid being caught, but "not being accustomed to the petticoats, he tripped and fell, and before he could recover himself, the strong grip of the law was upon him." The following year, a Third District policeman observed something suspicious about what the *Picayune* termed "a strapping female" and arrested her, only to discover that "she was a he." Finally, Daniel Neill received a fine of twenty-five dollars or thirty days in jail for wearing women's clothing. The newspaper accounts of men being caught in women's clothing do not indicate why they may have worn feminine attire. Three of the six arrests for this offense occurred during the Mardi Gras season, and so possibly these men wore these garments as a masquerade. Three other cross-dressers clearly wore Mardi Gras costumes. The *Picayune* reported in 1856 that two women and one man left prison after paying jail fees. The reporter observed that the three, all jailed for cross-dressing, were "belated masqueraders who had been keeping up Mardi Gras."[9]

Women arrested for the same offense present quite a different picture. For one thing, many more women faced arrest during the 1850s for cross-dressing. Twenty-one instances of arrests for wearing men's clothing occurred, and some involved more than one woman. According to one historian, cross-dressing was a long-lived tradition of Mardi Gras. Police arrested several women in men's clothing each Mardi Gras, women who "dressed in masculine apparel . . . beyond the boundaries of even Mardi Gras propriety and license." The *Picayune*'s reporters, all men, clearly enjoyed making fun of women caught for this offense. But the newspaper accounts also gave indications as to why women chose to cross-dress. Overwhelmingly, women assumed male attire as a survival strategy, to protect themselves, to make more money than they could as women, to go places they could not go as women, or to evade restrictive laws against women. The reason that cross-dressing aroused such disapproval was not so much that the women were overtly sexy but that they were assertive: dressing like men, smoking cigars, riding in open carriages. More than simply masquerading as men, the prostitutes were making savage fun of their customers. [10]

One of the most detailed accounts of feminine cross-dressing involved a woman named Charley, whom a Lafayette Square patrolman arrested because he suspected that Charley, attired in men's clothing and smoking "vigorously behind a twisted roll of the Virginia weed," was really a woman. "The disguised nymph" tried to convince the policeman that "he was mistaken as to the gentle character of her sex," to which the patrolman replied, "You can't fool me—you're no boy, or I never was one." When examined by the First District recorder, Charley confessed and told him the story of her life. It seems that her parents died when she was quite young, and her guardians lived in New York. They took her to Boston, where she had an love affair that did not end well. She claimed that after this disgrace her relations and guardians persuaded her to assume male attire and go to sea. She made three voyages from New York to Liverpool as a cabin boy, after which she worked in a barber shop, a grocery store, as a barkeeper in a taproom, and as a "spotter" for the New York police. She asked the recorder "to go easy on her." Surprisingly, the recorder stated that as she had committed no "impropriety of conduct . . . to dress was altogether a matter of taste. Especially among the 'strong minded women of the North,' and as she had no female apparel, he was sure that he would not force her to take off what she had—although she was sailing under false colors." He did advise her to return to "her own sex" and bade her "Godspeed." Six days later, Charley faced a much less sympathetic recorder, Peter Seuzeneau of the Third District, who sent her to the workhouse. The next day the *Picayune* observed, "Since Charley Smith, the celebrated female in pants, has been sent to the Work-House, another interesting female in like habiliments has been caught by the police. . . . She called herself Ellen Smith. Probably the Recorder will send her on a visit to Charley." The following year, another recorder, Recorder Fabre, fined Charley ten dollars for wearing male attire, which the recorder termed "sailing under false colors." The *Picayune* reported that Charley had returned to New Orleans after spending six months in New York. She claimed, the reporter stated, to have lived a "virtuous life" in New York, but he observed that she "is still dressed in masculine toggery and struts behind a cigar with the grace of an incipient gallant." The *Picayune* liked to blame women who cross-dressed on what one reporter called "the strong-minded women of the North." These northern women, the writer observed, "have lately elevated their ideas and skirts to a wonderful degree. Here some of the weaker sex have lately figured at one dash in breeches, several cases having been reported. Yesterday, Recorder Ramos fined Catherine Ware $10 for presuming to appear in public in man's attire." [11]

Two women who assumed male attire clearly did so as a method of economic survival. "Billy" came before Recorder Stith in 1856 for dressing as a man. She told the recorder that she had passed for a man for six years and had worked on several steamboats as a steward. She claimed never to have acted in any way to disgrace either her real or assumed sex. "Her desire to make an honest living alone prompted her to assume the breeches." Because she had not committed a criminal act, "the Recorder gallantly told her she could go. Billy is her boy name." Four years later, Minna Brown told Recorder William Emerson a similar story. When asked why she wore men's clothes, Brown stated that "she could not get along as a woman, making but small wages and not getting paid half the time." She also had shipped on a steamboat as a deck hand for the past six months and "liked it well." She stated that she was a "'good fellow' and had rather remain a man anyhow." Apparently Brown spoke from experience. In 1857 she had appeared before Recorder Stith charged with being "a loose character . . . being tight, vagrant, and abandoned." Stith had sent her to the workhouse for sixty days. [12]

One pathetic elderly woman assumed male attire to protect herself. Mary Smith, alias Mary Lynch, "a poor old haggard vagrant with but one eye," faced Recorder G. Y. Bright charged with wearing "masculine toggery." She told him that "she was a poor lone widdy," that she had just left Charity Hospital "with no one to protect her but herself." The recorder sentenced her to sixty days in the workhouse. [13]

One woman apparently dressed as a man to escape an unfortunate marriage. In 1856 the *Picayune* reported that "a sprightly female" came to New Orleans from Havana on her way to Spain. The newspaper reported that "the lady in question was married in Havana, and for some reason best known to herself, made her escape to this city in the guise of a cavalier." She foolishly entrusted five hundred dollars to one Pepe Limeño, alias José Gavino, who refused to return it to her. "A great deal of ire could be discovered in her sparkling Creole eyes as she was giving her testimony in the case, particularly when asked if she was not dressed in man's apparel when she first became acquainted with 'el Limeño.'" [14]

Some women dressed as men to avoid restrictions the law placed on them as women. In an article entitled "Wolf in Sheep's Clothing," the *Picayune* reported that police found a woman dressed as a man in a hotel "under suspicious circumstances." The woman, probably a public woman going to a customer's room, wore a "coat and breeches" to avoid detection. Recorder Clement Ramos fined her twenty-five dollars. As public women were not to frequent saloons and coffeehouses, they sometimes dressed as men to enter these establishments and drink there. The *Picayune* reported that a woman named Anna Linden traveled to New York and "donned male attire, visiting the theaters, hotels, and other public places, and passing herself off as a gentleman of wealth and fortune, under various assumed names." In 1859 several women dressed as men, "imagined that they could enjoy the prerogatives of the rougher sex, and after sundry libations in the *cafés,* became exceedingly noisy and troublesome, and were made to end their dream in the lock-up. The gallant Recorder set them free as soon as they came back to their senses, after extracting the promise that they would not attempt to assert women's rights within the limits of his jurisdiction." The reporter described the women's appearance the morning after as "droll." In 1861 Jennie Graham, "feeling like having a frolic," dressed herself in men's clothing and "went about in quest of adventures. Passing as a man, she decided to drink like one, and she became inebriated, after which she had indeed more adventures than she had bargained for, and at half-past 3 o'clock this morning, an officer capped the climax by arresting her." [15]

Public women sometimes wore male attire, and the authorities used their apparel as an excuse to arrest them and get them off the streets, at least for a while. Whether they chose to dress as men simply to flaunt convention or whether they hoped to disguise themselves and escape detection by the authorities is not indicated by the records. Newspapers regularly referred to public women as "frail." This word did not mean physically weak, as it might today, but morally weak. A "nymph" was another catchword for a public woman in the antebellum newspapers. And newspapers delighted in calling women cross-dressers "lambs in wolves' clothing" and making bad puns about them. For example, Madeline Balfour, "a frail but fair lamb in wolves' clothing, who was caught at the Lake decked out in the toggery of masculinity, was fined $5, and warned never to don the breeches again, as such conduct on the part of a woman was looked upon in the same light as breaches of the peace." Another reporter observed, "Two frail females who were found in the disguise of masculine habiliments were sent to the Workhouse." In 1857 a newspaper reported, "A fair nymph, who calls herself Jane Dunoyer, was last night found at the midnight hour, masquerading on the highways and byways in masculine habiliments." Two months later, police arrested one "Mrs. Green, who was verdant enough to don masculine habiliments, and was brought up, and after the impropriety of unsexing herself" received a fine of $10 "upon the lamb in wolf's clothing." Two years earlier, the *Picayune* had reported that "Louisa Babet, a young lady that *pants* for notoriety, was arrested . . . perambulating the street in male attire." The same year, under the headline "Mannish," the newspaper reported that "Sophia Hartman is one of the strongminded, and does not think even the Bloomer style quite significant enough of the strength within her. She, therefore, donned a complete set of unadulterated masculinity."[16]

On several occasions police arrested public women who were free women of color for the crime of "insulting a white person." As this crime could not be committed by white women, being a public woman of color meant added disabilities under the law and more harassment by officials. If a white person insulted another white person, the crime might be called assault, or assault and battery, but not "insulting a white person." Section 40 of the *Black Code* stated that free people of color "ought never insult or strike white persons, nor presume to conceive themselves equal to the white; but on the contrary that they ought to yield to them on every occasion, and never speak or answer to them but with respect under penalty of imprisonment." This warning demonstrated that lawmakers did not equate freedom with equality. The district attorney dropped some "insulting a white person" cases before trial, but if the case went to court and the jury found the person of color guilty, the fines or prison term (or both) proved minimal. Charging free people of color with insulting a white person constituted a way to let them know that they had stepped out of the bounds of acceptable racial etiquette and had to be punished for it. For example, a free woman of color, Louise Florian, called a white woman, Francisca Trystas, a "maquerelle," a French slang word for a pimp or procurer. She stood trial in the First District Court, and the jury found her not guilty. Perhaps the jury believed Florian's assessment of Trystas. In 1850 Jenny Gobet stood trial for insulting a white man, Pierre Conrolan, her landlord, by calling him "a damned rascal." Conrolan stated at trial that "she is in the daily habit of getting drunk and of receiving lewd and abandoned women and suspicious characters and of committing scandal and disturbances to the great annoyance of the whole neighborhood." This case never proceeded to trial. On several occasions, Armantine Boyard, a free woman of color, accused Mirida Gros of being a woman of color when she claimed to be white, which Gros considered a great insult. The same year, Mary Murdley accused a notorious public woman of color, Emily Eubanks, of being "a whore, a damn bitch, and other improper names." This case never proceeded to trial. The following year, a public free woman of color, Fanny Palfrey, insulted Theodore Blanchet, calling him "a white rascal, a thief and a swindler." Although she called him these names twice in two hours, she pleaded not guilty at trial. The judge found her guilty and sentenced her to one week in the parish prison. In 1855 Isaac Meyers, a white man, accused a free woman of color named True Love of using "the most vile and indecent language" to him, saying to him, "You are a damned black negro [sic] son of a bitch—a damned loafer." The district attorney dropped the case with a nolle prosequi (no prosecution) before trial, probably because Meyers dropped the charges. [17]

A nolle prosequi was a legal action in which the district attorney or prosecutor dropped the charges before the trial began and released the accused. Reasons triggering a nolle prosequi varied: the accuser withdrew the charges, no witnesses appeared to testify to the alleged crime, or not enough evidence existed to secure a conviction.

Quite often police arrested public women under the vagrancy statutes, even though most of these women clearly had places to live. Louisiana law defined a vagrant as an idle person who had no visible means of support and whom police found wandering about in public places such as groceries, beer houses, sheds, barns, uninhabited buildings, or in the streets. The definition also included habitual drunkards whose families complained about them. Most public women had residences, if only a rented room in a boardinghouse, and they did have a means of support, although not one considered honest or acceptable. Nevertheless, the New Orleans police picked up a steady stream of women whom they accused of vagrancy and brought them before the city's recorders. These charges constituted another method of temporarily getting public women out of sight, and the fines they paid amounted to a kind of sin tax, although city officials never referred to them as such. Arrests of women and men for vagrancy during the 1840s and 1850s became so common that the courts printed forms charging people with vagrancy, leaving blanks for the clerk to fill in the name of the vagrant and the date of arrest. [18]

Recorders sent a few women to the workhouse for vagrancy on valid grounds. For example, under the title "Cyprian Exiles," the newspaper reported that three "tattered and miserable looking women arrived on the Mobile boat yesterday, and were immediately arrested as vagrants." The women claimed that the Mobile authorities had expelled them and sent them to New Orleans. "Small favors are thankfully received and ought to be returned two-fold. What say our Mobile brethren? Shall half a dozen of our Workhouse beauties take their flight for Mobile Bay?" Recorder Webster

Long sent them to the workhouse for two months. Four and a half months later the mayor of Mobile sent a woman named Mary Sullivan to New Orleans. City authorities promptly sent her back to Mobile. One woman, Margaret Thorewith, went in desperation to the First District police station and asked that, "as she had no means of making a living," she be sent to the workhouse. The recorder obliged her with a sentence of ninety days. Aside from the fact that this sentence allowed her to live for ninety more days, one wonders how her condition could have improved upon her release. In 1852, Mary Miller, alias Mother Miller, "having no home, was furnished one in the Workhouse." [19]

Although some women arrested for vagrancy deserved the charge, city authorities often arrested public women as vagrants in response to outraged citizens' complaints or to harass the women and get them off the streets, even if only for a short time. The fines paid by these women enriched the city treasury. Often these women had well-known and talented legal representation, as the real estate owners who collected high rents from public women had a vested interest in getting them out of the workhouse and back to work as quickly as possible. Obviously, these women could not make any money to pay their rent while in the workhouse or the parish prison. For example, the *Louisiana Courier* reported under a headline of "The Cyprians": "The batch of disorderly females lately sent to the Workhouse by Recorder Blache, have sued a writ of *habeas corpus* before the Third District Court. . . . Col. A. P. Field is their attorney." Field had come to Louisiana from Illinois, where he had served as attorney general. He opened a law office in New Orleans and became one of the leading criminal defense attorneys in the city. He became attorney general of Louisiana after the Civil War. [20]

At times recorders charged public women with vagrancy but changed the charges when an attorney presented evidence that the women had residences. For example, the *New Orleans Daily True Delta* reported that ten "lewd and abandoned women" faced charges of vagrancy. After they proved that they had a place to live, the recorder fined them five dollars each for going to a grog shop in contravention of city ordinances. The *New Orleans Daily Crescent,* in reporting the same incident, stated that "Col. Field contended that the charge of vagrancy could not be sustained as the women had residences." Another case of women charged with vagrancy and represented by A. P. Field involved four "lewd and abandoned women," Catherine Yerger, Sophia Harper, Augustine Lambert, and Madelena Shorrell. Recorder Emile Wiltz had sent three of the women to the workhouse for three months for vagrancy and fined Shorrell fifteen dollars. The police officer who brought the women to the recorder testified that they lived in two houses on Burgundy Street between Bienville and Customhouse streets. He stated that the women "disturb the peace and create scandal in the neighborhood." Field contended that their imprisonment constituted an illegal and unjust violation of their constitutional rights, and he argued that the charge against them "is vague, uncertain, and insufficient to have justified their arrest." Field filed for a writ of habeas corpus. The judge of the Third District Court of New Orleans promptly discharged the three women. [21]

In 1848, Margaret Johnson sued for a writ of habeas corpus in the First District Court through her attorney, James Brannan. She claimed she could not be charged as a vagrant because she had a place to live. The judge ordered her release from the workhouse. Two other women, Elizabeth Grany and Josephine Acker, sued for a writ of habeas corpus after being charged with "being disorderly, lewd, and abandoned women." The recorder had fined them twenty dollars and, when they could not pay, sent them to the workhouse. They sued for a writ of habeas corpus, claiming that they "were illegally held in imprisonment." Judge John Larue of the First District Court ruled that "the forms of law had not been observed" and ordered their release. Ellen O'Keefe and Ann Hundly won release from the workhouse from the judge of the Fifth District Court on the same grounds in 1855. The same year, the *Picayune* noted the arrest of "fifty frail nymphs of Burgundy and other classic streets [who] were up on charges of following lawless avocations. . . . The Recorder, however, thought the charges . . . of too vague a nature, and so dismissed them." The reporter noted, "Such an array of frailties however filled the lobbies of the Recorder's office with a crowd of masculines . . . and when the result was announced, the accused and their friends rejoiced exceedingly." In 1860, A. P. Field once again sued for a writ of habeas corpus, this time for three dozen public women arrested as vagrants. The judge of the Third District Court released the women from the workhouse. [22]

One woman, Mary Ann Norman, successfully refuted a charge of vagrancy. Recorder Bright had committed her to the workhouse for one month for vagrancy. She proved that she had a place to live and, moreover, that she could support herself by honest means. She asked for a trial in the First District Court to prove her case. After hearing the testimony of witnesses, who said she kept house, did not "run about in the night," and "was taken in her own yard," the judge released her. Her landlord, who kept an oyster saloon next door, testified that she paid her rent regularly. Clearly the police has mistakenly believed her to be a vagrant. [23]

The *Picayune* described public women accused as vagrants with a variety of colorful language. Under the headline "A Shocking Vagrant," the newspaper reported that Mary Ann O'Brien, alias Lyons, alias Nolan, faced charges for "disturbance, scandal and being a vagrant." Margaret Reynolds, Mary E. McCann, Catharine Buckley, and Mary Campbell faced charges of being "confirmed vagrants." The newspaper described "Mary Hook, a hooker, Mary Ryan, Eliza Williams, Lizzy Hughes, Sarah Connelly and Henrietta Abyse" as "incorrigible vagrants." "Pittsburgh Mary" also received the description of an "incorrigible vagrant." A reporter described other women as "idle, worthless, vagrant and disreputable," others as having "vagrant tendencies," still others as "vagrants in the worse sense of the term," and another as an "obscene vagrant."[24]

Since prostitution itself did not fall under criminal statutes, police arrested public women on a variety of related and unrelated charges: for obscene language, indecent exposure, cross-dressing, and, the least related, vagrancy. The police force proved inadequate to suppress prostitution, even if politicians, real estate owners, and shopkeepers had truly wanted a serious effort made to eliminate or even curtail the proliferation of public women and their establishments. What police did resulted in mild and occasionally severe harassment, but not a genuine attempt to stop prostitution.

2

"DISGUSTING DEPRAVITY"

Sex across the Color Line

Sex across the color line in antebellum New Orleans was much more common than one might suppose. Recent scholarship has indicated that antebellum society, while not approving of sexual relations between the races, had a good deal of tolerance for these relationships. However, this research did not include New Orleans, where interracial sex (referred to at that time as *amalgamation*) often generated comment, disgust, and punishment. The Louisiana *Civil Code,* though it prohibited marriage between free people of any color and slaves and between whites and African Americans, did not forbid interracial sex. Nevertheless, couples engaging in sex across the color line found themselves prosecuted under general ordinances prohibiting gatherings that included white people and African Americans. Usually people charged with these offenses appeared before the recorders, who issued fines or whippings depending on whether the accused was free or slave. The people who were charged were almost always white women and black men, not because white men did not have sex with black women but because white men were generally protected from this kind of publicity.

Often white men in New Orleans had two families, a legal white one and a secret or not-so-secret one of color. By the antebellum period, these relationships had become institutionalized as plaçage, a form of concubinage in which a white man provided a house and support for his mistress and any children that might result from the liaison. Because the law generally pro-

tected white men and hid their indiscretions, concrete evidence of these relationships is scant, but some does exist. One of these arrangements came to
light in the trial of a free man of color, Victor Jourdain, who faced charges
of assault with a deadly weapon upon J. J. Krauss, a white man. The *New
Orleans Daily Picayune* described Jourdain as belonging "to a wealthy colored family, but slightly tinctured with Ethiopian blood." Jourdain had expressed his fury at Krauss, who he claimed had secured the affections of his
sister. Jourdain asserted that Krauss had promised to take his sister to France
and marry her. However, Krauss took her to live with him in New Orleans
"without any antecedent formality." Of course, Louisiana law would not
have permitted them to marry. Krauss's actions infuriated Jourdain. The
two men met on St. Peter Street, "and after a show of hostile gestures," Jourdain drew a loaded cane and struck Krauss. A struggle for the cane ensued.
Krauss got possession of the cane, and Jourdain drew a knife but was himself
wounded in the shoulder while Krauss fought to get the knife. According to
the newspaper account, Recorder Clement Ramos sent Jourdain to the First
District Court for trial, but no record of this case exists.[1]

Court records and newspaper articles do occasionally reveal relationships
between white men and African American women. In 1854 Mary Miller, a
white woman, charged her husband, J. O'Brien Miller, with bigamy, claiming that he had been married to a woman named Emma before her and
never divorced and, furthermore, that he had gone back to his first wife.
J. O'Brien Miller's defense consisted in claiming that he had never married Emma, and he produced Emma in court, heavily veiled, to prove his
claim. She raised her veil and revealed her face to the gasps of the spectators,
who could immediately see that "her face presented unmistakable evidence
of African descent." Emma's sister testified that Emma had African blood,
and another witness testified that she knew Emma's mother to be a woman
of color in Rapides Parish. Unfortunately, this case record has disappeared,
and only the newspaper account survives. However, as the *Civil Code* prevented whites and blacks from marrying, one assumes that the charge of bigamy failed because J. O'Brien Miller could not have legally married Emma.
In that case, Mary Miller would have continued to be married legally to
J. O'Brien Miller.[2]

A nonconsensual sexual relationship between a white man and an African American woman, this time a slave, surfaced in an 1858 lawsuit for libel
brought against J. P. Abrams by an attorney, A. J. Baer. Baer accused Abrams
of alleging that Baer "was in the habit of coming into Abrams's yard and
debauching [Abrams's] slave, who subsequently ran away." Abrams counter-

sued for the recovery of the slave or her value. Baer strenuously denied the charges. He filed an affidavit with the Fifth District Court stating, "This lye [sic] bill [was] contained in an answer to a petition filed by me against J. P. Abrams. The lye is that I am charged with debauching a slave of J. P. Abrams." This case record has not survived, so the outcome remains uncertain. However, the First District Court of New Orleans jury did render a criminal conviction against Baer for stealing a slave and aiding a slave to run away in that same year. Baer's appeal to the supreme court failed to reverse the conviction, and he went to prison for five years at hard labor.[3]

In another example, a white man named Prosper went before the recorder of the Second District and complained that his wife was drunk and disturbing the peace. The recorder dispatched a police officer to arrest her, and when he returned with her, the *Daily Picayune* noted "she was as black as the ace of spades." She gave her name as "Madame Prosper" and claimed to be married to Prosper, but under Louisiana law, the couple could not have been legally married because the law forbade marriages between the races. Sometimes the *Picayune* commented on relationships between black men and white women. In another article, a reporter for the newspaper wrote that Pauline Millas had accused a free man of color, Edmond Duval, of making "an indecently free use of his hands on her." The reporter archly observed that as Duval could not make bail, he "was sent where he will not be free to indulge in such freedoms, at least for a time."[4]

The following year, under the headline "Outrageous Depravity," the *Picayune* reported an incident in which a white man attempted to force himself on a free woman of color "as black as any of her ancestors . . . and old enough to be a grandmother for ripe men . . . he made advances to her, to which she replied, 'Go white man, I'se old enough to be your grandmother.'" He persisted and managed to throw her down, but her screams attracted assistance and he ran away. The recorder issued a warrant for his arrest.[5]

There are dozens of instances in which white women and African American men, free or slave, charged with "amalgamation" came before recorder's courts. Although the *Picayune,* in reporting an affair between a white woman and a slave, commented that "these occurrences are very rare," the newspapers' own pages and numerous court records prove the contrary. Often the newspaper reporters commented on the ugliness of the white woman involved, as if to give an explanation for a white woman lowering herself to have a relationship with a black man. For example, in 1852 "a miserable wretch named Ellen Gaines" and a slave named Ben received punishment for living together, "and the woman had the audacity to avow the connection." Ben received twenty lashes, and Gaines went to the workhouse for six months. The following year, the newspaper commented on Caroline Wilson, who associated with slaves, "The vile habits of this beast of a woman are too disgusting to relate." In 1853 Recorder Ramos fined Elizabeth Morgan fifty dollars "for indulging in habits of amalgamation of a disgusting character." Margaret O'Brien, described as "a coarse, degraded looking white woman," and a slave named Ned faced a charge of living together as man and wife. Margaret went to the workhouse for six months, and Ned received a whipping. The *Picayune* used an atrocious pun to describe Mary Lavelle, who also spent six months in the workhouse "for sinking to the level [a word play on her surname] of her status by indelicate familiarities with a negro." And in 1859 Recorder Henry M. Summers sent both Mary Griffin, "a horrible looking specimen of a white woman," and Nicholas Lanaux, a free man of color, to the workhouse for six months for "practicing amalgamation in a den on Dryades street." The same year, under a headline of "Amalgamation," the *Picayune* reported that Julia Hodges, a white woman, "took a fancy to a copper-colored beau . . . without reflecting that the laws of Louisiana do not admit such immoralities." Hodges went to the workhouse for six months, and her "dark gallant" received a fine of twenty dollars. Ordinarily whites and free blacks received fines and time in the workhouse for these offenses; slaves received whippings unless their owners paid the fine for them.[6]

At times the New Orleans newspapers seemed to delight in reporting these relationships. For example, in 1854 the *Picayune* reported that police arrested a slave named Frank and a "degraded white woman calling herself Mary Kinsella" for living together in a house on Burgundy Street. "The new Othello and Desdemona were locked up to await the punishment of their offence."[7] Three years later the newspaper reported that New Orleans police found Alice Crawford, "a dyed in the wool vagrant[,] suspiciously in company with a negro. . . . Her colored companion was of the darkest type of human kind." In a similar instance, an Irish woman named Margaret Beard and "a negro slave as black as the ace of spades" faced the recorder charged with "improper intercourse." The same year, Catherine Mannacks had to go to the workhouse for three months for being "found in bed with a negro." In 1854 a free man of color, F. Deda, a barber, faced charges along with Catherine Markey, a white woman, for "being more intimate than the law allows." Sometimes neighbors who observed interracial relationships reported them to authorities. For example, in 1858 W. J. Freret reported his neighbor, Catherine Manning, "for amalgamating and incorrigibly vagrant tendencies." Recorder Gerard Stith sent her to the workhouse for six months. In 1860 the *New Orleans Daily Delta,* under a headline that read "An Ace of Spades and His Lily White Wife," reported that Henry Wilson, a cook on a ship docked in New Orleans, "is married to an Irish woman who serves as the stewardess on the vessel."[8]

Under the headline "Practical Amalgamation," the newspaper reported that the police had found Jane Todd, a white woman, and Thomas Renny, a free man of color, in bed together in her house. Recorder Ramos fined them both fifteen dollars. The following year Margaret Murray, "charged with general depravity and amalgamation," tried to escape arrest, but police caught her. The record does not indicate her sentence. The newspaper also reported the fixing of a trial date for "the amalgamation case of Margaret Nolan, a wicked looking *Irlandaise,* and John Parker, f.m.c. [free man of color]." Police arrested Margaret Maher "for indulgence of the vagrant comfort of taking a drunken snooze in a cotton pickery with a negro man." The newspaper observed, "Margaret will have to suffer for this. Recorder Adams does not allow such characters to pollute the Garden District."[9]

As we saw in some of the cases mentioned earlier, not only did a number of white women have occasional sex with black men, slave and free, but many actually lived with black men. In 1855 the *Daily Picayune* published a list of crimes committed in March of that year. It listed two females under "white persons cohabiting with males," and one male under "negroes cohabiting with white persons." For example, under the headline "A Degraded Woman," the newspaper reported that "a white woman named Charlotte . . . who is in the habit of disturbing the whole neighborhood by her riotous conduct . . . lives in a state of concubinage with a free negro named Eugene Warlung." Police arrested both of them. In 1858 a free man of color named S. Molar, who "lived in a house on Perdido street with a white woman named Margaret Golden on particularly intimate relations," faced the recorder charged "with malice aforethought." The recorder found them guilty and sentenced both to the workhouse for six months. The following year, Ann Smith, "an amalgamation vagrant who cohabits with a negro man," also received six months in the workhouse. The following month the *Picayune* noted that "only one little bit of scandal was created" by the arrest of Clement Purcell, a free man of color, and Anna Smith, "a lily white daughter of the Emerald Isle, charged with living together, contrary to the statutes." The reporter archly stated that "the Recorder disposed of them, but whether he sent them to Massachusetts, or to the Workhouse, we did not exactly learn." In another sarcastic article, the newspaper reported that

Stephen Nelson, a free man of color, and Josephine Smith, a white woman, "forgot that they lived south of Mason and Dixon's line, and agreed to cohabit as man and wife." Their "vagrant habits" brought them into court; both received six months in the workhouse.[10]

Evidence of sex across the color line also came to light when a white woman bore a mixed-race child. In July 1852 an Irish woman named Ann Cassidy faced Recorder Peter Seuzeneau charged with "having harbored, concealed and lived" on Love Street with a runaway slave named John Johnson, the property of Mr. E. Canon. The article began with the headline "A Wretched White Woman." When arrested, she had a mixed-race child with her, upon whom she "bestowed . . . all the endearments of a mother." When asked how long she had resided in New Orleans and whether Johnson fathered the child, she answered that she had been in New Orleans seven years and that the father of the child was a "Spanish man," who left her to go to Mexico. The reporter noted that she appeared pale and consumptive. "She appears intelligent, her manner is quiet, and she has evidently been good looking. . . . There is only one other instance of a white woman having so debased herself in this city, and the issue of her unnatural connection still lives and claims to inherit from his mother the privileges of a free white citizen." The newspaper described Johnson as "a stout negro, dark as ebony, and about as ill favored a specimen of the *genus homo* as one can see anywhere." Three months later, Cassidy faced Recorder Joseph Genois on the same charge. The newspaper reporter commented: "She must have been living in this way for several years, as she had a mulatto child, three or four years old with her." Surprisingly, Recorder Genois released her, "there being no law to punish such a crime."[11]

While investigating the case of Cassidy and Johnson, a deputy sheriff told police that he knew where another mixed-race couple lived. Recorder Seuzeneau ordered an inquiry, and police found the couple living together in a house on Bagatelle Street. The newspaper commented: "The Recorder considers that such connection is a violation of good morals and public decency, but we know of no law which imposes a penalty on the offending parties."[12]

Later in 1852 a free woman of color, Elizabeth Noel, charged with killing a mixed-race infant, cleared herself by implicating the real mother of the baby, a white woman named Margaret Brennan, in the crime. Noel testified that four weeks before, Brennan had come to her house with a newborn mulatto infant to which she had given birth. She rented a room from Noel, but eight days later she left Noel's house, leaving behind her baby, who appeared to be injured. Noel brought the child to a physician, who informed her that the injuries were such that the child could not live. The infant died soon after. When questioned, Brennan admitted that she was the mother of the baby. No record exists of a trial for Brennan. Another white woman, Catherine Rutledge, charged with stealing a mixed-race child, admitted that she was its mother. The court dismissed her, satisfied that the child was hers.[13]

In one instance a charge of blackmail revealed sexual improprieties between a slave and a public woman. Louisa Niles, "a frail but fair young lady of No. 76 St. John street," charged a policeman, William Tennant, with extortion. She claimed to have been sitting in a public carriage waiting for an assignation when the curtain in her carriage dislodged and she asked the slave driving the carriage to enter the carriage and reposition it. According to Niles, while the slave was fixing the curtain, Tennant spotted the pair together in what he believed was a compromising situation, and for his silence he demanded ten dollars from the slave and from Niles her gold watch, valued at twenty-five dollars. Although Louisiana law prohibited slaves from testifying against whites or free people of color in court, other testimony proved that the slave gave the watch to his master, claiming that Tennant had given it to him. As the slave "is of notoriously bad character, and may have received it from someone else, this was not accepted as evidence." Tennant enlisted three witnesses, all fellow policemen, to establish that he could not have been anywhere near the carriage when the incident occurred. But the most telling testimony came from Paul Burges, who kept a coffeehouse next door to Niles's residence. Burges testified that "Miss Louisa is in morals no better than she should be, and that he would not believe her under oath. Catholic priests," he went on, "and coffee-house keepers were very much alike . . . as far as being repositors of secrets was concerned." He testified that often men coming from Niles's establishment "had lately left the amorous arms of the handsome plaintiff," and often she confided in him "with how much pecuniary profit she had played the hypocrite of love with certain silly youths or gray-haired lechers." At this testimony, Niles flew into a rage and told the court that she could reveal some illegal activities of Burges in selling liquor to slaves. There is no record of further action of this case; Niles probably dropped the charges. It is not indicated whether she ever recovered her watch.[14]

Often evidence of sex across the color line surfaced when one party or the other was accused of a crime. For example, a free man of color named Crick, a British subject, stood accused of aiding and abetting a runaway slave and also being in the state in contravention of the law. The newspaper noted that Crick "had a white wife." In 1855 the First District police recovered $212.50 in stolen money from a man identified only as Joe and later found $1,700 under a brick in his room. The article does not make clear whether Joe was a free man of color or a slave. In searching his room, the police found that Joe had been living with a white woman, Mary Riley, and had purchased some new furniture, believed to have been bought with some of the stolen money. The case never went to trial. Under a headline of "Practical Amalgamation," the *Picayune* reported that police caught two "abandoned" white women living with a slave named William Jackson, who claimed to be free but who police suspected was a runaway. The women received fifty lashes and thirty days in the workhouse, and Jackson went to prison until he could prove his status as a free man of color. This is a rare case in which free white women received a whipping, a punishment usually reserved for slaves.[15]

A violent altercation between a white man, Adam Rapperlie, and a free woman of color, Maria P. Gray, revealed a relationship between the parties. Rapperlie faced a charge of assault with a dangerous weapon after he cowhided Gray and then stabbed her with a sword. In the fight, Gray had a small pocketknife, with which she gave Rapperlie a superficial wound. The account of the incident stated that the pair had been living together "on terms of affectionate intimacy, but the relationship dissolved. They met by accident on Rampart street, and after harsh words, Rapperlie proceeded to use a cowhide on her." His case went before the First District Court of New Orleans, but the records do not indicate whether the matter ever went to trail. In a similar case a free woman of color, Caroline Williams, became jealous of her live-in lover, A. Q. Carey, a white man and the bartender aboard the steamboat *Princess,* and hit him over the head with a broomstick. Carey took the broomstick away from her and knocked her down, at which time she called for help to her white servant, Mary Burns. With Burns's assistance, Williams broke free and immediately drew a knife from under her bonnet. Carey ran away, and Williams could not catch him. Carey went for the police, who arrested Williams and Burns, charging them with assault with intent to kill. The records do not indicate the outcome of the case.[16]

In 1855 John Chandler came before the First District Court of New Orleans charged with murder. Chandler lived with a white woman next door to C. W. Highams, who lived with a free woman of color. The two women quarreled, and Chandler's lover reported the free woman of color to the police. This made Highams furious, and he decided to attack Chandler. First he went to Chandler's place of business, an infirmary, where Chandler worked as a pharmacist. He tried to get Chandler to fight him, but

Chandler refused. After Highams left, Chandler expressed fear to one of the physicians at the infirmary that some great bodily harm might come to him that evening from Highams. The doctor gave Chandler a pistol and, as Chandler did not know how to use it, instructed him in its use. Highams returned home and proceeded to curse Chandler and threaten him, walking up and down the street in front of Chandler's house. Chandler came home from work and sat on his steps, brazenly smoking a cigar. Highams approached him and said, "I hate a d——d coward." Chandler told Highams to go away, threw his cigar in Highams's face, and then shot at him. Highams ran away, and Chandler pursued him, shooting him again, this time fatally. The police who found Highams said that he held a sword cane in his hand and that he had a Bowie knife in his breast pocket. Chandler's attorneys claimed self defense. The trial resulted in a hung jury. [17]

Jealousy caused a slave woman who lived with a white man to kill him. Adeline, the property of Mr. Forsyth, became jealous of her lover, John Blakesly, a carpenter, and stabbed him in the back with a sword cane. He died a few days later. Police immediately became suspicious of Adeline, and she confessed the crime to police. She told the police that she would have killed them if she had as much trouble with them as she did with Blakesly. After twelve year of living with him, he left her for another black woman, telling her he would "do as he pleased," and kicked her, at which point she stabbed him and threw the sword cane down a well. The reporter observed, "There is nothing attractive about her whatever. Her dress, if not slovenly and dirty, was but little removed from it, and she looked much as any house servant just from her day's work." She stood trial before the First District Court of New Orleans. The special tribunal found her guilty and sentenced her to twenty-five years at hard labor in the penitentiary. Her owner hired an attorney to represent her at the appeal to the Supreme Court of Louisiana. The attorney, Franklin Clack, argued that her confession should not have been admitted as evidence and that the length of the sentence was unreasonable. He argued that twenty-five years constituted most of Adeline's remaining life and would consume her labor but that Forsyth could not gain compensation, since the court did not order her to be executed. Chief Judge Edwin Merrick realized that Forsyth's interests were more grounded in the monetary loss of his slave's labor than in justice. He wrote: "As the punishment of imprisonment is more merciful, perhaps, than any corporal punishment that the jury could inflict commensurate with the offence committed, the argument appears to be more in the interest of the master than the accused." Forsyth lost the appeal. [18]

Not uncommonly, the *Picayune* reported sexual relations between slaves and white women. For example, in 1854 the New Orleans police arrested Rosa McCann, a white woman, for "knowingly, wilfully, and maliciously concealing, harboring, and living with the slave Tom Peterson, belonging to F. M. Fisk." Two weeks later under a headline of "More Amalgamation," the newspaper reported that police arrested a white woman named Phoebe Moran and a slave named George, belonging to Mr. Finay, at the request of a neighbor, Mr. Dunn, who found them in bed together. "This disgusting pair" came before the recorder, who sent Moran to the workhouse for six months and ordered a whipping for George. In June 1855 "a rather good-looking young Irish woman named Theresa Lee arrived at the Third District Guard House . . . strapped to a cart." She had in her possession a letter from the overseer of the Battle Ground plantation to Recorder Seuzeneau. The letter stated that the young woman had been living in a small shed on his property and that "she had succeeded in demoralizing the larger number of the negroes on the plantation." The overseer had ordered her off several times, but she refused to leave. Therefore, he seized her and strapped her down to a cart, sending her to New Orleans to be dealt with by Recorder Seuzeneau. The recorder examined her and, finding her "totally depraved," sent her to the workhouse for two months. Four days later, under the headline "Disgusting Depravity," police found Bridget Smith and her daughter "in common embrace" with Simon, property of Overton and Bell and Sidney, the property of Captain Holmes. [19]

A great deal of evidence exists, in both the city newspapers and court records, that sex across the color line was not unusual in houses of prostitution in New Orleans, and racial integration seems to have been accepted both by the women who staffed these houses and by the brothel keepers and customers. Even slaves appeared as customers. On numerous instances, slaves actually managed brothels, turning over the proceeds to their owners. In 1849 the *New Orleans Bee* reported that the New Orleans police had arrested the slave Adeline for "keeping a house of ill fame at the corner of Frenchmen and Greatmen streets." In 1851 the *Picayune* reported the arrest of the slave Eliza for "keeping a disorderly house." Eliza came to the attention of the police because she ran a house of prostitution in which a male customer, Abraham Parker, shot and killed a white woman, Eliza Phillips, a public woman who lived in the house. The following year, Melanie, slave of R. A. Lefebre, faced charges of keeping a disorderly house on the corner of Rampart and Toulouse streets. She came to the attention of the police because she insulted and abused a white woman. The *Picayune* described Melanie as a woman "of very extensive proportions." Four months later, police descended on a "house of ill fame" run by the slave Louisa, the property of Mr. Kokernot. "The house is a resort of slaves of an abandoned character, and two slaves were found there who had passes from their owners and baskets of flowers to hide their evil deeds [pretending to be flower sellers]. Such establishments should be thoroughly broken up." Police caught two "lewd and abandoned" women, Julia Frances and Mary West, in "close companionship" with a slave named Aaron, property of Mr. Flood. In 1855 police charged Mary Short, a slave belonging to J. Green, with keeping a brothel on Perdido Street and having an illegal pass. The next month, police arrested the slaves Margaret, Patsey, and Josephine, property of Mr. Taylor, for "keeping a disorderly brothel." One month later, police caught another slave, Madeline, property of Mr. Stiles, for "committing scandal." The *Picayune* reported: "Madeline is a perfect monster: when we say she must weigh 400 pounds, and is black and ugly in proportion, we give but a very imperfect idea of this ebony fat girl." One year later, police again arrested the same slave Madeline for keeping "a house of bad repute" on Burgundy Street and two white women named Mary Collins and Mary Morrison, who "lived in Madeline's den." Recorder J. L. Fabre sent them all to the workhouse for a month. Six months later, Recorder Stith charged the slave Cassey, the property of Dr. Rivet, with "keeping a disorderly and improper house on Rampart street." In 1857 the *Picayune* reported that Mary, a slave belonging to Mrs. C. Canonge, faced charges of keeping an establishment on Lafayette Street for the "accommodation of white women of bad reputation." The same year the newspaper noted the arrest of two slaves for keeping "an improper establishment" on Franklin Street. Mary Wheeler, a white woman, faced arrest for living in that house. Another slave woman, named Ann, property of Mrs. Gaudet, also kept "a vile house" on St. Philip Street. Another Eliza, slave of D. Falzo, paid a twenty-dollar fine for keeping a disorderly house on Dauphine Street. In one case the owner of a slave who kept a brothel received punishment as well as the slave. The court required the slave Sarah to "be the recipient of a material application" [whipping] and her owner, Mrs. Bonsigneur, to pay a fine of twenty-five dollars. Finally police arrested another Ann, the slave of L. Genart, for "keeping a house of bad repute on Rampart street."[20]

In 1848, Mathilda Raymond, a white woman, came before the First District Court of New Orleans, charged with keeping a brothel. Police had arrested "four light colored negro wenches" for living in Raymond's brothel on Gravier near Phillippa Street. Raymond owned these four slave women, whom she "kept in her house for the vilest purposes."[21]

At times, free women of color ran brothels, some staffed with other free women of color, others with white women, and still others with women of both races. In 1851 police arrested a free woman of color named Suzanne, who kept a brothel for other free women of color on St. Peter Street. When police searched her residence, they found two slaves, Isaac, slave of Mrs. Hutchinson, and Caroline, slave of Mr. Fosdick, on the premises. A First District Court jury inexplicably found Suzanne not guilty. In 1855 Pierre Soulé, a respectable attorney, made an affidavit in which he charged that the house next to his on Basin Street constituted a house of prostitution kept by a free women of color. He alleged that "white and blacks meet indiscriminately and indulge in the most scandalous practices . . . that the people frequenting the house are most disorderly . . . making the night the accomplice of their vices and the time for their hellish amusements." In 1857 police arrested Mag Thompson, "a frail female of color," and another free woman of color, Martha Harris, for keeping a brothel, the former on Customhouse Street and the latter on Marais between Bienville and Customhouse. During the same year Recorder J. Solomon ordered "a lot of colored frailties" fined five dollars for causing a row in their brothel. Rose Morris, a free woman of color, kept as boarders in her house "certain white women of a lewd and abandoned character." The recorder fined Morris fifty dollars and the white women twenty-five dollars each. "The amount was promptly paid, and the females went their way rejoicing." One white man, William Gottz, kept a brothel staffed by three free women of color and one slave prostitute. Police booked Gottz for keeping a disorderly house at 14 and 16 Franklin Street and the women for being the "scandalous inmates" of the houses.[22]

Spanish law had a specific stipulation unrelated to *coartación*—the practice of allowing slaves to purchase their freedom—that held that placing a slave in a brothel where her master could make a profit from her meant that the slave would automatically gain her liberty. This benefit disappeared under American rule, and evidence exists that slaves often worked in brothels as prostitutes in the period before the Civil War. For example, in 1857, police arrested "three free darkies and four slaves" in a disorderly house on Bienville Street. The free blacks had to pay a fine of twenty-five dollars and the slaves "in an other manner [whipping]." Sophia, the property of Laurent Millaudon, a prominent New Orleans businessman, had to pay a fine of twenty dollars for violating "the lewd and abandoned ordinance." The most unusual evidence of a slave living in a brothel was an advertisement for a runaway slave named Emey, property of the widow of E. Louis Lebeau. Emey's owner described her as "5 feet high, pretty stout, has no eyebrows, teeth all decaying, stutters when spoken to, a very good seamstress; she is supposed to board in one of the prostitute houses in this city."[23]

Perhaps the saddest case of a slave being forced into a life of prostitution is the case of the slave Carmelite, who sued for her freedom in 1850. Carmelite had originally belonged to a free woman of color, Françoise E. Doubrère, whose child she nursed with great care through a serious illness. After the child recovered, Doubrère sold Carmelite to Jean Lacaze for eight hundred dollars with the stipulation that he would free her after seven years. Lacaze, an unscrupulous businessman and a brothel owner, first took Carmelite into his home and lived with her. Witnesses testified that Lacaze and Carmelite slept in the same bed. After a time he grew tired of her and brought another slave woman into his home as his "wife." He then put Carmelite into his brothel to work as a prostitute. Witnesses testified that they had seen Carmelite dancing "in a complete state of nudity" with white and black men. After seven years, Carmelite sued for her freedom under the terms of the act of sale. The *Civil Code* required slaves to have been of good character for at least four years prior to the manumission. Lacaze objected to manumitting her; he claimed that because she was a prostitute she obviously did not present a good character. He had her shackled and put in prison for safekeeping. Testimony at trial indicated that Lacaze had put her in the brothel "for profit" and corrupted her mind and character. At the trial level, Carmelite won, and Lacaze appealed to the Supreme Court of Louisiana. The high court reversed the decision of the lower court, even though Lacaze had purposely caused her to have a bad character. As Chief Justice Eustis wrote in his decision: "We cannot permit a man to falsify his title by his own infamy . . . the question before us is one exclusively of property, and must be determined according to the rules of law." Carmelite remained Lacaze's slave and probably continued to work as a prostitute. [24]

Often court cases and newspaper articles give evidence of racially integrated houses of prostitution. In *State v. Reynolds, f.w.c.,* Eliza Reynolds, a free woman of color, stood trial for "keeping a brothel." The affidavit against her stated that Reynolds "was in the habit of receiving disorderly persons both white and blacks [*sic*], slaves and free, who were in the habit of committing scandals and of disturbing the peace and tranquility of the neighborhood . . . last night a number of free persons of colour, a white man, and several colored women were committing some noise." As soon as they saw police officer Ferrari coming, they scattered and could not be caught. The incident occurred on 24 July 1846. The court record indicated that numerous attempts by the sheriff to find Reynolds to bring her to trial failed. She probably left town or at least moved her residence. [25]

One day later the same police officer arrested Ferdinand Sanadet for keeping a brothel. Officer Ferrari entered this brothel, located on the corner of Burgundy and Customhouse, and found slaves acting as prostitutes in the house. He also found two young white girls, about ten and twelve years of age. A witness stated that the girls had been "taken to the house to sleep with men." He also found four or five white men and three or four black men in the house, who escaped. Despite the strong evidence, the district attorney dropped the case with a nolle prosequi on 9 September 1846.[26]

In 1852 the *Picayune* reported the arrest of a free woman of color, Caroline Long, for keeping a disorderly house on Burgundy, between Customhouse and Bienville. The policeman who entered the house found four women, two mixed race and two white. Long claimed that the two women of color were her slaves. One of them claimed to have come from Mobile and had been placed under Long's charge. No trial record exists of this case.[27]

In 1853 the *Picayune* reported the arrest of two public women, "Sugar Mary" and Adeline Duncan. Catherine Williams, another prostitute, told the police that the two women had "been in the habit of provoking and insulting her in terms too gross for the modest regions of Burgundy street." Williams particularly charged Adeline with insinuating that Williams "was indifferent to the race of the purchaser of her embraces as she is easy in her virtue." The reporter archly suggested that the recorder would no doubt settle the disputes between the "fair rivals with characteristic wisdom and sagacity." In 1855 police arrested a runaway slave named Ben, the property of Mr. Brown, in a house occupied by three white women, with whom he was drinking, gambling, and shouting. The arresting officer stated that as near as he could tell, "the whole crowd lived together in a disgusting state of filth." Police arrested Ben as a runaway and arrested the women for "harboring" him.[28]

A notorious public woman, Emeline Gibson, a free woman of color, pressed charges against John Whitlow for breaking up the furniture at her brothel on Customhouse street. Three other men had smashed all her furniture just the year before. The reporter for the *Picayune* showed no sympathy for Gibson, commenting, "She keeps a vile and amalgamating den, which should be 'abated' as a nuisance." Five months later, Gibson, whom the newspaper described as "a free and fair female of color," faced charges of attempting to choke a white woman who worked for her. At Jane Luck's brothel, also on Customhouse Street, police found "all the females being colored and the males amalgamating whites." A fight had broken out at the brothel, and when the police arrived, the combatants turned on the police, badly beating two of them. The police withdrew, and the "soiree" went on until 3:00 AM. Violence in brothels occurred with some regularity. In 1859 police found George W. Duval suffering from serious and probably fatal stab wounds he received in a "house of ill fame" on Customhouse Street. The police arrested the inhabitants of the brothel—three white men, one white woman, three slave women, and two free women of color—as being implicated in the stabbing. They also found two revolvers in the yard of the premises. [29]

Other police reports published in the *Picayune* provide further evidence of sex across the color line in brothels. For example in 1857, Mary Carey faced charges of keeping an establishment at 140 Conti Street, "where colored men and white women familiarly, habitually, and unlawfully associate." The same year two white men and two free women of color paid a fine of ten dollars each for keeping a brothel where "unlawful assemblages of free negroes and slaves are allowed." A month later a "lot of white and colored rowdies, who habitually insult decent people when they pass their den on Girod street," came before Recorder Solomon. Two days later, police arrested Harriet Johnson, a free woman of color, for "keeping a brothel on Gravier street, where disreputable white women are accommodated with rooms." She paid a twenty-five-dollar fine. [30]

One of the more remarkable cases heard by a special slave tribunal involved a slave named Sam Scott, slave of Samuel Stewart. The special tribunal tried Scott for assault with intent to commit a rape but found him guilty of assault and battery and sentenced him to one year at hard labor and fifty lashes. His attorney, Franklin H. Clack, argued that the special tribunal had allowed "illegal and improper testimony" to go to the tribunal trying the case and that its verdict was contrary to law—that the tribunal had no right to convict a slave of assault and battery when the charge was assault with attempt to commit a rape. Clack requested an appeal to the Supreme Court of Louisiana, but on the same day Scott withdrew the request, asking instead that the sentence be carried out. Whether Scott's owner did not want to pay for an appeal or whether he feared that the Supreme Court would reverse and remand the case for a new trial that might result in a harsher sentence we cannot know. The alleged victim, Euphremia Willis, testified that Scott had entered her house and assaulted her as she was sitting on the sofa. He pushed her down, and in the ensuing struggle, both Willis and Scott fell on the floor. Another woman, Cornelia Charles, testified that Scott had entered her bedroom while she was asleep, raised the mosquito bar, "caught her by the wrists, held her down in the bed, forcibly kissed her on the side of the neck . . . previous to and since that time he has taken improper liberties with her and her sister, such as passing his hands over their persons, feeling them, etc. etc." On the very day of trial the two alleged victims found themselves charged with keeping a disorderly brothel, "the resort of slaves and idle persons," and selling liquor to slaves. The fact that their attorney, A. P. Field, the most prominent criminal defense attorney in the city, defended them indicates solid financial backing behind Charles and Willis. Field managed to get the brothel-keeping charges against Willis and Charles dropped without explanation, but Charles had to pay a hundred-dollar fine. The lesser charge and the relatively light sentence for Scott indicated that the members of the tribunal felt that the women were not hostile to Sam's advances and that the attempted violation of women of their reputation did not constitute a crime serious enough to condemn a slave to death or life in the penitentiary. In fact, as one historian has observed, white women caught in the act of having an intimate relationship with a black man often leveled accusations of rape to salvage their self-respect. [31]

This case first came to light when another public woman, Alice Darthenay, alias Constance LaFabre, who claimed to be a milliner and a mantua maker, went to Recorder G. Y. Bright and accused Cornelia Charles and her sister Ophremia Willis of violating the rules of public decency by "having indulged with a negroe slave, certain indecent familiarities which it is here useless to specify. This certainly constitutes a gross outrage upon public decency, the culprit being a white woman." After the recorder sent Charles to jail because she could not pay the hundred-dollar fine, Charles retaliated by charging her accuser with having sex with Sam Scott, whom the *Picayune* called a "salacious darky." She claimed that she had caught the couple in the act and that "her breasts were his." She also testified that Scott paid for her services. Thomas Jefferson Earhart, himself a convicted felon, served as Darthenay's attorney. Earhart often represented prostitutes, free people of color, and others considered the lowlifes of antebellum society. After his conviction for embezzlement, respectable people probably would have avoided him. Why the Louisiana Bar admitted him to practice a year after his release from prison remains a mystery. [32]

Although sex across the color line was viewed with disapproval and even disgust in antebellum New Orleans, it happened frequently. And the evidence in the court records and newspapers probably constitutes only a fraction of incidents that occurred; others were either never discovered by the authorities or were hidden from view, especially those involving white men and women of color, free or slave.

3

THE SEXUAL EXPLOITATION OF CHILDREN

One of the most disturbing aspects of the sex trade in New Orleans during the antebellum period was the number of children who became prostitutes or were otherwise sexually exploited at an early age. This phenomenon was hardly unique to New Orleans. One historian states that child prostitution was so widespread that it constituted a major concern in antebellum New York. Some Manhattan brothels actually specialized in prostitutes between the ages of ten and fourteen years. One source of evidence that reveals children selling themselves, being sexually abused, or being forced into prostitution in pre–Civil War New Orleans is the newspaper reports of the daily workings of the recorder's courts. The recorders heard dozens of complaints from frantic parents and other relatives who stated that their daughters or, less commonly, sons had fallen under the influence of people of suspicious and malevolent reputations. As another historian has pointed out, relations in working-class families were often troubled, and parents of poor children expected them to work and turn over their earnings to help support the family. Boys had more freedom, but prostitution was one of the only ways girls could get away from home, keep their wages, and escape parental discipline. Girls' wages for respectable work were even lower than adult women's wages, leaving prostitution as an avenue for a young girl to escape parental discipline, leave home, and support herself. For some children, as with many women, it was an issue of economic survival.[1]

The Louisiana *Civil Code* stipulated that the age of "full majority" was twenty-one. Minors in Louisiana—children under twenty-one years of age—could marry only with the consent of both their mother and father.

However, the law set the age of consent at twelve years old. Under Louisiana law, a person who had sex with a child under that age was considered to have raped the child, whether the child consented or not. In *State v. David, slave of Drake,* the Louisiana Supreme Court heard an appeal of a case in which the slave David stood accused of assault with intent to commit a rape of a white girl under ten years of age. The slave's attorney implied that, although the child had resisted at first, she had ultimately consented to the act and that resistance was an essential element in finding the slave guilty. The presiding judge held that under Louisiana law a child under the age of ten could not consent to such an act, and the slave tribunal found David guilty. The Louisiana Supreme Court agreed and affirmed the judgment. Although Louisiana law set twelve years as the age at which a young woman could choose to be sexually active, judges and recorders in New Orleans usually set the age of consent closer to sixteen years. As we will see, judges and recorders usually did not require girls who were around sixteen to go to the workhouse or return home if they were already working in a brothel. [2]

Numerous incidents of girls and young women becoming prostitutes appear in the New Orleans newspapers. For example, in 1854, a distraught father made an affidavit stating that his daughter Josephine, age fifteen, had left his house and "is at present consorting with abandoned prostitutes." He requested that she be arrested and sent to the house of refuge (a reformatory, usually for younger people and not requiring work, as did the workhouse). The same year, a father took his young daughter to the police station. He told the presiding officer that the young girl "is becoming very depraved, and he is fearful that she will become lewd and abandoned." In 1853 Mrs. Catherine Oldenburger swore an affidavit that her daughter, age sixteen, had left her home and "is concealed in a house of prostitution in Gallatin street." She asked for the brothel to be searched and her daughter returned to her if found there. The same year another young girl, age fourteen, ran away from her mother for eight days. Her mother found her "concealed in a house of ill repute." Mary Jennings, a thirteen-year-old, went to the house of refuge at the request of her mother, who claimed her daughter was "an abandoned woman." [3]

Sometimes these scenes in the recorder's courts could be quite poignant. In 1852 the *New Orleans Daily Picayune* reported that a "fair girl with a pretty face was arrested at the request of her mother, for visiting a house of bad repute. The mother, however, proved forgiving when she saw her weeping child in the Recorder's dock, and took back the wanderer to the maternal bosom." The same year Ellen Sullivan made an affidavit that her daughter, age fifteen, had wandered off and visited houses of prostitution. Following her arrest, she went home with her mother. Another young girl, age twelve, came before a recorder with her mother and stepfather, who claimed that she had been away from their house for several months and had lived in brothels. "The affliction of the mother seemed deep, and she cried piteously over the degradation of her child." The recorder said he would send her to the work-house if she left her mother's house again.

In at least one case, city officials decided that a young girl could not continue to live with her mother. One of the city's recorders had ordered the daughter of Elizabeth Piper to the house of refuge, as the mother kept a brothel in which the child lived. Piper sued for a writ of habeas corpus to recover her daughter, Catherine, but the judge of the Fifth District Court of New Orleans ruled against her, stating that Piper "was not a fit person to have custody and guardianship of her daughter."[4]

In some instances, the city's recorders refused to order teenagers accused of having become "lewd and abandoned" to either return to their mother's residence or go to the workhouse or the house of refuge. In 1856 a mother complained that her daughter had left home to reside in a "house of ill re-pute." Recorder Gerard Stith ruled that the law afforded the mother no rem-edy, as the daughter had reached the age of sixteen and had chosen her own way of life, and he discharged her. "As she left the court room, an expres-sion dropped from her lips which shows pretty conclusively that all efforts to reclaim her will prove in vain. The mother followed at a distance with big tears rolling down her cheeks." The same year, Maria Scheyer, whom the *Picayune* described as "a decent looking German woman," asked for the arrest of her daughter, Marie, who ran away six months before "for the purpose of leading a life of lewdness." She stated that she believed her daugh-ter, age seventeen, "is now concealed in a disorderly den on Elysian Fields street, known as 'Stadt Amsterdam.'" There is no record of the disposition of this case, but considering the girl's age, she probably remained in the brothel. In 1859 the *Picayune,* under a headline that read "Among the Col-ored Folks," reported that a free woman of color, Catherine Albert, make an affidavit in which she claimed that Josephine Joubert, a fifteen-year-old girl of color, "was harbored in a certain house of ill fame kept by another colored woman." She asked for the girl's arrest, but Recorder Henry M. Summers established "her right to take care of herself" and discharged her from custody.[5]

One mother blamed a slave for leading her daughter astray. Margaret Hal-ney procured a warrant for the arrest of her daughter for "walking in the way of wickedness." She also asked for the arrest of the slave Cassy, whom she accused of "teaching Mrs. H.'s daughter to walk as aforesaid." Another mother, Bridget Murphy, stabbed one John Shanolinburg with a dirk (a type of dagger) for having seduced her young daughter, Bridget Quinn. Police arrested her, but there is no record of the trial.[6]

Occasionally the parents of young boys went to the recorder to regain their sons from what they perceived to be a life of vice. Police arrested Constantine Stallberger for "abandoning his domicile, keeping bad company, and visiting places of bad repute." One year later, a parent requested the arrest of Louis Kraus, age fifteen, for "frequenting houses of bad repute, and aping the evil ways of older vagabonds." In 1854 the *Picayune* reported that a distraught father took his son, Anthony Martin, to the Second District police and requested that he be locked up, "as he had gone entirely beyond his control, and was in the habit of frequenting bad places, with dissolute companions. A sad picture."[7]

But mothers complaining about their daughters most often appeared in the New Orleans newspapers. In addition to the instances mentioned above, twenty-five more reports involving mothers asking for the arrest of wayward daughters in the 1850s appeared in the *Picayune* under headlines such as "Youthful Depravity," "A Sad Case," "An Abandoned Child," "A Bad Child," "Juvenile Depravity," "Badly Inclined," and, most often, simply "Bad Girl."[8]

In three instances, the parents of young women encouraged their daughters to become public women or at least accepted that they had done so. In one case, the father of a young girl had his wife arrested on a variety of charges, including getting drunk, beating their children, threatening to poison him, and encouraging their oldest daughter "to commence a life of lewdness." Recorder Solomon sent the mother to prison. In another instance two policemen faced charges that they had sexually assaulted Marie Auguste Vogelsang, age thirteen. Testimony proved that "she had already entered fully on a life of lewdness, and had previously had relations with one of the accused." Her parents offered to drop the charges against the two policemen if they paid the parents twenty-five dollars. In light of this development, the recorder dismissed the case. In 1858 the *Picayune* reported that Special Officer Ben Leggett had "forcibly violated the person of a German girl, thirteen years of age." The girl, Caroline Fay, testified against him in front of an "excited crowd," and the recorder set bail for a thousand dollars. The defense presented evidence that the girl could not be proved either "modest or innocent." However, the recorder sent Leggett to the First District Court of New

Orleans to face trial for attempted rape. At this point, Caroline Fay appeared before the recorder and told him "that Leggett never had anything to do with her; that she was never at his room; that her former statement was false, and she had been forced to make it by her mother in order to get money . . . that she had been criminally intimate with several persons whom she named, and that her mother had left the city and gone to parts unknown." Upon hearing this testimony, the recorder dismissed the case.[9]

Evidence exists in court records and in the New Orleans newspapers that a number of young women and girls visited or lived in houses of prostitution. The *Picayune* reported two instances in 1849 in which police found eight girls, age nine to fourteen years old, in brothels. In a case that went before the First District Court of New Orleans, Ferdinand Sanadet faced a charge of keeping a brothel occupied by several slave women. Testimony proved that every night "disorderly persons, both black and white, free and slave, are in the habit of meeting in said house and committing scandal and disturbances." Police raided the house and found two white girls, Mary Forbes, age ten, and Mary Ann Neele, age twelve, "said girls being taken to the House to sleep with men." The case never went to trial. In another incident, police took two little girls, age nine and ten, from a brothel on Customhouse Street because they believed "that [the] little girls were to become prostitutes." The recorder discovered that the girls were already prostitutes, and he fined the brothel keeper fifty dollars and sent the girls to the workhouse. In 1856 police arrested Nannoune Montignac, a free woman of color, for keeping a brothel, for threatening the arresting policeman with an ax, and for "keeping in her establishment a white girl, under age, for purposes of the vilest character." One year later, "an old witchlike female," Mary Musser, faced charges of having enticed away an orphan girl, age eleven, from a respectable family "for purposes of the vilest character." Another eleven-year-old, Christina Pauline Oride, took up residence in a brothel because her sister turned her out of doors. Two other girls, Catherine and Ellen O'Hara, faced arrest for "frequenting houses of bad repute." The newspaper warned, "Those who enticed them there may also consider their personal liberty to be in danger."[10]

Evidence abounds that young girls and women often faced enticements to become public women. This evidence appears both in court records and in the New Orleans newspapers. For example, Recorder Ramos ordered the arrest of Madame John, whom he charged with having enticed away from her mother a little girl named Catherine Murphy "for improper purposes." The recorder further charged her with assault because she beat Catherine's

mother when she went "in quest of the little wanderer." Under a headline "Abduction and Seduction," the *Picayune* printed an editorial that condemned the abduction of young girls "for the worst of purposes. . . . The
victim in one of these cases is but a little over thirteen . . . the daughter of a
widow. She was sent out to purchase a pair of shoes, and during her absence,
was enticed into a den of infamy on Gravier street, and there ruined. As yet
she is concealed somewhere. . . . The other case is that of a girl, fourteen
years old, the daughter of a poor but honest and respectable man. She . . .
was enticed away into a den of infamy by a fast clerk in a dry goods store,
and in this place her father found her." The next day the newspaper reported
that the brothel keeper who enticed her away, John Fields, alias Pappy John,
a free man of color, often enticed girls "with a view of leading them into
the ways of lewdness. It was in this establishment that one of the little girls,
else where referred to, was found by her father, after she had been seduced
by a heartless clerk." Recorder Bright, who stated that testimony proved
that Fields attracted young girls and "initiated them into the worst mysteries
of vice," sent the case to the First District Court, which dropped the case
with a nolle prosequi because no witnesses appeared for the prosecution. In
1856 Benedict Rőhm, a married man, committed an offense that the newspaper reporter considered unusual for a man of his age—he "enticed away"
a woman seventeen years of age "and induced her to commence a life of
lewdness." [11]

The *Picayune* reported numerous attempts by various people to entice
young girls into prostitution. For example, Charles Whitney faced arrest for
attempting to entice a nine-year-old girl "for supposed improper purposes."
The recorder sent him to prison for six months. Enraged by this sentence, he
"undertook to swallow a policeman, but he failed and was himself swallowed
by the Black Maria" (the horse-drawn paddy wagon that conveyed people to
jail). In 1856 Mary Page, a free woman of color, faced charges of "keeping
an establishment where young girls are enticed for improper purposes." The
same year police arrested Catherine Bowman on a charge of "keeping a disorderly den at No. 171 Burgundy street, into which young girls are decoyed,
in order to be trained in the lowest ways of wickedness." [12]

Sometimes young women left their homes and went to houses of prostitution of their own volition. Police arrested Martha Bannon for having
abducted a little girl of twelve years. The prosecuting witness dropped the
charges after authorities found the girl and determined that "she left on her
own accord." Some young women chose to leave their homes and seek refuge in houses of prostitution because of ill treatment at home. Certainly

there is ample record of children fleeing from abusive situations. In 1855 the *Picayune* reported the story of Mary Brown, who left her home because of cruel treatment by her stepfather. He had sent her out to collect some money for him, and when she found she could not, she feared returning home to his wrath. Instead, she accepted the offer of police officer Hatch to sleep in his room while he was on the night shift. The reporter noted: "She shows marks of severe cowhiding, and stated to the ladies at the House of Refuge, she could show yet more. She also shows that several teeth have been knocked out of her jaws by a blow . . . from a stick of wood thicker than an officer's staff." Her stepfather had knocked out her teeth because she had run outside for a moment to see a parade, abandoning his boots, which he had given her to shine. Sobbing before the recorder, she stated that his cruelty had caused her mother to commit suicide the year before by stabbing herself in the throat. As she lay dying, he continued to curse her. The young woman begged the recorder not to return her to "endure the cruelties of her stepfather." There is no disposition of this case and no evidence that the stepfather faced criminal charges. Since the girl's mother had died, the recorder probably returned her to her stepfather. Another young woman faced charges for being a "juvenile vagrant" for running away from her home to a brothel, though the incident seems to have been one of enticement rather than fleeing an abusive home life. The young woman's mother, Bridget McGinn, swore an affidavit that a free woman of color, Madame Young, had decoyed her daughter to a "house of ill fame on Gravier street." Her attorney pointed out that "whatever might be her frailty, she was in this case sought to be made a victim of a desperate attempt to defeat justice." The girl was a material witness in a murder case, and some people involved in the case wanted to prevent her from testifying. When she returned home, her mother beat her severely. Again, there is no disposition of this case and no evidence of criminal charges.[13]

Young women and girls sometimes faced arrest for being "lewd and abandoned." In 1852 the *Picayune* reported the arrests of two little girls, Suzanne Bryne and Mary Quin, as juvenile vagrants. "There are many such little girls straying about the city, and practicing all sorts of vice, whose arrest and confinement would be a blessing to them and the community." A few months later, the newspaper reported the arrest of Mary Ann Miller, "aged only twelve years . . . for visiting disorderly brothels." There are several other instances of authorities arresting young girls for frequenting brothels. The recorders sent the youngest of them to the house of refuge and the older girls to the workhouse.[14]

Why would young girls be drawn to prostitution? Certainly their economic situation provided a motivation. If women's wages fell beyond subsistence, children's proved even lower. Poor families expected their children to
work and contribute to the family's income—and not always through lawful
occupations. In 1852, police arrested twenty women and children for stealing goods from the levee. The *Daily Picayune* commented: "The worst part
of this habit is that the parents oblige their children to follow this means of
gaining a livelihood, thus training them up to a life of robbery." For many
girls, prostitution provided another way to escape more dangerous activities
and backbreaking labor. Girls found that they could trade their sexual favors
for a chance to live independently of their families, keep their own earnings,
and even purchase fancy clothing. One young New York prostitute stated
that she preferred the "merry" life of a prostitute to "scrubbing up in public
houses in exchange for food for her family." Even if a girl sold herself for a
shilling, she earned more in an hour than a seamstress earned in a day. Becoming a public woman freed girls from dependency on wages and from the
drudgery of domestic work. [15]

Of course, men had to demand the services of young women and girls
to support their entry into prostitution. In the nineteenth century, young
women did not usually reach sexual maturity until the age of fifteen, and
young women below that age could become prostitutes without them or
their customers fearing pregnancy. This automatic form of birth control and
the likelihood that a very young girl would be free of sexually transmitted diseases made them attractive to men. Also in the nineteenth century
many believed that having sex with a virgin would cure the man of any
sexually transmitted disease that he might have contracted, and they would
pay a premium for such girls. Of course, this practice only infected the
young woman. [16]

In the 1840s and 1850s, Mary Thompson used her cigar store as a front
behind which she sold young virgins to male customers for $250 to $500.
Her operation came into public view when she sold one Mary Fozatte to an
elderly man for $350. Fozatte reneged on the deal at the last minute and es-
caped as she was being delivered to a house of assignation. Enraged, Thompson had her arrested on the charge of stealing her own body. Thompson
pressed charges, the case actually went to court, but the judge dismissed the
case. Fozatte then brought suit against Thompson for injuring her character,
and the court awarded her $50. [17]

Salvador Viosca, a Spanish immigrant, also sold virgins. In 1852 Viosca
faced trial in the First District Court of New Orleans for "keeping a disorderly tippling house" and "keeping a brothel." Viosca managed two of

the city's most infamous ballrooms, the Globe in the First District and the Whitehall in the Third District. The prosecution described the balls held at these establishments as "Whore Balls" and "Strumpet Balls." Ordinarily the police did not interfere with the Globe, as Viosca managed it for a anonymous member of the New Orleans City Council. However, he did face prosecution for his brothels. He owned and operated four: the Sign of the Lion, the Mobile, the Pontchartrain House, and the Whitehall, all located on Elysian Fields Avenue in the Third District. Prostitution was rampant in the Third District, thanks in no small part to the leniency and semiofficial tolerance of it by its recorder, Peter Seuzeneau. This case before the First District Court accused Viosca of running a "sink of iniquity, hell's dark domain . . . [where] young girls are decoyed, drugged, and while in a state of stupefaction, their persons sold to the highest bidder—when they awake to a sum of their depredations, they are then told they can do no better—they are lost." The prosecution also referred to Viosca's establishment as a "boiling caldron of hell . . . where Satan presides over the society of the damned" over "midnight orgies," and it berated the authorities for doing nothing. Three and a half months after the case came before the First District Court, the district attorney dismissed the case, almost certainly because of political pressure. Viosca had powerful connections in high places. He also had connections in low places. The following year, the person who put up a bond for Viosca's appearance at trial, José Quintera, faced trial in the First District Court for raping Ellen Winters, whom the *New Orleans Bee* described as a "child." The four-year-old girl's mother pressed charges against Quintera. She alleged that he did "commit a brutal act upon the person of her said daughter . . . did rape her." An Orleans Parish grand jury declined without comment to indict Quintera for the act, and the judge had no choice but to dismiss him. [18]

One case of enticing a young girl to reside in a house of prostitution involved an attorney named Benjamin F. Haughton. On 29 April 1854, the father of a fourteen-year-old girl, Jacques Leon, charged Haughton with abducting his daughter, Emilie, and hiding her in a brothel at 185 Gravier Street kept by a free woman of color, Cynthia Davis. After looking for her for two days, Leon went to the brothel on Gravier Street. Davis at first told him that the girl was not in the house, but Leon said he knew she was there, and he forced his way in to rescue his daughter. Police arrested Leon for forcing himself into the house, but as the newspaper reporter commented, "It will be shown that the proceedings were only the result of his very natural anxiety to recover his child." Police arrested Davis for keeping a brothel, but the court subsequently dismissed her. [19]

One historian estimates that a full one-third of all rape cases in New York between 1810 to 1876 involved girls age twelve or under. Although the New Orleans sources do not reveal actual numbers, child rape in New Orleans occurred with some regularity. Because the city newspapers openly reported the names of the alleged victims, the young women could not escape notoriety and were thus victimized twice. At times these incidents happened in brothels, at times in family homes. In 1849 the *Picayune* reported that Cornelius Holland "enticed" Mary McLaughlin, thirteen, into a house, where he raped her. No evidence exists of a subsequent trial. In 1850, H. B. Taylor, his wife, and a slave named Pony faced the recorder for having "conspired to assault and commit a rape on the persons of Isabelle Thompson and Augusta Nesbitt, two young girls, who state that they were decoyed into the house of Mrs. Taylor, in Phillippa street, by the slave Louisa." The "scandalous conduct took place there." The recorder discharged the accused on the basis that no law existed to punish a conspiracy to commit rape, "although the evidence was strongly against them in that particular."[20]

In 1852 T. J. Bonnand, a free man of color, faced Recorder Jacob Winter on the charge of "having made a brutal assault upon a poor immigrant girl, Catherine Kennedy in his house." The newspaper reported that Bonnand, described as "a wealthy man," had hired the girl as a servant. He first showed her some "obscene prints" and offered her money before he attempted to sexually assault her. The newspaper noted that "he is an aristocratic looking genmen [*sic*], and is said to have been educated in Paris." Bonnand faced Recorder Winter on a charge of assault and battery on 17 April. No explanation exists as to why he did not face charges of attempted sexual assault. Kennedy testified before Recorder Winter that Bonnand had "seized hold of me around the body, after having first showed me obscene pictures & offering me a dollar for immoral purposes . . . accused wanted to force me by exhibit, obscene pictures, taking and catching me around the body and offering me money to accomplish his purposes." Kennedy testified that Bonnand "took hold of me violently with the view of throwing me down." No other people witnessed the incident, as his wife and his mother were in an adjoining room. "Accused asked me if I knew how to ———, and I answered no." As she attempted to get away, Bonnand got between her and the door, but she managed somehow to escape. The recorder sent the case to the First District Court, where the district attorney dropped it with a nolle prosequi without explanation. The following month, Henry Fouchemohn went before Recorder Seuzeneau and charged Charles Barthelemy, a free man of color, for attempting "to violate a negress of about age 8," the slave of Fouchemohn. Seuzeneau issued a warrant for Barthelemy's arrest, but no trial record can be found. [21]

One month later, an outraged father made a complaint to police "that a gross outrage had been perpetuated upon his daughter, a girl of twelve years, in a house on Barracks street." A free woman of color, Fedora Monk, had hired a white girl, Elizabeth Benoist, as a live-in servant. Six weeks after she began to work for Monk, she awakened in the night to find someone "tickling her about the thighs." Pedro Dalbaret seized her hands, and despite her repeated cries for help, he "violated her person and succeeded in taking her virginity by penetrating and rupturing her hymen." During the rape, Monk, her mother, her sister, and a woman named Mary Healy stood in the doorway, laughing. At one point Monk came into the room and put her hand on the child's head to silence her. Benoist accused Dalbaret of rape and the women as accessories. Police went to the house and arrested Dalbaret and two of the women. Recorder Joseph Genois sent the case to the First District Court for trial. A witness for the defense, Dr. Alcée Chartant, testified that he had examined the girl and found no evidence of penetration. Whether the defense attorney made the selection of this expert a case of expert witness shopping is impossible to determine. It is difficult to discount the detailed testimony of the child. However, six months later, the district attorney dropped the case with a nolle prosequi with no explanation, and the judge dismissed the accused. [22]

In 1856 another angry father reported that one Joseph Leclerc had "taken violent and felonious liberties with the person of a little girl about ten years of age." The father claimed the accused called his daughter into his house, "placed a handkerchief over her mouth, and violated her person." The newspaper reported rather salaciously the rumor that "the child is actually *enciente* [pregnant]." No record of a criminal proceeding exists. The same year a mother reported an attempt by her husband to sexually assault her daughter by a former marriage. Although the stepfather faced charges and the judge set bail at five hundred dollars, no record of a criminal prosecution exists. The same year, another father charged Conrad Fay with raping his nine-year-old daughter. Although Recorder Solomon sent him to prison without bail to await trial, no evidence of a trial exists. In 1858, another mother complained that James Barkus had attempted to rape her daughter, a girl of nine years, at the corner of Rampart and Perdido. Recorder James T. Monroe set bail at a thousand dollars, but no record exists of a subsequent trial. [23]

Most of the child rape cases have survived only in fleeting newspaper reports or in a few cases in which the district attorney declined to prosecute.

However, one extremely detailed and deeply disturbing case exists in the records of the First District Court of New Orleans: *State v. Vorygrumbler* (1854–55). The first page of this court record consists of an impassioned letter from jail from John Vorygrumbler, manager of the Tivoli Beer Garden on Elysian Fields Avenue, to his relatives in New Orleans. In his letter, written in nineteenth-century German, Vorygrumbler begged his relatives to "take the child away from here so that it will not serve as a witness against me." He wrote that he has been unable to eat or sleep in prison for fear of being incarcerated for life, "for which I would of course not be able to survive for even a year." He depicted himself as "lying on the bare earth" in prison, surrounded by arsonists and robbers. He offered to pay all expenses necessary to get the child out of town. The letter ended, "May the Almighty soften your hearts."[24]

Vorygrumbler must have written the letter, dated August 1854, shortly after his arrest. The *Picayune* reported the case on 1 and 2 September 1854 and the *Louisiana Courier* on 3 September 1854. Both papers briefly stated that police arrested John Vorygrumbler for raping his nine-year-old stepdaughter, Anna Elizabeth Jackaway. On 2 September 1854, the little girl appeared before Recorder Seuzeneau and charged her stepfather with multiple acts of rape. She testified that her mother lay ill in a room upstairs at the time the rapes occurred. She also claimed that she still suffered "cruel pains" from the incident. Seuzeneau sent the case to the First District Court of New Orleans on 13 September 1854.[25]

The second page of the court record of the case, dated 7 October 1854, consists of a statement sworn before Recorder Seuzeneau by the child's grandparents, who testified that Vorygrumbler's wife, the mother of the child, had offered them two hundred dollars either to take the child away to prevent her testifying, or to get her to contradict her statement under oath charging Vorygrumbler with rape. The grandparents asked the recorder to take the girl under protective custody "to protect her from any sort of violence, which otherwise will be made against her to defeat the ends of justice." It cannot be determined whether Seuzeneau acted on this suggestion, but there is no evidence that he did. The girl went to live with her uncle after she gave her testimony.

On 13 November an Orleans Parish grand jury indicted Vorygrumbler for the crime of rape. He pleaded "not guilty." In the indictment the Orleans Parish grand jury charged that Vorygrumbler "violently and against her will feloniously did ravish and carnally know." The next page of the trial consists of a motion submitted by Vorygrumbler's attorney to Judge John Robertson, judge of the First District Court, in February 1855. In it the attorney stated that although Vorygrumbler's arrest had occurred in August 1854 and his indictment in November, the First District Court had yet to set a trial date, "a novel form of imprisonment [that] is currently unknown to the Constitution and law of the Republic and of this Commonwealth." He asked for a "speedy and impartial trial."

The next pages of the court record consist of a list of eligible jurors for the trial and then a four-page statement of testimony by Anna Elizabeth Jackaway. In chillingly graphic detail, the child, described as being between three and four feet tall, told the court of not just one act of rape but a pattern of abuse that had taken place over several months. She described in great detail how Vorygrumbler had "used" her at least twenty times with his fingers and actually raped her at least twenty more times. She also claimed that she had told no one, not even her mother, about the abuse because Vorygrumbler had forbidden her to do so.

Several physicians examined Jackaway after her testimony. All found her genitals inflamed, but they could not state with certainty that a rape or numerous rapes had caused the inflammation. One of the physicians stated that the irritation might have resulted from masturbation. "Children masturbate themselves," he stated.

The Vorygrumbler case appeared to be proceeding to trial in a regular fashion when, without any explanation, the district attorney dropped the case with a nolle prosequi on 19 March 1855 and released Vorygrumbler from prison. We have no way to determine what happened. The *Picayune* noted the nolle prosequi without comment. Either someone forced the child to retract her charge, or someone removed her from the jurisdiction of the court. The New Orleans tax records show Vorygrumbler still living at the Tivoli Gardens, a property assessed at one thousand dollars, in 1856.[26]

Although some young girls chose to reject boring and backbreaking work for the seemingly easy life of a public woman, it is clear that some young women found themselves forced into the sex trade and others suffered sexual exploitation, some by family members. The city's newspapers condemned such actions, but repeated demands for reform did not accomplish much. Even the individuals who raped children seldom received punishment. And the city's newspapers' policy of publishing the names of the child victims further victimized them.

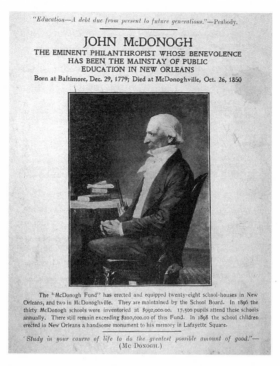

"*Education—A debt due from present to future generations.*"—Peabody.

JOHN McDONOGH
THE EMINENT PHILANTHROPIST WHOSE BENEVOLENCE HAS BEEN THE MAINSTAY OF PUBLIC EDUCATION IN NEW ORLEANS
Born at Baltimore, Dec. 29, 1779; Died at McDonoghville, Oct. 26, 1850

The "McDonogh Fund" has erected and equipped twenty-eight school-houses in New Orleans, and two in McDonoghville. They are maintained by the School Board. Oct. 26, 1896 the thirty McDonogh schools were inventoried at $992,000.00. 17,500 pupils attend these schools annually. There still remain exceeding $200,000.00 of this Fund. In 1898 the school children erected in New Orleans a handsome monument to his memory in Lafayette Square.

"*Study in your course of life to do the greatest possible amount of good.*"—
(Mc Donogh.)

John McDonogh, the "eminent philanthropist" who endowed public education in New Orleans in the antebellum era. The thirty public schools built in the New Orleans area through the McDonogh Fund were valued at $992,000 in 1896. *Courtesy Special Collections, Tulane University Library*

M Donogh's last trip and last picayune saved for the poor lawyers.

Drawing satirizing John McDonogh, who rented property to a number of brothels. McDonogh lived on the west bank of the Mississippi River at McDonoghville. When he had to contract business on the east bank, he was so cheap that he had one of his slaves row him across the river rather than spend a picayune to take the ferry. *Courtesy The Historic New Orleans Collection*

The beautiful Tivoli Gardens, managed by John Vorygrumbler, who repeatedly sexually molested his nine-year-old stepdaughter. *Courtesy The Historic New Orleans Collection*

"The Carondelet Canal Separating the Crust from the Crumb of Old New Orleans." Public women are shown on one side of the canal calling and gesturing suggestively to "respectable" people on the other bank. *Courtesy The Historic New Orleans Collection*

"A Peaceful Evening on Gallatin Street," an ironic reference to the often chaotic, rowdy atmosphere on the street known for its prostitutes. *Courtesy The Historic New Orleans Collection*

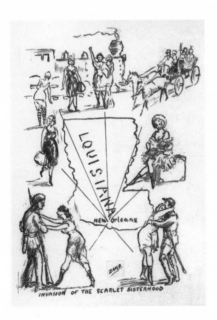

"Invasion of the Scarlet Sisterhood," a depiction of some public women plying their trade in New Orleans. *Courtesy The Historic New Orleans Collection*

John Randolph Grymes, the flamboyant defense attorney for Abraham Parker in *State v. Parker* (1851). *Courtesy The Historic New Orleans Collection*

One of the two horse-drawn paddy wagons that took public women from the recorder's courts to the workhouse, or parish prison. The wagons were called the Red Maria and the Black Maria. *Courtesy The Historic New Orleans Collection*

Gerard Stith, who served for many years as the recorder of the First District in New Orleans. He also served one term as mayor of the city just before the Civil War. *Courtesy The Historic New Orleans Collection*

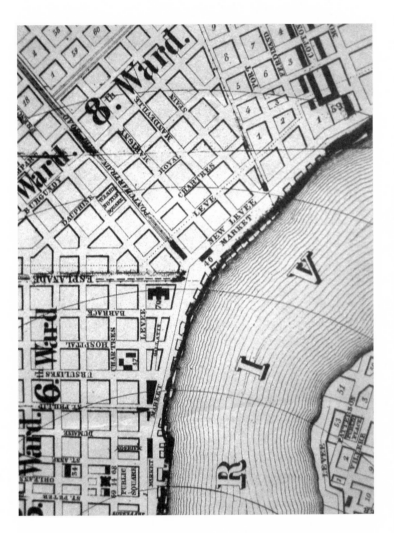

Detail of *Norman's Plan of New Orleans & Environs* (1854), showing Gallatin Street near the river. *Courtesy Special Collections, Tulane University Library*

4

INFAMOUS PUBLIC WOMEN

Antebellum New Orleans newspapers and court records reveal that many public women had nicknames or aliases. Taking a colorful name probably constituted an attempt to appear flamboyant, and aliases may also have been adopted to confuse the police as to one's true identity. Often these names identified the women with a location—perhaps where they had resided before coming to New Orleans—or they indicated some signature trait. For example, the *New Orleans Daily Picayune* and court records contain names such as "Hoozier Mary," "Charleston Pet," "Cincinnati Mary," "Boston Kate," "Irish Mary," "French Mary," "Royal Mag," "Red Mary," "Petruchio's Kate," "Irish Susan," "New York Mary," "Shell Road Mary," "Baltimore Jenny," "Biddy Ryan," and "Pittsburgh Mary." Perhaps the most inexplicable alias belonged to Ellen Flemming, also known as "Judy Come Home with the Soap."[1]

Although many public women faced arrest for various crimes and misdemeanors, several prostitutes appear in the newspapers and in the court records over and over: Delia Swift, alias Bridget Fury; sisters Emily and Nancy Mayfield; Belle Thompson; mother and daughter Emily and Elisabeth Eubanks (both free women of color); and another free woman of color named Emeline Gibson. Swift, alias Fury, a flaming redhead who had a particular fondness for stabbing men, became a prostitute in Cincinnati at the age of twelve. She came to New Orleans in 1856. In Cincinnati, she had worked as a pickpocket in the local dance halls as well as a public woman. After coming to New Orleans, she joined up with other tough and violent prostitutes, notably Mary "Bricktop" Jackson, a reference to her shock of flaming red hair, in one of the first female street gangs in the United States. Her first appearance in the pages of the *Picayune* chronicled a pattern of violent acts that would eventually land her in prison, albeit for a short time. Under the headline "Probable Murder," the *Picayune* reported an altercation on the new shell road near the lake. It seemed that four "Burgundy street women," one of whom was Delia Swift, alias Bridget Fury, got into a fight with two men. One woman slapped one of the men in the face. Angered, he struck her with a carriage whip, and "while he was so engaged, he was stabbed in the back. He received two other wounds, one in the head and one in the hip. Bridget Fury alias Julia [*sic*] Swift mortally wounded the victim." The newspaper observed that Swift had been arrested in New Orleans as a fugitive from an Ohio penitentiary, where she was serving time for having murdered a man. She remained in prison for ninety days to await a requisition for extradition from the governor of Ohio, but none came, and the court released her.[2]

The following year, the newspaper reported that Swift stabbed one Thomas J. Dolan with a sword cane in a house on Phillippa Street. Swift claimed that Dolan had choked her. The reporter noted that "frequently before she has been up on similar charges." Two weeks later the newspaper reported that Dolan had left town to avoid "the necessity of prosecuting; thereupon Delia was discharged, as she had previously been on one of two occasions when brought up for similar offences." The reporter observed that Dolan had been living with Swift in a house on Phillippa Street when the stabbing took place.[3]

Swift led a life punctuated with violence. Three months after she defeated the charge of stabbing Dolan, one James Hornsby faced charges before Recorder Lucien Adams for attempting to strike Swift, and he "threatened to terminate the existence of the celebrated Delia Swift alias Bridget Fury." The reporter observed that Hornsby "must be bold indeed who would dare attack Delia." A week later the court dismissed Hornsby with no explanation. Perhaps Swift dropped the charges.[4]

The next month, Swift and Mary McCoy came before Recorder Gerard Stith charged with having stolen ninety dollars from Hugh McKeever in Swift's house on Phillippa Street. The *Picayune* observed that Swift and McCoy had stolen the money from McKeever's "pantaloons" while he slept. "It appears that McKeever, who was a sojourner from Mobile, was verdant enough to trust himself in the same room with Bridget Fury, and while sleeping, perchance dreaming, his money disappeared." No record of a trial exists. McKeever probably dropped the charges because he did not want to go into open court and testify that he had been in a brothel or because he had returned to Mobile.[5]

By August Swift had moved from Phillippa Street to Basin Street. That month, she and Alice Cunningham faced Recorder John E. Holland charged with "keeping a house of ill fame on Basin street." Holland fined both women twenty-five dollars, after which Swift and Cunningham "complained of the frequency with which fines were imposed on them, and coolly observed that it was but little use for them to make money if it were all extracted from them in the shape of fines."[6]

In November police again arrested the "notorious" Delia Swift, alias Bridget Fury, for stabbing another man. The officer testified that she had a dirk in her possession when he arrested her. "This is the third or fourth time that Bridget has been arrested for similar offences." Then the reporter noted: "She came here originally from Ohio, and was first arrested as a fugitive from the Ohio Penitentiary." This case also failed to go to trial because the alleged victim did not appear to testify against her. Perhaps she threatened these men to prevent them from appearing against her. Recorder Stith fined her ten dollars. The *Picayune* termed her a "fast female who was mulcted $10 for furiously effulging on Basin street."[7]

In 1858 Swift moved back to her old Phillippa Street neighborhood. Police arrested her and Isabella Marshall in June for "having thrown gross abuse and rotten eggs at the person and premises of Catherine Williams, another public woman, on Phillippa street." Once more, the recorder dismissed them, as Williams dropped the charges. In August Swift, Kate Brunel, and Margaret Gilmore, "all frailties," faced charges of instigating a fight against another public woman, Belle Thompson. Swift drew a knife on Thompson and threatened to kill her. Police brought all of them to Recorder Henry Summer's court, and Thompson made a comment in open court that she should have had more sense than to expect anything like justice there. Not amused, Recorder Summers fined Swift and Thompson each five dollars. When Thompson heard his decision, she "stormed in a most gross and vulgar manner, so much that we . . . were obliged to close our ears."[8]

The following month Swift committed a crime for which she could not escape prosecution: murder. On 3 September 1858 Delia Swift, "in one of her characteristic paroxysms," mortally wounded Dennis Croan, a native of Ireland, age twenty-two, in the Poydras Market. He died of peritonitis several days later. The *Picayune* reported that as Croan walked through the Poydras Market, he made some remarks to his companions concerning "women of a certain class." Some of the women standing nearby overheard him, and one of them jumped up, saying "there is no ———— here" [whore?] and stabbed him in the abdomen. The trial transcript contained more details. Apparently a somewhat intoxicated Patrick Croan went up to Delia Swift and "her women," slapped her on the shoulder, and said: "You are my prisoner." The three women walked off toward Phillippa Street, and Croan followed, calling the women a "parcel of bitches." At this, Swift stabbed Croan. After the stabbing Croan reportedly said, "It serves me right, I ought to die. I am of no use to myself or the world." The arresting officer saw Swift drop something in the gutter and found her dagger there. Swift alleged that Croan had attacked her with a loaded cane. One of the other women, Kate Brunel, alias Boston Kate, stated that Croan had called the women "d———nd bitches and rats" and said he would burst Swift's head: "'As for you, you old slut, I would not strike you with my fists, I will burst your head open with this,' twirling the cane in his hand." He continued to follow them, calling them "old bitches." Another witness stated that Croan was leaving when Swift lunged at him, stabbing him. The *New Orleans Daily Crescent* reported the murder with this comment: "Bridget Fury has stabbed a number of men since her residence in New Orleans, but Croan is the first one she has killed. We have been told that when Bridget first came here, she was just out of the Ohio penitentiary, where she had been serving a term for manslaughter." The reporter continued with this observation: "We have seen her several times before the Recorder, and always wondered at the wildness and good-humor expressed by her face, and the politeness of her demeanor in Court. Though so smooth and smiling outside, it appears that she is in reality another Lucretia Borgia; that is a fiend incarnate when insulted." [9]

The First District Court found Swift guilty without capital punishment on 28 April 1859. She received a sentence of life at hard labor in the penitentiary two weeks later. Her attorney appealed on the grounds that the killing had been justified as self-defense. The Louisiana Supreme Court ruled that just the belief that someone is going to do one great bodily harm did not make homicide justifiable. The court affirmed the judgment of the First District Court. However, Swift did not have to serve her entire sentence. One source states that her "popularity among local politicians . . . allowed her to secure a pardon in 1862." Another source states that in September 1862 the military governor of Louisiana, George F. Shepley, emptied the state penitentiary by wholesale pardons. After her release she stayed in New Orleans for another decade, often being arrested and sent to the workhouse for public drunkenness. [10]

If Delia Swift, alias Bridget Fury, had a peculiar fondness for stabbing men, Emeline Gibson, a free woman of color, seemed to enjoy assaulting and attacking white women, although she was also the victim of violent acts directed against her. Attacking white people put Gibson on the wrong side of section 40 of the *Black Code*, which held "that free people of colour ought never to insult or strike white people, nor presume to conceive themselves equal to the white; but on the contrary they ought to yield to them on every occasion, and never speak or answer to them but with respect, under the penalty of imprisonment." [11]

In May 1850 Gibson spotted Elizabeth Williams, a white woman, passing by her Dauphine Street residence. According to a witness, Williams "without any just cause or provocation whatever . . . was grossly insulted and abused by the defendant [Gibson]." Furthermore, a witness stated that Gibson "violently assaulted her with pitchers, saucers and tumblers which she threw at her, wounding the aforesaid [Williams]." Her wounds were so severe that Williams remained confined to her bed under a physician's care for some time. Apparently this episode of flying crockery and glassware began as Williams passed Gibson's house and Gibson called her a "bitch." Williams "enquired wheather [*sic*] she was addressing her, was not only answered in the affirmative but was furthermore assaulted by the aforesaid Emeline Gibson, free woman of color, who violently struck this deponent and severely wounded her on the face with two tumblers which she threw at her." The First District Court jury found her guilty, and the judge sentenced her to four months in the parish prison and court costs. Apparently dishes and glasses were Gibson's favorite weapons. Between the assault on Williams and her trial and conviction for the incident, Gibson "dangerously wounded" another white woman, Mary Ann Mallary, "with blows from articles of crockery." No record exists of a trial in this instance. [12]

Three years later Gibson came before the First District Court once more, charged with assault and battery on another white woman, Frances Thompson, after Gibson beat her with a broomstick. This case ended in a nolle prosequi; either Thompson withdrew the charges, or the district attorney did not have enough proof to proceed to trial. The same year, Gibson faced Recorder Clement Ramos charged with keeping a brothel on Dauphine Street between Customhouse and Bienville streets. The newspapers did not report the outcome of this charge. The same month, Gibson faced charges of stealing a dress valued at ten dollars from Mary McVey. After hearing the evidence, the recorder dismissed the charges. [13]

Gibson herself fell victim to violence. Groups of men perpetrated a rash of what some historians have called "brothel riots" on her. These riots, common in New York and in other antebellum cities, sought to close brothels and put them out of business. Generally this violence aimed at destroying property, not at individual women. The "brothel bullies" sought to destroy the prostitute's property and the tools of her trade—beds, mirrors, and other furniture. Sometimes these brothel riots reflected neighbors' resentment of having the nuisance of a noisy brothel located in the neighborhood. Another historian contends that brothel riots may have been the result of excessive alcohol or male resentment of the independence of self-supporting and sexually active women. [14]

The first instance of an attack on Gibson's brothel occurred in 1854. Just after midnight on 19 August, a group of fifteen men forcibly broke into her house, smashed her windows, and destroyed all her furniture, including her piano. Witnesses heard one of the ringleaders, Victor Duprat, say, "Let's burn down the damned shanty." Another witness testified that Duprat said, "All we want is the goddamn bitch and her pimp; if we don't get them we will set the goddamn shanty on fire." Gibson stated that one of the men had placed a lighted candle under one of the beds in an attempt to set fire to her house, but she had put it out. The rowdies severely beat several women in the house, black and white, who were asleep when the riot began. When the police arrived and tried to arrest some of the rioters, the hoodlums ran them off. [15]

The recorder determined that Duprat and Charles Reeves, alias Long Charley (later murdered by "Bricktop" Jackson), were the ringleaders, and he sent them to the First District Court charged with riot, trespass, assault and battery, and attempt to commit arson. An Orleans Parish grand jury returned an indictment against them for riot only. The case came up for trial in June 1855, but the district attorney dropped the case with a nolle prosequi. There is no explanation in the records as to the sudden end of the case. [16]

The following year, Gibson had her furniture destroyed in another brothel riot, this time by one John Whitlow. As the *Picayune* reported, "Emeline is unfortunate in the furniture line, for, it will be remembered, all her effects were smashed last summer by a riotous gang." The writer commented: "She keeps a very vile and amalgamating den, which should be 'abated' as a nuisance." [17]

Gibson continued to be involved in violent acts, as both victim and perpetrator. In 1856 G. Henry faced charges of assault and battery on Gibson and also for attempting to "violently and forcibly" take possession of a slave woman who was walking with Gibson. Henry's case never went to trial. Two weeks later Gibson found herself charged with knocking down and attempting to choke a white woman who was one of her employees. The newspaper reporter referred to Gibson as "the free and frail female of color." The following month, the city newspapers reported that Gibson, "a brazen female," had knocked down and choked another employee, a white woman named Julia Donnelley, who worked for Gibson as a servant. The *Picayune* described Gibson as being "noted for assaults on white people." This case went before the First District Court, but the prosecutor dropped it with a nolle prosequi the following year.[18]

On the day after the assault on Donnelley, the *Picayune* reported that Gibson, "who is in trouble oftener than any other resident of that celebrated street [Customhouse], still has another little difficulty on her hands." The rent collector accused her of snatching the receipt for the rent from his hand and then refusing to pay the full amount owed, leaving the collector responsible to the landlord for the balance.[19]

In 1856 Gibson charged another free woman of color, Ann Thompson, with stealing fifteen dollars' worth of jewelry from her. The *Picayune* referred to her as "the notorious Emeline Gibson, f.w.c." The following year she returned to court, this time to sue the city of New Orleans for one hundred dollars for not protecting her property. Apparently she had caused a man to be sent to jail, and his friends disguised themselves and attacked her house in revenge, destroying her furniture and her piano (again). Gibson must have kept the city's furniture merchants happy, as rioters smashed her furniture with some regularity. The record of this case has been lost, so we cannot know the outcome.[20]

The same year, Gibson charged Samuel S. Smith, "the hero of a hundred police items," with shooting at her with intent to kill. Gibson claimed that Smith came to her residence and began to quarrel with one of her servant girls, named Louisiana. He pursued her into the yard and was about to beat her when Gibson ordered him off of her property. In response, he drew a pistol and stated that he would shoot Louisiana if he had a chance. He fired one shot at her and one into the parlor window. Smith alleged that he had been shot at by one Henry Philips, the owner of the brothel in which Gibson resided, and that Gibson had aided and abetted Philips. There is no transcript of this confusing case, as the record does not exist.[21]

A few months later, Gibson charged John F. Collins, alias Jack Shepard, with trying to induce a group of men to break into her house "for the amiable purpose of murdering her." They entered her house and smashed all her furniture (once more), after which they hurled rotten eggs and other putrid substances at her house, causing a fowl odor. Apparently the night ended in a brawl, as the morning newspaper reported that one man suffered a knife wound in the chest and one a gunshot wound. Others had various injuries.[22]

Gibson exhibited more of her usual behavior in 1858. In May "the notorious Emeline Gibson, f.w.c.," faced charges for "having grossly black-
guarded a white man." Four days later Gibson and Bridget Mahoney had to
post peace bonds of five hundred dollars each. At the end of May, Gibson
went once more before the recorder charged with "grossly abusing a white
woman." In June, "for gross impertinence and misconduct," the recorder
required her to pay a fine of ten dollars and furnish "solvent" peace bonds.[23]

In 1859 and 1860 Gibson appeared in court charged with fighting with
two other public women, one a free woman of color and one a white
woman. In 1859 she had an altercation with Nancy Bell on Rampart Street.
Bell and Gibson, who the *Picayune* described as "high-blooded colored ladies," fought, falling to the ground, and in the process one of them (the
paper does not say which one) bit off part of the other's lip. In 1860, Gibson
assaulted and beat Ellen Lewis, a white woman, and "tore off from her fair
shoulders a costly cape worth at least $45, which she bore off as a trophy of
her victory." The recorder sent Gibson to be tried before the First District
Court, but the case never went to trial.[24]

If Emeline Gibson lived a violent life, Nancy Mayfield and, to a lesser extent, her sister Emily gave a new definition to the word *violent*. Emily first
appeared in the records of the First District Court of New Orleans in 1849,
when another prostitute, Sarah Meyers, accused her of assault and battery.
All the witnesses in the case, all women who lived on Girod Street between
Magazine and Camp (a neighborhood in which many prostitutes resided),
testified that Mayfield had struck Meyers. No record exists of a criminal
trial. The following year, Henry Shadrick accused Emily Mayfield of "stabbing with intent to kill." Shadrick claimed that he was "unprovokedly and
dangerously stabbed in the abdomen with a knife." His wounds proved serious enough for him to go to Charity Hospital, where a reporter for the *Picayune* described him as "lying very ill." Three witnesses, all public women
(including her sister Nancy Mayfield), testified for her at trial. Their testimony has not survived, but it must have been convincing, as the jury found
her not guilty.[25]

But Nancy Mayfield far outdid her sister both in terms of living a violent
life and in the number of her court appearances. She first appeared in the
records of the First District Court in 1848, charged by Rachel Leese with
assault and battery. Witnesses testified that Mayfield came to Leese's house
and bit her on the arm "without any just cause." Leese alleged that Mayfield
"constantly threatened her life and that she is in fear of some bodily injury."
A jury found Mayfield guilty, and the judge sentenced her to two weeks in

jail. The judge gave no reason for the light sentence. Perhaps he felt that the case was simply another squabble between two public women.[26]

In 1852 Nancy Mayfield and another public woman, Hannah Kenner, stood trial for a more serious charge: assault with intent to kill. A police officer testified that he had heard Mayfield's lover, William Bonfield, alias Wilkinson, curse her and say, "I will knock Nancy's brains out." As the *Picayune* reported, Bonfield "has distinguished himself in the affairs of the Mayfield family." He had served as a witness for the state in a case in which Emily Mayfield stood accused of the murder of her lover (the case record of this trial is missing). Nancy Mayfield and Bonfield had an on-and-off relationship, and on 13 October, Bonfield went to Mayfield's house on Phillippa Street. Mayfield refused to see him, but he came in anyway and walked through Kenner's room. She called him a "son of a bitch and other epithets." She told him to get out, at which time Mayfield said, "God damn him I'll move him." Mayfield entered the room wielding a knife with an eight-inch long blade (described as a Bowie knife) and stabbed him twice in the face as Kenner screamed "stab him." Kenner armed herself with a "chandelier." Mayfield stabbed Bonfield once more and cut him twice, then stabbed him in the side. Bonfield gave her a blow, and she fell, breaking a carafe. Kenner then attacked him twice with the chandelier, cutting his coat, after which Mayfield recovered and stabbed Bonfield in the side in what witnesses descried as a "mortal wound." Bonfield attempted to leave the house, followed by Mayfield and Kenner, who attacked him again with the chandelier. He collapsed on the sidewalk, and passersby took him to the hospital. Bonfield survived, and when the case came to trial before the First District Court, Bonfield admitted to the district attorney that he had lived with Nancy Mayfield "on friendly terms" both before and after the attack, and the prosecutor abandoned the case. On the instructions of Judge John Larue, the jury found her not guilty and discharged her. Authorities later arrested Bonfield for kidnapping Mayfield's child and threatening to kill her if she did not marry him. The following year, Mary Anne Warren faced charges of assaulting and cutting Mayfield.[27]

In 1854 Recorder Jacob Winter sent Mayfield to trial for keeping a "disorderly brothel on Phillippa Street, the resort of lewd and abandoned persons." New Orleans police officers served as the only witnesses, but the district attorney dropped the case with a nolle prosequi the following year because the sheriff noted "no residence given not found [*sic*]." Between the time that Mayfield stood accused of keeping a brothel and the nolle prosequi, Mayfield went on a violent spree and found herself once again before the First District Court charged with three separate incidents of assault and battery. The first involved and assault and battery on Sarah Douglas, another resident of Phillippa Street, whom she "knocked down and cut in the head." The second charge involved and assault and battery on a police officer on Phillippa Street, who testified that Mayfield tore his clothes. In the third case, Mayfield stood accused of assault and battery on William Hite and his sister. In the melee, Mayfield smashed Hite's violin. The *Picayune* reported that Mayfield, "a woman of the lowest class," had been drunk on the day of the three incidents and "she attacked several persons with the fury of a tigress, beating, wounding and tearing them." The district attorney inexplicably dropped all three cases on the same day with a nolle prosequi. [28]

The following year Mayfield appeared once again before the First District Court, this time charged with larceny. Elbert G. Davis accused Mayfield of robbing him on Christmas Eve of a $500 bill and a $20 gold piece at the Globe Ball Room, a venue where prostitutes regularly solicited customers. Davis, the overseer of a plantation near Baton Rouge, had entered the ballroom with $600 in his pockets. He spent $80 "in treating the denizens of that place, and got exceedingly drunk." He went home with Mayfield and, before going to bed, laid his wallet on the wash stand. In the morning he found that the wallet was still there but his money was gone, and he had Mayfield arrested. The police found $100 in her possession, but he did not recognize the money as his. Presumably they were notes issued by a different bank than those that had been in his wallet. Nonetheless, the *Daily Picayune* observed, "Nancy will stand a fair chance of spending the ensuing summer in Baton Rouge" (meaning in the state penitentiary). However, when the case came to trial, Davis failed to appear to press charges, and the district attorney dropped the case with a nolle prosequi. [29]

In 1855 Peter Freeman faced charges of beating Mayfield and wounding her in the head with a knife. Several months later, Mayfield almost became a victim of violence once more when Bridget Feenan attempted to stab Mayfield with the intent of killing her. Mayfield escaped injury, however. The reporter for the *Picayune* noted that the altercation occurred because of the "insidious workings of the green-eyed monster." [30]

In 1856 Mayfield narrowly escaped being stabbed by one Peter Feenan. Attracted by her frantic cries of "murder," a police officer, George W. Place, found Feenan "engaged with one hand in holding down a courtezan [*sic*] named Nancy Mayfield, and with the other attempting to open a spring knife, apparently with intent to stab her." The officer attempted to arrested Feenan, and Feenam turned on him, striking him, choking him, and "savagely biting his hand in two or three places, with a supposed attempt to maim." Recorder G. Y. Bright sent the case to the First District Court to have Feenan answer for attempting to stab Mayfield and for the attack on the police officer. The district attorney dropped the charge of assault with intent to kill with a nolle prosequi. [31]

Less than a year later, Belle Golding, alias Lucy Loo, faced charges of stealing fifty-three dollars in gold and silver coins and bank notes from Mayfield's house on Dryades Street (the city council had changed the name of Phillippa Street to Dryades Street). The *Picayune* noted that both parties "belong to the frail sisterhood." Golding appeared before the First District Court charged with larceny. The district attorney dropped the case with a nolle prosequi, stating, "I am satisfied from the evidence furnished me that his case grows out of a whore's malevolence against one of her own frail sisterhood." [32]

In 1858 Mayfield made an additional appearance before Recorder Summers, once again for assault and battery. According to the *Picayune,* she knocked down Ellen Mahony with brass knuckles. Mayfield testified in court that she had used nothing but her "natural knuckles, and as it was in proof that Ellen had given her great provocation," the recorder fined Mayfield ten dollars for the attack by "Nancy's mauleys." Recorder Summers required Mahony to furnish three hundred dollars to keep the peace for six months or go to the workhouse for three months for "assaulting and threatening her neighbor Nancy Mayfield [with a knife] . . . to the great terror and fear of the complainant." Mahoney could not post the bond, and she went to the workhouse. [33]

Four months later, Mayfield herself was again a victim of violence when she and Mary Coulter, described as "two frail females," got into "a difficulty about their moral status." Coulter drew a knife and stabbed Mayfield in several places, the worst wound being in her thigh. Her wound proved serious enough that police took her to the Circus Street Infirmary and arrested Coulter. The *Picayune* reporter observed, "Heretofore, Nancy has had the reputation of being quite expert in the use of knives." Four days later Mayfield's physician pronounced her out of danger. "The quarrel was about a dress, which, during days of friendship, Nancy gave to Mary. Finally they disagreed, and after exchanges of words, bantered each other for a fight." Recorder Summers sent the case to the First District Court. Coulter, facing charges of assault with a dangerous weapon, pleaded guilty. Judge Randell Hunt sentenced Coulter to three months in the parish prison and the costs of prosecution. [34]

The next month, Mayfield was again the victim of violence and theft. William Wills received a sentence of thirty days in the parish prison for assaulting Mayfield on the stair leading to Recorder Summers's court. He threatened to cut her throat if she filed a complaint against J. B. Wills (his brother?), against whom she had made an affidavit for assaulting her. J. B. Wills had to post a $250 bond to appear to answer charges that he had entered Mayfield's room and stolen "sundry household linen and furniture, rings, earrings, a breastpin, etc, all valued at $76. The parties had occupied quasi-marital relations with each other, it is said, but had dissolved them." Apparently the relationship soured further, as in 1860, in the Crescent Oyster Saloon, Mayfield drew a knife on Wills and stabbed him. In response, Wills took out a revolver and fired three shots at her. The bullets missed her, but one pierced the shoulder of the proprietor of the oyster house, wounding him grievously. The newspaper account is the only evidence of this incident, the case record being lost.[35]

In 1859 Mayfield once again appeared before Recorder Summers. This time she faced charges of "pitching into Rhodes Hardin and breaking his glass." Summers fined her ten dollars or thirty days in the workhouse. In 1860 the *Picayune* reported, "Nancy Mayfield, Kate Hector and Kate Hussey (what a name that last! One can't pronounce it without insulting the owner)" came before Recorder Emerson charged with assaulting and beating one Mike Cunningham. Perhaps fault existed on both sides or perhaps Emerson thought the evidence insufficient, as he dismissed the case after hearing the testimony of those involved.[36]

Emily Eubanks and her daughter, Elisabeth, alias Lizzie, free women of color, also had a fondness for insulting and assaulting white women. In 1852 Emily faced charges of insulting and assaulting Mrs. E. G. Ritter, a white woman. Ritter alleged that Eubanks "unprovokedly assaulted, abused and insulted and threatened her with personal violence." Ritter claimed that she feared that Eubanks would carry out her threats if not restrained by law. Eubanks pleaded not guilty before the First District Court, but the case ended in a nolle prosequi. Two weeks later, Eubanks again faced charges of insulting a white person, this time Mary Murday, who alleged that Eubanks "was in the habit of calling me a whore, a damn bitch." This case also ended in a nolle prosequi. In 1856 Eubanks and her daughter came before Recorder Bright charged with throwing brickbats at the residence of one of her neighbors, "thereby endangering human lives." No trial record exists.[37]

In 1861 Emily and Elisabeth Eubanks came before the First District Court in two separate trials, both for assault and battery on a white woman. In the first, Maria Stahl testified that Emily and Elisabeth had "thereby struck and beaten, being struck in the face and her hair pulled and otherwise abused." The First District Court jury found the mother and daughter guilty but must have felt that fault existed on both sides, as they recommended both women to the "leniency" of the court. Elisabeth received a fine of ten dollars or four days in jail, Emily a fine of twenty dollars or eight days in jail and costs of prosecution.[38]

In the second case mother and daughter faced an accusation by Mary Culican for assaulting and striking her "with a large pole on a stick, with intent to kill and murder." The clerk of the First District Court set the trial for 12 November 1861, but a note in the case indicated that just before the trial the sheriff could not find the either Emily or Elisabeth Eubanks. They either went into hiding or left New Orleans.[39]

Belle Thompson first appeared in the *Picayune* in 1857, when she tried to kill herself by jumping off a steamboat into "the muddy bosom of the Mississippi." A police officer who witnessed the incident jumped into a skiff and saved her by grabbing her by the hair. Thompson, described as "a woman of the town," recovered from the attempt and went on to live a violent and tumultuous life. Just three weeks later, she faced charges of bombarding Jean Rollerle with "glasses, flower pots, and other offensive weapons." Rollerle did not appear at the hearing, and the recorder discharged her. Just one month later, Recorder Stith fined her twenty dollars for "gross abuse of one of her neighbors on Gravier street."[40]

In 1858 the *Picayune* reported that Belle Thompson stabbed John Phillips "in a house of bad repute" on Basin Street. "A difficulty appears to have occurred between Phillips and a woman named Belle Thompson, who keeps the house, when she drew a knife and stabbed him." Thompson claimed she acted in self-defense. Three months later, Thompson and Isabelle Marshall stood charged with attacking another public woman, Ellen White. The *Picayune* reported that one of them held her down while the other pulled her hair and kicked her in the face and elsewhere in "an exceedingly savage manner." Just three months later Thompson faced charges of having assaulted Mary Ann Rider, "striking her several blows about the face, severely bruising her, and knocking out two of her teeth." No record exists of any of these cases going to trial.[41]

In 1859 Thompson had to pay a fine of ten dollars for "insulting an officer in discharge of his duties." Late that year, she became a victim of violence when Edward Banker faced charges of "pummeling" Thompson at the lake on the shell road. She failed to appear at his hearing, and Recorder Summers dismissed the charge against him.[42]

Finally, under the headline "A Virago," the *Picayune* reported an incident in which Thompson attacked "a mild and weak man," Myer Lund, a perfume and cosmetics peddler. Lund walked down Basin Street to sell his wares to the "denizens" of that street when he met Thompson and offered her his wares. He must have said something to anger her because "she pitched into him *a la Heenan,* bruising his face badly and blackening his eyes in a twinkle" (italics in original). She then threw his basket of wares into the gutter. Thompson faced Recorder William Emerson, but no record indicates the disposition of this case.[43]

Many prostitutes lived violent and tumultuous lives in antebellum New Orleans. They fell prey to assaults by their customers and their pimps, but they also on many occasions attacked each other. If a sisterhood existed among public women in antebellum New Orleans, as one historian has alleged, evidence of it proves difficult to find. Most often, prostitutes lived by their wits, struggled to survive, and hoped to escape as much violence as they could.[44]

5

———⊗⊗⊗———

LARCENY AND ROBBERY
AMONG PROSTITUTES

Louisiana law defined larceny as "the felonious taking and carrying
away of the personal goods of another." Glancing through the docket
book of the First District Court of New Orleans indicates that the
two crimes of which New Orleanians most often stood accused were assault
and battery and larceny. Literally hundreds of cases of both crimes clogged
the docket books of the court in the 1840s and 1850s. Prostitutes committed
many of these criminal acts, especially larceny. These women, after all, lived
by their wits, seizing opportunities for profit whenever they arose. They
frequently robbed their customers and quite often stole from each other, although what they took from their counterparts differed from what they stole
from the men who bought their sexual services. From other public women
they sometimes stole money, but most often they took clothing and jewelry.
This behavior is not surprising. Prostitutes in the antebellum period lived
in an age in which ready-made clothing had not become widely available,
making hand-constructed garments expensive. As prostitutes depended on
looking flashy and attractive to lure their customers, stylish and eye-catching
apparel would have been a necessity. Withholding or stealing money or clothing was a time-honored way for brothel owners and pimps to control public
women who worked for them. And taking attractive apparel away from a fellow prostitute could make it harder for the victim to compete for customers.[1]

One instance in which a brothel keeper stole money from one of the
women living in her house occurred in 1856. Mary McGlove went before

the First District Court charged with taking a ten-dollar gold piece from the carpetbag of Anna French. Although three other public women living at the same address testified in the case, the district attorney dropped the case with a nolle prosequi. On the same page of the docket book, Mary McGlove appeared again, this time charged along with her husband with "keeping a disorderly brothel" and "entertaining thieves and vagabonds . . . the said house is a nuisance to the whole neighborhood." Although four neighbors testified in the case, the district attorney also dropped this case with a nolle prosequi.[2]

Two of the strangest cases of prostitutes committing larceny involved one victim who was a slave and one who was a twelve-year-old boy. Mary Cox came before the First District Court charged with stealing three dollars from a slave woman. The jury convicted her, and the judge sentenced her to six months in the parish prison and ordered her to pay court costs. An all-white jury willing to convict a white prostitute who stole from a slave says much about how antebellum society viewed prostitutes. In the second case Ellen Flemming, alias Judy Come Home with the Soap, stole twenty-nine dollars from a young boy, the son of a widow whom the New Orleans Fire Department supported because her husband had been a member of the department who had died in the line of duty. His widow recovered the money, and the case never went to trial.[3]

Occasionally men took money, jewelry, or clothing from public women. In 1854 Frank Dorsey, alias Murphy, came before the First District Court charged with breaking into the house of Mary Ann Kearner with four other men and forcibly taking fifty dollars from her. The only evidence to support the charge was given by Kearner, who the *New Orleans Daily Picayune* noted "was of notorious character and lived in a room over a dance house where a public ball was held on the night in question." The newspaper reporter expressed surprise that anyone would believe Kearner, as she had been in the workhouse several times for drunkenness and vagrancy and was now incarcerated in the parish prison on a charge of larceny. Despite these circumstances, the jury found Dorsey guilty. In 1857 C. H. Foster, a former police officer awaiting trial for "negro stealing," faced charges of stealing a trunk containing $250 and "a quantity of clothing" from Mary Ann Green. At the same time and place Green accused him of stealing a number of dresses and other articles said to be worth $350. Green received permission from the chief of police to inspect Foster's luggage, in which she found many of the stolen articles. Quite likely, Foster served as Green's pimp. Although the recorder sent the case to the First District Court, it never went to trial. Also in 1857 Ellen Mahoney accused Ephraim S. Dailey of coming to her room on Perdido Street and stealing a pair of gold bracelets, three finger rings, and a breast pin from her. She subsequently saw one of her rings on his finger, and when police arrested him, two other rings, identified as hers, were in his possession. Recorder Stith sent him to the First District Court to be tried for the thefts, but no record of trial exists. The same year, J. T. Millan and J. E. O. Wingfield came before Recorder Stith accused of attempting to extort fifty dollars from "a fair frailty named Mathilda White." Millan had impersonated a police officer. The two men also assaulted her and took a gold watch and chain valued at seventy-five dollars from her. No record exists of a trial.[4]

As already mentioned, most often when prostitutes stole from each other, they stole clothing or jewelry. Elizabeth White testified in court that before retiring she put some jewelry on the mantelpiece of her room. After she went to bed, she saw Ellen Dorman sneak into her room and take the jewelry. She said that she could not get out of bed to stop her because she was naked under the covers. The district attorney dropped the case with a nolle prosequi. In 1852 Harriet Kennedy accused Catherine Osnaburg of going to her Phillippa Street room and taking dresses, chemises, a quilt, sheets, pillow slips, mosquito bars, and petticoats valued at seventy dollars. The court issued a search warrant, and the sheriff found the property. Other items taken in other thefts included silk dresses, bonnets, a mantilla, a white linen shawl, and corsets.[5]

In 1857 a prostitute named Kate Williams faced Recorder Gerard Stith charged with having forcibly taken a silk dress on a public street from another public woman, Catherine Yonker. Williams claimed that the dress actually belonged to another prostitute, Adelaide Balfour, who had lent it to Yonker. Williams claimed the dress "and ordered her either to strip off the dress or expect to have her heart cut out forthwith." A frightened Yonker disrobed on the spot and surrendered the dress. Balfour swore that the dress was hers and claimed that she had never given it to Williams. Williams claimed that Balfour had given her the dress as a gift. As there was no disposition of this case, the real owner of the dress cannot be determined.[6]

One of the most unusual instances of theft involved a light-fingered prostitute named Anna Marie Kelly, alias Ann Moore. The *Picayune* described Kelly as having a large "organ of acquisitiveness," stealing "whatever her eye covets" and not understanding the difference between "*meum* and *teum*. Ann, in short is a g'hal." The newspaper noted that Kelly had spent several terms in the workhouse. During her last incarceration, she "concluded that the city owed her something more than a living—undergarments, for instance."

Just before the end of her sentence, she cut up several of the city's blankets and converted them into petticoats. When she prepared to leave, her "bulky appearance" engendered suspicion; upon inspection officials discovered the theft and sent her to Recorder G. Y. Bright to face charges of theft. The recorder dismissed the case, saying, "Let the officers of the Work House do their duty and the prisoners cannot take away clothes and blankets when they are discharged."[7]

In 1858 two prostitutes who were free women of color faced Recorder Henry Summers for stealing "fabulous quantities of female apparel" from free woman of color Kate Parker, a public woman, while she was in jail awaiting trial for killing her female slave. The *Picayune* reported that "almost everything that she left in her house was stolen during her involuntary absence." Some of the stolen articles turned up at a local pawn shop, others at the home of one of the accused. Although the recorder sent the case to the First District Court, no record exists of trial. Incidentally, the Orleans Parish grand jury refused to indict Parker for the murder of her slave, and the judge of the First District Court discharged her.[8]

Instances of prostitutes stealing from their customers occurred more often than any other type of larceny cases involving public women. Most often the man went to bed with the prostitute and awakened some time later to find that his money, and often his watch, had vanished. Occasionally, however, public women stole clothes and other items from their johns. For example, in 1846 Catherine Myers, alias Augusta Myers, alias Mary Myers, came before the First District Court charged with stealing money, two gold chains, two gold rings, a gold pencil, and "sundry wearing apparel," valued at two hundred dollars, from George Griswald. The case ended in a mistrial. In 1849 Sophia Montgomery, who lived on Phillippa Street, took a variety of items from one Hamilton McKee, including one pairs of pants, one pair of kid gloves, one black vest, one handkerchief, two sheets, one tumbler, one knife and two forks, two bowls, and one painting. The most expensive item was the painting, estimated to be worth fifteen dollars. Although the case went to the First District Court, the judge dismissed it without explanation. Another public woman, Julia Wood, leased two beds, two mattresses, one mirror, feather pillows, an armoire, and four chairs from Maurice Stevens for five dollars a month. Stevens accused her of selling his furniture and bedding, delivering it to a man who lived on Canal Street, and skipping town. The case never went to trial because the sheriff could not find her to arrest her.[9]

In the overwhelming majority of cases involving larceny and public women, however, it was the prostitutes who stole money from their customers. Usually the thefts occurred either when the men disrobed, leaving their wallets in their trousers pockets or under the mattress, or after they had fallen asleep following their having sex with the prostitute. When they discovered their loss, some of them called for the police and reported the theft. These matters would first come before one of the recorders, who would send the case to the First District Court for trial. Most often, when the district attorney called the case, the customer, not wanting to appear in a public courtroom and admit that he had been in a brothel, or being a visitor to the city who had since departed, did not appear to testify, and the district attorney had no choice but to drop the case with a nolle prosequi for lack of a prosecuting witness. Many minor variations on this sequence of events occurred, but this basic scenario happened repeatedly.

For example, in 1846 a man named Daniel (last name illegible) went to a brothel on the corner of Customhouse and Tremé streets and went to bed with a woman named Suzanne Hubbard. Before getting into the bed, he placed a "purse" containing $12.00, a $5.00 bank note, a $5.00 gold piece, and $2.00 in silver under the mattress. He awakened to find the money gone. After searching the room and examining Hubbard, he found the bank note in her hair and the gold piece in her mouth. This incident occurred on 26 June 1846; the district attorney dropped the case with a nolle prosequi on 28 July 1846, as the prosecuting witness did not come forward to testify. The same month, Mary Ann Golden, alias Hoozier Mary, came before the First District Court charged with larceny for stealing fifty dollars from a customer, John H. Lambert, who gave his residence as a flatboat at the foot of Julia Street. Lambert had gone to the room of Golden on Customhouse street. He admitted that he "took off his pantaloons and went to bed" with Golden. Upon awakening, he discovered that his money and Golden had vanished. The case ended in a nolle prosequi. [10]

In 1847 Willard Stevens and John Chambers accused free women of color Margaret Butterwick and Caroline Taylor and their pimp, James Perry, for stealing fifty-five dollars from them while they slept in a Customhouse Street brothel. The owner of a coffeehouse on the ground level of the building testified that Butterwick and Taylor were "women of ill fame" and that he saw James Perry, who was probably their pimp, with a key to their rooms. Chambers and Stevens must have failed to appear to testify at trial, as the case ended in a nolle prosequi. A few weeks later, as John Davis strolled down Marais Street, Mary Reid, who was sitting on her stoop, called him over and asked him, among other things, if he liked oysters. The couple then went to a "private and separate room" in an oyster saloon, where Davis took out a purse containing two hundred dollars. Reid told an apparently trusting Davis that "as they were going to sleep together," she would take care of the purse and give it back to him in the morning. Upon awakening, he found the money and Reid gone. This case actually went to trial, but the jury inexplicably found Reid not guilty, and the judge discharged her. In a similar case Thomas Dixon went to a brothel on Customhouse with a money belt around his waist containing $150. He went to bed with Cecilia Sloan, after which they went out to a restaurant for dinner. While dining, he discovered that he had only a coin and a few dollars in the belt. Police searched Sloan, but she only had $44.25 on her. Dixon must have declined to prosecute, since the case ended in a nolle prosequi.[11]

Often pimps and public women worked together to steal from the women's customers. In 1848 Robert Jackson met Elizabeth Moran at the Louisiana Ball Room (a favorite place for public women to solicit customers). She took him to her room on Marais Street, where he undressed, and the two went to bed together, after which Jackson fell asleep. When Jackson had first entered the room, he placed his gold watch and chain, which he valued at $150.00, on a table in the room. When he awakened, his watch, chain, and Moran had disappeared. The missing items turned up in possession of Charles McDonald, Moran's pimp, who said that Moran had given the watch and chain to him. Moran faced charges of larceny, and McDonald faced charges of receiving stolen property, but the case ended in a nolle prosequi.[12]

In 1851 a public woman named Mary Ann McLaughlin, alias Mary Ann Doris, came before the First District Court charged with stealing twenty dollars from William McCluskey. A man named T. Gilmore (her pimp?) wrote to the judge in the case that McLaughlin was a "prudent woman" who had never before appeared in court. He appealed to the judge's "humanity," asking him not to sentence her to a long prison term, as it would deprive her young children of their mother (and perhaps deprive him of his income if she could not work). This plea fell on deaf ears; the jury found her guilty, and the judge sentenced her to six months in the parish prison and ordered her to pay court costs.[13]

In 1851 three public women used what the *Picayune* described as "an opiate" to separate a man from his money. Upon entering a "house of ill fame or brothel" on Elysian Fields Avenue, Margaret Royal, Ellen Jackson, and Elizabeth Wilson offered Charles Thompson a cup of coffee. After drinking the coffee, he became "immediately stupefied." When he recovered his senses, he found himself on the sidewalk outside the brothel with his coat and his overcoat on his arm but missing the seventy dollars he had in his pants pocket. Under the headline "Depraved," the *Picayune* reported that Recorder Peter Seuzeneau, who had a reputation for being less than rigorous in trying to repress prostitution, sent the three women to the First District Court on a charge of "keeping a house of the vilest character on Elysian Fields street." Seuzeneau often sent cases of this kind to the First District Court, knowing from experience that they would end in a nolle prosequi. In this way, he could please his reform-minded constituents while at the same time not disturbing the lucrative business of prostitution. In other words, he could seem to be doing something to discourage the sex trade, knowing it would have no effect. In this case only Margaret Royal faced charges of "keeping a disorderly brothel" before the First District Court, and the case, as with almost all such prosecutions, ended in a nolle prosequi. [14]

The same year, François Desplante charged Elizabeth Blaise of stealing two hundred-dollar notes from him in a brothel. He claimed that he had "got into a conversation with her" (a nice euphemism for sex) when he noticed his money gone, and he named another inhabitant of the brothel, Mary Matus, as an accomplice. Desplante obtained a search warrant, and the police found the money in Blaise's room. Having recovered his money, and not wishing to admit in court that he had gone to a brothel, Desplante declined to prosecute, and the case ended in a nolle prosequi. [15]

Reading these cases, one finds it difficult not to wonder at the naïveté and gullibility of the men who frequented brothels. No doubt alcohol often clouded their judgment. For example, in 1852 Jean Porres was returning at daybreak from the Globe Ball Room when Mary Williams called him into a house on Burgundy Street. He said that "he was quite overcome with fatigue" (and perhaps intoxicated?), so he entered the house and went to sleep. When he awakened, he discovered that Mary Williams had her hand in his pocket, and his watch and his money had vanished. He accused Williams of robbing him, they got into an argument, and she called the police to arrest him for disturbing the peace. He subsequently obtained a search warrant, and he found his property in an armoire in her room. Satisfied, he declined to prosecute, and the case ended in a nolle prosequi. The same month Elizabeth West "invited" John Minor, a guest at the Commercial Hotel, into her Customhouse Street brothel, where he spent the night. When he awakened, he found his watch and money gone from under the mattress, where he had placed them before retiring. This case also ended in a nolle prosequi. [16]

Often men who went to a brothel did not want to admit that they had sex with a prostitute. Charles Courtney told the recorder that "he had occasion to go to her [Juliana Lucy's] house on St. Charles and Julia." While he was sitting down and having a conversation with her, "she thrust her hand in my pocket feloniously" and took twenty-five dollars in gold and notes. When he asked her to return the money, "she seized a broomstick" and assaulted and battered him. The case never went to trial. In another instance James Gilroy went to a brothel on Julia and Tchoupitoulas streets, where he told Bridget Horn that he wanted to "lie down for an hour." After about fifteen minutes, Horn came to him and said that she "wanted to be taken. She was feeling around my belt." She then unbuttoned his suspenders, after which he dozed off. When he awakened his pants were open and the money gone. Horn stood trial before the First District Court, and the jury found her guilty of larceny. The judge sentenced her to one year in the parish prison. This case is a rare instance in which a public woman faced conviction and a prison term for larceny. The same year George André stated that Elizabeth Wilson "induced" him to enter a brothel on Barracks Street near Gallatin. When he went in, Wilson asked him what time it was. He showed her his watch, and she took it and left the room, stating that she would return. When she did not, he went out and found her in a house across the street. He asked her for the watch, but she said she did not have it. This case also ended in a nolle prosequi. [17]

In 1853 Mary Ann Jones came before the First District Court charged with stealing John Moran's gold watch and chain, valued at one hundred dollars, in a Burgundy Street brothel. Moran claimed that he saw Jones picking his pocket. Jones testified that Moran came to her house "much intoxicated," that she could not get him to leave, and that he had no watch when he came to the brothel. The manager of the Globe Ball Room and a man well connected to city hall, Salvador Viosca, put up bail for Jones, but the case never went to trial. The same year, Benjamin Whitback alleged that he had gone to the brothel run by Phoebe Black, a free woman of color, where Cecilia Hulsey, a white woman, invited him to her room, and "they agreed to go to bed together." Before retiring, Whitback locked the door of the room from the inside with a key and put the key into his pocket. He had $145.00 in gold pieces in his pants pockets. When he awakened, he found the door open, his pants on the floor, and the money gone. Phoebe Black, the madam, put up bail for Hulsey, but the case never proceeded to trial. A few days later, William Lattimore and Mary Johnson, alias Cincinnati Mary, went to the First District Court charged with stealing $150 from one of Johnson's customers in a Perdido Street brothel. The jury found Lattimore guilty of larceny, and the judge sentenced him to five years at hard labor in the penitentiary. The jury found Johnson not guilty. [18]

In August 1853 Adam Miller charged Edward Gorman and John Sheehan with shoving him into a house on Girod Street, where two public women, Mary Kelly and Margaret Kearny, robbed him of his watch and his money. The two men ordered him out of the house after the women relieved him of his property. Recorder Jacob Winter dismissed the men but sent the women to the First District Court for trial, charged with robbery. The jury found them guilty, and the judge sentenced them to one year in the parish prison and to pay court costs. The men, probably their pimps but certainly their accomplices, never faced charges. [19]

Often visitors to New Orleans fell prey to being robbed by public women. In 1854 Elizabeth Hickey "enticed one Daniel McCarty into a house of ill fame in Phillippa street." McCarty accused her of stealing a money belt containing two hundred dollars in gold. The *Picayune* reported that McCarty was on his way to Texas, when he planned to purchase a farm, and the theft had deprived him of much of his money. Police found no money on Hickey, and she claimed that he had none when he arrived at the brothel. Recorder Bright nonetheless sent her to the First District Court for trial, but no record of a trial exists. The same year the *Picayune* reported that police arrested "three frail women" for robbing a discreetly unnamed man, described by the *Picayune* as an "old gentleman, a planter from up the coast," of more than eight hundred dollars when he visited a brothel on Burgundy Street near Customhouse. He apparently went to bed in the house, and when he awakened, he discovered that the money had disappeared from his pantaloons. Police found three hundred dollars on the three women, but they claimed that the money was theirs, and the gentleman was not able to identify the particular notes as his. One of the women actually alleged that the gentleman owed them money! Police then charged the free woman of color who ran the brothel, Catherine Robinson, with the theft, but the case never proceeded to trial. [20]

Sometimes violence accompanied acts of larceny committed by public women and their pimps. In 1855 an unidentified man in a Perdido Street brothel struck Thomas Evans on the back of the head with a blunt instrument. Elizabeth Perrit assisted him in the attack, and together they robbed him of a gold watch and chain and a pocketbook containing thirty dollars. No record exists of a trial. Three months later a fruit seller in the Beef Market, Joseph Bodge, "not having the fear of consequences before his eyes," went to a Perdido Street brothel. Upon retiring, he put his vest containing fifteen dollars between the mattresses. Upon awakening, he found his money gone, and he accused Ann Hauley of stealing it. The recorder dismissed the case a week later, as Bodge did not appear to testify. [21]

On occasion public women took possession of things other than watches and money that did not belong to them. A free man of color named Charles Poree accused Catherine McGin and Mrs. Neal with taking possession of his house on the corner of Josephine and Rousseau streets, thereby committing a trespass. "Here they lived a riotous sort of a life, following no honest occupation, and making the nights hideous with their drunken orgies." In another instance two men and "three abandoned women" stole J. J. Patterson's horse and cart from the door of his house on Customhouse Street. When he pursued them, they turned on him and beat him severely. In another instance, a white prostitute, Bridget Boyce, and a free woman of color who was also a prostitute harbored seven "negro burglars" who broke into a house and stole $150 worth of jewelry and money. Although neighbors reported the incident, there is no record of any action taken by Recorder Bright.[22]

The same year, John Davis, whom the *Picayune* described as "a verdant one," accused Mary Eldridge, alias Irish Mary, of threatening to cut his heart out if he did not give her twelve dollars, and he told the recorder that he gave her the money to save his life. He further claimed that she "had daggers in her eyes and in her hand and put him in great bodily harm." This case went to the First District Court, but no record exists of trial. A few days later, Louise Schrader faced charges of robbing James Howard "and of being an abandoned and disreputable vagrant . . . the story, in full, is a very old and a very nasty one." The same year the *Picayune* reported that Ann Hyman, alias Ann Welsh, alias Ann Hannahan, and Jane Boyce "had taken in and done for" (an expression for robbing) one Matthew Murphy. The reporter noted that the women had taken all of Murphy's money. A few days later Recorder Bright sent Mary Smith, "an abandoned vagrant," to the workhouse for stealing five dollars "from a man who did not wish to be known in the transaction."[23]

Often the victims of larceny by public women were visitors to New Orleans who came to the city for business or pleasure. In 1856 Bridget Dunn, Elizabeth Burnett, and Washington Johnson appeared before Recorder Bright charged with having 'taken in and done for" a man from Attakapas Parish named Binly D. Hanger in a brothel on Perdido Street. Bright sent Dunn, whom the *Picayune* described as "one of the frail nymphs of Perdido," to stand trial in the First District Court, but no trial record exists. The following month Margaret Kelly stole four hundred dollars from "a country planter" in a brothel on Gravier Street. The planter left the city before the hearing took place, and the Recorder Bright had no choice but to discharged Kelly. However, a few days later, Recorder J. L. Fabre fined her twenty dollars for disturbing the peace. A short time afterward Margaret Kelly and six other prostitutes came before Recorder Stith charged with stealing Celestine Joly's watch "in a den on Gallatin street where the abandoned congregate." One month later Bridget Mallory, "one of the Dryades [Phillippa] street ladies of the night," came before Recorder Bright charged with having "taken in and done for" a young Mississippi man named Joseph Williamson. The *Picayune* commented, "The robber nymph is not over 18 or 20 years of age—as fair as she is felonious." A few days later Margaret White stole seventeen dollars from Alex Pigeon "in Bill Spriggin's den on Gallatin street." Pigeon left New Orleans for Nicaragua before the case came to trial, and Recorder Bright dismissed White.[24]

On at least one occasion a public woman was bold enough to steal from a police officer. While officer Peter Conway was on patrol on Perdido Street, Bridget Jane Casey somehow took one hundred dollars from his pantaloons. The *Picayune* subsequently reported that Officer Conway faced three charges of assault with a deadly weapon. Apparently he became angry when he realized his money had vanished, and he went looking for the thief. "As it was election day and he had been imbibing pretty freely he went to the wrong house" as he searched for the thief, and he assaulted the inhabitants. No record exists of a trial for Casey or Conway.[25]

In 1856 Kate Winters, alias Irish Kate, a notorious public woman, came before Recorder Fabre charged with bilking Michael Schmidt of a taxi fare after he drove her all about the city. According to the *Picayune,* "she grossly and insultingly swindled him out of his fare." Recorder Fabre fined her five dollars. On the same day, Ann Brown, described as "the partner and copeer of Kate Winters in all descriptions of wickedness," and her accomplice and probably her pimp, Frank Cosia, alias Fleming, described as "a Sicilian," appeared before Fabre charged with stealing ninety dollars from the pants pockets of François Tesidore in a Burgundy Street brothel. In a similar case Kate Davenport, another alias Irish Kate, took forty dollars from the pants pockets of Thomas Jackson while he slept in a brothel on Burgundy Street, "but the heart of Jackson was some how or other induced to relent and he withdrew the charge he had made." However, Recorder Stith sent Davenport to the workhouse for three months for "keeping a disorderly house."[26]

Upon arriving in the city, some travelers went directly to a brothel, where they immediately had their money stolen. F. J. Felraith came to New Orleans on Christmas evening on the Jackson railroad. An unnamed man directed him to a Phillippa Street brothel occupied by Lena Smith, "an establishment . . . of the most notorious description." After he had gotten into bed, a man sprang out from behind an armoire and beat him until he fell, unconscious. When he awakened, his $150 had disappeared, and so had Smith and the man. A few days later, Smith came before Recorder Stith charged with larceny, but she was able to prove that she had an alibi for her whereabouts that evening. Testimony also proved that Felraith was intoxicated at the time he lost his money, "and he was probably mistaken as to the female who had placed him in the hands of a bully and robber, who beat him when he was in bed and snatched from him his purse." Three years later the *Picayune* reported that Lena Smith appeared before Recorder Summers charged by the chief of police with "frequenting disorderly places, having no visible means of maintenance, being unable to produce creditable testimony of her good conduct and morals, and being an incorrigible vagrant." She also faced charges of robbing a Mr. Sacket of $170. [27]

On occasion, public women worked together to rob men who entered their establishments. Isabella Godfrey, Margaret O'Neill, and an unnamed woman "forcibly and feloniously" robbed William Cahill of forty dollars in a brothel on Phillippa Street on the evening of St. Patrick's Day, 1857. The *Picayune* reported that Cahill said "he was taken in and done for . . . after the most approved fashion, being held and fondled while his pockets were rifled of their contents." Recorder Stith sent the case for trial to the First District Court, but the district attorney dropped the case with a nolle prosequi without explanation. [28]

Travelers who visited New Orleans often seemed to have left their common sense at home. In March 1857 two residents of Pike County, Mississippi, B. F. Johnson and William Foil, described as "cattle drovers," left their rooms at the Arcade Hotel to inspect some cattle that they were considering for purchase. On the way back to the hotel, Kate Brunel, alias Boston Kate, and Caroline Miller hailed them from the second-story window of a brothel on Gravier Street and invited them to enter. They went in and, because the night was cold, went by the fire. Johnson said that immediately a "proposition was made to trade, or to go to bed with the two," for a price of five dollars each. As Foil had no money, Johnson handed him his pocketbook containing $150 and then retired to another room to give Foil and Miller some privacy. A few minutes later Johnson "saw Caroline Miller on top of Foil and fondling with him." Within a few minutes Foil called out, "Johnson, I am robbed, and witness [Johnson] saw Caroline Miller escaping from the house." Foil and Johnson appeared before the recorder, and both testified that they had not had sex with Brunel or Miller. Neither, apparently wished to appear in court and admit to having had sex with a prostitute in a brothel.

Foil stated, "Caroline Miller soon desired witness to trade, but witness said he did not do anything of the sort." They also stated that they had never recovered Johnson's money. Only Miller stood trial for larceny before the First District Court. The jury convicted her, and the judge sentenced her to one month in the parish prison and to pay court costs of $22.30. Not a bad exchange for $150. [29]

In July 1857 Kate Jones came before the First District Court charged with stealing $125 from two flatboatmen in the infamous John Swan's house on Gallatin Street. Swan, perhaps overcome with a rare case of honesty, or more likely fear of trouble with the law, returned $105 of the money. A week later, the *Picayune* carried a notice that the First District Court judge had discharged Jones "to renew her career on Gallatin street." There is no explanation for the nolle prosequi; perhaps Swan paid off someone to have her released, or the boatmen left town and could not testify against her. [30]

At times men seemed to have little sense of self-preservation when it came to protecting their money from public women. In August 1857 Thomas Gorman accused Mary Burns of stealing $510 from him. After spending the evening at the Globe Ball Room and then having breakfast at a restaurant on St. Charles Street, Gorman took a walk down Customhouse Street and went into the house of Mary Burns. "There he went to bed with his money around him." He awakened at four o'clock in the afternoon and discovered that his money had vanished. Although he could not swear that Burns had taken it, he felt certain that she had done so. Sam Smith, the proprietor of the Globe Ball Room, and his bartender both testified that Gorman was very drunk and was looking for a place to sleep, "which proposition was accepted by Mary Burns, who happened to be present at the time." According to Smith and the barkeep, when Gorman awakened, he initially claimed that he had lost only ten or twelve dollars. The bartender also testified that he had brought liquor to Gorman while he was staying in Burns's room. The recorder decided that the testimony was not sufficient to charge Burns, and he dismissed the case. However, he charged her with vagrancy. Most likely, Smith, the bartender, and Burns were all in on the robbery, but only Burns received a punishment, probably a term in the workhouse. The same day Eliza McKay faced Recorder John Holland charged with stealing Henry Haselbusch's money in a "den" on Gallatin Street. As the *Picayune* noted, "the verdant young man failed to make his appearance, he having in all probability been frightened away from the city by Eliza's pals." Here we get an explanation of why so many larceny cases against public women failed to proceed to trial; it was not just that men did not want to appear in open court and admit that they had been in a brothel. Some were actually frightened into leaving so that they would not testify. However, in McKay's case, as in the case of Mary Burns, the recorder could not just let McKay go. He stated that she was "of bad repute, a habitual drunkard and a vagrant," and he sentenced her to six months in the workhouse.[31]

The following year three public women, Mary Ann Holt, Elizabeth Williams, and Mina Larkin, fleeced Joseph E. Jones of $140 in a brothel on Gravier Street. Apparently, as the *Picayune* reported, Holt "induced [Jones] to trust himself within the den." After a while. "the two other girls began to romp with him and managed to extract from the pockets of his pantaloons $140." Although the case went to the First District Court, it never proceeded to trial.[32]

In 1859 four public women, Eliza Collins, Mary Morrison, Mary Smith, and Catherine Carroll, worked together to rob John Pfeiffer of $110 in the notorious Archy Murphy's establishment on Gallatin Street. The *Picayune* described the women as "four of the numerous and chaste nymphs of that poetical region" (Gallatin Street). Apparently Pfeiffer slept with Eliza Collins on the night of 11 March 1859. When he went upstairs into her room, she told him to undress. While he was disrobing, she saw that he had a handkerchief tied around his leg that held several gold pieces. After staying in her room all night, Pfeiffer awakened early and returned to his boardinghouse for breakfast. At this point he still had his money, but he was foolish enough to return to Murphy's brothel about seven-thirty in the morning, and he ordered a glass of whiskey. The four accused women sat near him, and suddenly they jumped on him, held him down, forced his mouth open, and poured the glass of whiskey down his throat. He felt ill immediately and vomited, and the women took him upstairs to bed. Once in the room, they held him down, rolled up the leg of his pants, and cut off the handkerchief containing the gold pieces. The women immediately ran out of the room and locked him in to prevent him from following them. After a few minutes the door opened, and he returned to the downstairs barroom, where all the women, except Collins, were sitting. He charged them with having robbed him, but they denied it. The *Picayune* commented that the moral of the story was that "your left leg is not the proper place to carry your purse." Recorder Webster Long sent the four "syrens" to the First District Court for trial, and took the precaution of locking up Pfeiffer to make sure he would be available to testify. Notwithstanding, the district attorney, perhaps paid off by Archy Murphy, dropped the case with a nolle prosequi two weeks later.[33]

In 1859 the *Picayune* took to reporting larceny in a sarcastic manner. In

March the newspaper reported that Daniel Conway charged Mary Ann Higgins and Margaret Daily with stealing his pocketbook containing six dollars from his pantaloon pockets. He failed to appear in Recorder Summer's court because he "did not care to divulge how he gave the women the chance at his pantaloon pocket, and Summers dismissed the case." Six weeks later, the newspaper reported that Ann Wilson stood charged with "extracting from Wm. Clark's pantaloons pocket a purse containing $150, whilst the owner of the unmentionables was in bed." [34]

In July 1861 Nelly Gray, along with two other public women, faced charges of robbing Charles Couch of his gold watch and five dollars as he slept in their "den" on Phillippa Street. This case did not proceed to trial, and Gray and her pimp, John Leonard, alias Monkey Leonard, "on account of his peculiar style of beauty," also faced charges of stealing $120 from a Red River barkeeper, who "unfortunately strayed to Perdido street." No trial record exists for either incident. The same year, Louisa Giggons, a free woman of color and a public woman, came before the First District Court charged with receiving stolen property and larceny. Jose Rusillo claimed that Giggons received $150 over a six-week period from the slave Antoinette, who had stolen it from him. He also accused Giggons of harboring the slave Marie, the property of Mrs. Bougère, and he demanded a search of Giggons's room. The result of the search does not appear in the record, but the First District Court jury found Giggons guilty, and the judge sentenced her to a term in the parish prison and to pay the court costs. [35]

Whether prostitutes were stealing from each other or from their customers, the records of the First District Court of New Orleans and the Crescent City's newspapers show a systemic pattern of public women taking advantage of situations in which they could help themselves to others' property. In the case of robbing their customers, no doubt these women knew that the chances of being convicted and punished for such actions were slim, as many of their victims were travelers to the city who were long gone when the cases came to trial. Those who were locals would not have wanted to go into open court and admit that they had been with a prostitute. Some were frightened or bribed into silence. Under the circumstances, public women had little to fear from law enforcement officers, which undoubtedly encouraged them to continue stealing with impunity.

6

VIOLENT LIVES

ntebellum New Orleans was home to a society permeated by violence. Prostitutes were often the victims of brutal acts, sometimes by their customers, sometimes by brothel bullies, and frequently by other prostitutes. A few public women turned on themselves and tried to commit suicide. For example, in 1855 Augusta Smith, a seventeen-year-old German immigrant, used laudanum "as a means of fleeing from the ills she suffered." Three months later, Fanny Palfrey also used laudanum in an attempt to end her life, but someone discovered her intent and administered an emetic. She survived the incident. The same year, Lena King jumped into the Mississippi River in an attempt to commit suicide. An onlooker jumped in and saved her, and "she was sent back to her disreputable home." The *New Orleans Daily Picayune* noted that this attempt was Lena's second try at ending her life. [1]

The following year, "one of the frail daughters of Gallatin street," Ann Doyle, jumped into the New Canal and drowned. The *Picayune* observed: "Hard, indeed, must be her lot, if her prospects are darkened by the change." Three weeks later a free woman of color named Eliza leapt into the "Father of Floods" (the Mississippi River) in a suicide attempt. A passerby grabbed her by the hair and saved her life. She told him that she had been distraught because her lover had deserted her and enlisted in the "Nicaraguan movement." [2]

In 1861 Mary Ann Winters, an "abandoned woman," tried to commit suicide in the First District Lockup by hanging herself from the upper bunk in her cell. The clerk of the institution observed her actions and cut her down. The *Picayune* noted that the clerk had saved her life, "casting her once more adrift on this wide, wide tempestuous world."[3]

Men who associated with prostitutes sometimes took their own lives. In 1856 twenty-three-year-old Washington Johnson, who "was much addicted to strong drinks and the use of opium as a stimulant," took a large quantity of laudanum in a brothel and died. Originally, police thought that some of the women in the brothel had poisoned him, but an autopsy proved that he had caused his own demise. Two year later, Frank Ringler, a German immigrant, went to a brothel on Gravier Street, wrote a suicide note, and swallowed a fatal dose of laudanum. He wrote, "An unfortunate love affair brings me to this determination. . . . The enclosed miniature will indicate the person for whom I die." The following year, a twenty-year-old French immigrant named Eugene Lacoste killed himself in a brothel on Burgundy Street. He had spent the previous night there, as well as some other nights, and upon awakening, he asked one of the women of the house to go for coffee for him. When she returned, she found him dead with a gunshot wound to the head. Before his death, Lacoste had been a vendor at the cigar stand in Santini's Coffee Saloon. He left a note addressed to Joe Santini the day before he died telling him that he would not see him again and that he would find some money missing when he checked his accounts. Santini denied any discrepancies in his accounts. He said he had always known Lacoste to be honest and upright and felt his death must be the result of some family trouble. In 1861 another man, not identified by the *Picayune,* "out of respect for his family, which is a very respectable one," killed himself in a brothel on Tremé Street.[4]

Some public women drank prodigious, and sometimes fatal, amounts of alcohol. City authorities had to put "Shell Road Mary alias 2.40" (the price of her favors?) into a taxicab to take her to the lockup because they found her in the gutter of Perdido Street in an advanced state of inebriation. The recorder sentenced her to three months in the workhouse, calling her "idle, worthless, lewd and abandoned." Police arrested Ellen Flemming, alias Judy Come Home with the Soap, on Perdido Street so drunk that they brought her to the watch house in a furniture cart. The recorder sent her to "her old quarters in the Workhouse." Catherine Kennedy, aged thirty-one, died in a brothel in 1856. The coroner's verdict: "died of intemperance. Deceased was a poor, frail, fallen creature." Police arrested Ellen O'Brien, "who ever since she crossed the ocean brine has been athirst and has made unsuccessful attempts to quench the cravings . . . by spirituous imbibings," for being a confirmed drunkard and for carrying a dangerous weapon: "a doubled barreled pistol being her bosom companion." The following year, Ann Cassidy died of alcoholism in a "shanty" on Phillippa Street.[5]

In 1858 Laura Williams, "a young and beautiful woman of the town," died in a brothel on Tremé Street. The *Picayune* reported: "For some time past she has shown signs of dissatisfaction with her mode of life, and has sought relief, as too many unfortunately do, in the intoxicating bowl." Some of the women of the brothel where she lived found her dead in her room. The same year, police found Rachael Craft, alias Fanny Brown, dead in a brothel on Penn Street near Phillippa. A physician attributed the death to the effects of intemperance. The following year, Margaret Nelson died in a brothel on Girod Street. The coroner declared intemperance as the cause of death. Catherine Pierson, an Irish immigrant, also died of alcohol abuse in a house on Perdido Street in 1862.[6]

Men who frequented brothels in the Crescent City and the men who ran them often became embroiled in extremely violent acts. In 1852 James F. Dunn went before Recorder Peter Seuzeneau and charged that Frederick Henson had assaulted him in a brothel, nearly biting off his nose. Henson had been arrested with a number of public women, and he suspected that Dunn had informed on him to the police. The *Picayune* reporter observed that "the lower part of Henson's nose looks as if it would drop off if not restrained from such desertion by numerous bandages." Henson claimed that he had hit Dunn with his fist, but 'the appearance of the useful member does not substantiate his statement." No record exists of a trial.[7]

In 1856 Dan Kelly suffered fatal wounds after being stabbed by Bastien Antin on Gallatin Street. When police arrested Antin, they found a knife concealed in his shoe. The *Picayune* reporter observed that "of late such occurrences on Gallatin street have been less frequent than usual," despite all evidence to the contrary. The same year, Mary Ann Mulder became drunk on Perdido Street. She began screaming "so as to be heard for half a mile," and she bit police officer Peterson when he tried to arrest her and also attempted to gouge out his eye. In 1858 Robert Gallagher, "the Gallatin street buffer," faced charges of shooting William McGinn with intent to murder him. Apparently Gallagher accused McGinn of beating his brother at Quebee, a game, and he fired at him. The *Picayune* noted that the act was "entirely unprovoked." The same year, three men, H. Johnson, Mike Gallagher, and Dick Diamond, faced charges of "setting up a grand row on Gallatin street . . . and of having drawn weapons with the savage intent of shedding human blood." However, the witnesses, perhaps intimidated, failed to appear, and Recorder Gerard Stith discharged them.[8]

Two proprietors of establishments on Gallatin Street engaged in a quarrel that resulted in the death of one of them. Apparently William Clark made derogatory remarks about the wife of Cornelius Keegan, who "kept an establishment of notoriously bad repute" on Gallatin Street. Testimony proved that Keegan had attacked Clark with a knife and that Clark had killed Keegan in self-defense. Friends of Keegan testified that on the night of the incident Keegan saw Clark coming across the street and said, "Here comes that son of a bitch and I am going to kill him." He then walked toward Clark, and as Clark passed by, he attacked him. The recorder discharged Clark, ruling that he acted in self-defense.[9]

Senseless violence took the life of another man just outside a house of prostitution. As John Dougherty sat in a brothel with Mary Robertson, a man on the street began to curse at him through an open window. Dougherty went outside the house, punched the man, and knocked him down. A passerby, John Kennedy, asked Dougherty why he had slugged the unidentified man, and Dougherty told Kennedy that it was none of his business. Dougherty then drew a revolver. In response, Kennedy drew a knife and stabbed Dougherty, killing him. The coroner's inquest found that Dougherty first struck Kennedy before he stabbed him in self-defense. In another violent incident, Edward Keating suffered near fatal wounds, inflicted by George Mills, in a house on Love's Lane, an alley that connected Baronne Street to Phillippa Street.[10]

Three men, all of whom owned establishments on Gallatin Street, lived particularly violent lives apparently with impunity: John Swan, George Kent, and Archy Murphy. John Swan, described by a *Picayune* reporter as "a leader on that classic thoroughfare," often found himself entangled in dangerous acts. In 1856 "Gallatin street was enlivened by a grand row, in which the police were roundly berated and somewhat vigorously handled." Led by John Swan, a group of rowdies "dared the Knights of the Crescent [the police] to combat . . . a terrible fellow is John Swan and a bruiser withal." Police arrested Swan and some of his friends, male and female, on the next day for the brawl and also for extorting seven dollars from one J. C. C. Downs. The *Picayune* reporter wondered how Downs, apparently an otherwise respectable citizen, happened to be on Gallatin Street. No record exists of arraignment or trial. The following year, Recorder J. L. Fabre sent Swan to the First District Court for trial for making an assault on William Kane with a knife in a coffeehouse on Gallatin Street and, in a separate incident, for assaulting and beating Mary Ann Linton. Once, again, no record exists of a trial in either case. George Kent's wife attacked and kicked the wife of John Swan in

1858. The *Picayune* noted that both women were denizens of Gallatin Street. Swan's wife lived a dangerous and precarious life. A month later, the *Picayune* noted that "a vile woman named Mary Ryan alias Brockey Mary attacked and nearly beat to death the Gallatin street wife of John Swan."[11]

On 8 June 1857 one of the public women who worked in John Swan's brothel, Mary Jane, met her death at the hands of a drunken immigrant, Francisco Brunetto. The *Picayune* gave this description of Mary Jane: "Though the victim in this case was frail, she was fair, and even in her degradation, had modesty enough to conceal her family name. She lived, died, and was buried under the simple name of Mary Jane." The *Picayune* characterized the murder as being of "the most bestial description" and stated that "it had in connection with it features which are wholly revolting to human nature, and such as cannot be described in decent print." The trial record of the case indicates that Brunetto brutally stabbed Mary Jane between the second and third ribs, puncturing her lung and severing an artery. She explained, just before she died, that she had provoked his rage by refusing to satisfy Brunetto's particular wishes, saying, "I did not want to stay with him as he wanted." The proprietor of the Gallatin Street brothel, John Swan, testified that Mary Jane had told him before she died that Brunetto "wanted to commit sodomy upon her." Mary Jane, age twenty-five and a native of Ireland, died of her wound two hours later.[12]

The case went to trial before the First District Court on 15 July 1857. Several eyewitnesses, including John Swan, testified against Brunetto. The jury retired to deliberate in the late afternoon. After two hours the judge decided to allow the jury to leave the courtroom in order to have dinner at Victor's Restaurant, which was about three blocks away from the courtroom, accompanied by two deputy sheriffs. During the course of the dinner, the twelve jurors ate heartily. They also drank absinthe and anisette as aperitifs, followed by six bottles of claret. Toward the end of the meal, the proprietor of the establishment presented the jurors with a complimentary bottle of brandy, which some of them drank. Then two jurors made a bet guessing about the amount of the forthcoming bill (paid by the state), and the wager was a bottle of champagne, which several of them consumed. After more than two hours of drinking and dining, the jurors returned to the courtroom and resumed their deliberations, finally rendering a verdict of "guilty without capital punishment" about 11:30 at night. A few days later, Judge Theodore Hunt sentenced Brunetto to life at hard labor in the state penitentiary.[13]

Brunetto's attorneys filed motions for a new trial as well as an appeal to the Supreme Court of Louisiana. Judge Hunt denied the motions for a new trial. The supreme court appeal rested on two arguments: the first was that the dying declaration of the deceased murder victim should not have been admitted as evidence. The high court rejected this argument, holding that knowledge of impending death by the victim ensured "that the declaration is in accordance with the truth." The second argument was that there were irregularities committed by the jury while considering their verdict. On this count the supreme court split 3-2 against Brunetto and voted to sustain the verdict of guilty. The chief justice, Edwin Merrick, was one of the dissenters. He stated that in light of the amount of alcohol consumed by the jurors at dinner, "one or more of the jurors were not in the possession of that unclouded intellect which the accused had a right to demand. The possibility that this might have occurred, I think entitles the prisoner to a new trial." [14]

If violence seemed to follow John Swan, George Kent had a particular fondness for stabbing and shooting others. In 1853 Recorder Seuzeneau sent him to face trial before the First District Court for stabbing John Kelsey in the shoulder. No trial record exists. Two years later, police arrested Kent, "the keeper of a notorious brothel . . . called the Lion's Den," for committing a brutal assault on Catherine Ring, "an inmate of his house," who attempted to leave against Kent's wishes. In 1856 Kent, described once more as the proprietor of the notorious "Lion's Den" and the "Stadt Amsterdam," faced accusations of drawing a revolver with intent to shoot Charles Thomas. Recorder Webster Long sent the case for trial to the First District Court, but no record of a trial exists. The same year Kent faced charges of carrying a concealed weapon and disturbing the peace. "A number of depraved females, who were found in Kent's establishment, were held to answer for leading immoral lives." He also faced charges the same year for beating Ann Schwam and also knocking down and choking John Fealy, drawing a knife on him with intent to kill. None of these incidents resulted in a criminal proceeding. The following year, Kent's wife of two years, Johanna Loettman, sued him for divorce, alleging habitual drunkenness and cruel treatment. She claimed that she feared for her life and also that Kent had committed adultery within the past six months. She asked for alimony of twenty dollars a month. A search of the records of the Fourth District Court failed to find the trial record. The same year, Kent came before the First District Court charged with assault and battery on Ann Lehmann, but the district attorney dropped the case with a nolle prosequi. Two years later, Mary O'Donnell, who resided in Kent's brothel, charged him with having cowhided her. The same year, a public woman named Kate Baker accused three residents of George Kent's Gallatin Street establishment, Mary Hickey, Dutch Kitty, and Jenny McNaff, of striking her in the face with their fists and also over the head with some blunt instrument. The district attorney dropped the case with a nolle prosequi for unknown reasons. In 1861 Kent once more faced charges of assault with a dangerous weapon with intent to kill, this time from Charles Devlin. Again, no record exists of a trial. [15]

Newspaper accounts and court records show Archy Murphy to be a thief as well as a violent thug. In 1848 John Swan, described in court records as the keeper of an oyster saloon on Gallatin Street, reported that Murphy, along with his friend Hamilton Rowan, had stolen a piece of cloth worth fifty dollars, the property of John Laville, from his establishment. The record of this case ends with no indication of the outcome. In 1851 Murphy came before the First District Court again under a charge of assault and battery. Again the case record ended with no indication that it ever came to trial. Two years later Murphy once more faced charges of assault and battery before the First District Court. For unknown reasons, the case never went to trial, and the district attorney dropped the case with a nolle prosequi three years later. The most likely explanation for the delay and the nolle prosequi is that the alleged victim either declined to prosecute or had left the city. In 1855 Murphy, "the bold knight and buffer of Gallatin street," appeared before the First District Court charged with "brutally kicking in the stomach" of Mrs. Leopold Graethel. Although the woman was pregnant, and although the court record described her condition as "dangerous," the case was also dropped with a nolle prosequi. [16]

Under the headline "Another Gallatin Street Notoriety," the *Picayune* reported in 1855 that the First District Court had required Archy Murphy to give a five-hundred-dollar bond to appear when notified to answer to two charges. The first involved Murphy's beating of Anderson Clark and then kicking him while down. The second was a charge of assault with intent to kill on Emelia Schaddle. No evidence of a trial of either matter exists. [17]

The same year just before Christmas, Murphy and Tom Piner faced charges of burglary and receiving and being in possession of stolen property. Thieves had entered the "Uncle Sam" coffeehouse and made off with about a thousand dollars' worth of pistols, knives, jewelry, and other items. Police, armed with a search warrant, "penetrated into the felonious precincts of Gallatin street." There they discovered in Archy Murphy's establishment a "plunder *placer*," in which they found a number of gold rings, a bracelet, a locket, a pistol, and some other articles said to be stolen from the "Uncle

Sam." By that afternoon, Murphy and Piner, described in the *Picayune* as "the good men and true of Gallatin street," faced Recorder G. Y. Bright, who set bail at one thousand dollars each. The newspaper reporter observed wryly, "There will be grief along the shadows of Gallatin when the result is known." At the hearing before Recorder Bright, a surprise witness, a peddler, swore that he had sold the goods in question to Murphy and Piner. Three other men, all vagrants, then faced charges of committing the burglary, but no evidence came before the recorder against them. Nonetheless, two of them received terms in the workhouse for sixty days. It is not clear whether the sentences meted out constituted punishment for the alleged burglary or for vagrancy. It is also questionable whether the peddler spoke the truth or whether Murphy and Piner paid him to supply an alibi to protect themselves. Four days later, the *Picayune* reported that Murphy smashed a number of articles at another coffeehouse. [18]

The following year Murphy, referred to in the *Picayune* as "the celebrated Archy Murphy of Gallatin street," faced charges of stabbing a man twice in the back with intent to commit murder. Although initially Murphy did not realize it, the man's wounds proved to be superficial, but when police caught Murphy, he had armed himself with a Bowie knife and a revolver. According to the police, he appeared to be heading toward the back part of town to escape capture. [19]

At times it seems that Murphy and his cohorts delighted in enhancing their reputations as hell-raisers. In 1857 Murphy, Hamilton Rowan, and Dave Kinney visited two coffeehouses near Gallatin Street. They entered, drew handguns, and fired at their reflections in the coffeehouses' large mirrors that were hung behind the bar, shattering the mirrors. The incidents "caused the keepers of the respective houses to fear and tremble." The *Picayune* observed that there was supposedly a reason for the actions of the trio— that the mirrors reflected "the ugly faces of customers [who] stare at those which are better favored. . . . Besides, they accuse the mirrors of an imposition in multiplying illusively the number of decanters and glasses in front of them, and of repeating and exaggerating the contortions of intoxicated individuals." [20]

Violence abounded in and around Archy Murphy's establishment. In 1857 Walter Bell, alias Scotty, shot William McGinn outside Murphy's brothel. The two men had been arguing inside Murphy's place, and Murphy threw them out, threatening to "blow the roof of [his] head off if he tried to stab the other man." A year later Murphy's brothel (politely called a "boarding house" in the local newspapers) was the scene for what the *Picayune* termed a "deadly cutting affray, which will probably result in the death of four men," two of whom were police officers who tried to prevent the stabbing. Apparently Murphy also tried to stop the carnage, not because he loved law and order but, as he said, because he did not "care to see the amusements of the evening broken up by the interference of the police."[21]

One of Murphy's most violent enterprises, a brothel riot, involved a public woman named Elizabeth Myers. Under the headline "Gallatin Street Rangers," the *Picayune* reported that Archy Murphy, James Dillon, John Smith, and Thomas Bell had attempted to set fire to Myers's brothel. The also beat her and smashed her furniture. The recorder fined them each fifty dollars, and Murphy and Dillon received fines of an additional twenty-five dollars for smashing the furniture in a nearby oyster saloon. In 1858 Hamilton Rowan, Dave Kinney, and Archy Murphy assaulted and brutally beat one Yacinto Marino with brass knuckles for unknown reasons. Police arrested them, but the case never went to trial. The *Picayune* noted: "They have long ruled in Gallatin street, and laughed at the law and its administrators. Possibly the time may arrive when their rule may no longer be recognized as beyond the pale of legitimate authority." Apparently brothel riots occurred with some frequency in New Orleans, as they did in New York. The same year, two men smashed in the lower sash of Adelaide Balfour's window, took the pin out of her front door, took the door down, entered the brothel, and beat a man within with a chair, smashing several chairs and an armoire in the process. According to the newspaper reporter they also shattered her glasses, "yelled like 10,000 Choctaws, and cursed worse than Job's wife." They also resisted arrest. At times prostitutes, rather than property, served as the targets of violence. One month later, another man faced charges of kicking Balfour under her chin and dragging her by the hair "in a most fiendish manner"; he "beat her on her body, and attempted to choke her by squeezing her in his vice-like hands." Phoebe Black, a free woman of color and a public woman, survived an attack on her and the inhabitants of her house by five men, at least one of whom, Eugene Suchet, was a pimp. Several police officers who came to break up the affray received severe injuries from being beaten by the men.[22]

Public women themselves sometimes led dangerous lives and found themselves victims of violent acts by their customers. In 1855 John Regan, alias John McCarty, stabbed and seriously wounded Mary Lynch "in that famous locality known as Corduroy Alley" on St. Thomas Street. Apparently another public woman, Catherine Hays, had planned to testify against Regan in a criminal case, and in a darkened room, he mistakenly stabbed Lynch, believing her to be Hays. The *Picayune* reported that Regan "was determined to assassinate her, in order to get rid of the evidence." Two days later, police arrested Regan for threatening Hays with a pistol. One wonders why the authorities had not already incarcerated Regan, as the newspaper reported that he was a member of a "gang of murderers who had killed two men and severely wounded two others in Corduroy Alley some weeks since." [23]

In 1856 Ellen Flemming, alias Judy Come Home with the Soap, suffered a beating "in a most fiendish manner by some inhuman monster" on Gallatin Street. Two months later, John Doyle faced arrest for beating and perhaps mortally wounding a Mrs. McPherson by beating her on the head with a paving stone in Corduroy Alley. The same month, Joseph Bowman faced charges for drawing a loaded pistol on Ann Doyle and threatening to shoot her in a house on Gallatin Street. Also in 1856 John Oufknoch beat two public women, Sugar Mary and Ellen Anliz, and had to face charges for "having disfigured the countenance of one of the frail sisterhood." [24]

In 1857 police found a woman, Margaret Keif, "badly cut and beaten by Tim Meagher, who, without doubt, designed to kill her." The *Picayune* reported that jealousy was the alleged cause of the attack. A few months later, François Despeau had to answer charges that he had "severely beaten a colored woman who is supposed to live too loose a life on Toulouse street, a thing which Despeau despises, when he is so disposed." In November Philip Brady faced charges of beating and kicking Margaret Holmes in her room on Phillippa Street. Recorder Fabre fined him ten dollars. [25]

Prostitutes abused each other verbally as well as physically with great frequency. If the recipient of abusive language happened to be white and the abuser a person of color, the slave or free person of color ran afoul of the *Black Code,* which prohibited "insulting a white person." This crime was one that only a person of color, free or slave, could commit. If a white person insulted another white person, the crime might be called assault or assault and battery, but not "insulting a white person." By city ordinance, the punishment for a slave for "insulting a white person" was twenty-five lashes. Consequences for a free person of color accused of the same offense varied according to the discretion of the judge or recorder. Most often it constituted a week in the parish prison or the workhouse, a low fine, and the payment of court costs. If the complaining witness declined to prosecute when the case came to trial, the district attorney had no choice but to drop the case with a nolle prosequi, but the accused still had to pay court costs. The payment served as a reminder that the free person of color had stepped out of his or her place and had to be punished for it. [26]

An accusation involving "insulting a white person" that came before the First District Court of New Orleans in 1847 involved one Elizabeth Parsons, alleged to be a free woman of color. Two white public women, Elizabeth Hatfield and Margaret O'Brien, claimed that Parsons "did grossly insult, defame and abuse one Elizabeth Hatfield, a white person," on Phillippa Street "contrary to the statutes regulating the conduct of free persons of color toward white persons." Parsons countered the charges by alleging that Hatfield and O'Brien had threatened her with personal violence and that she feared bodily injury from them unless restrained by force. She further claimed that they had "maligned and slandered her" by falsely asserting that she was a person of color. Apparently Parsons was telling the truth about her race, as a man from Richmond came forward to testify that he knew Parsons's mother and grandmother and that they were both white. Perhaps O'Brien and Hatfield thought that Parsons was a person of color because, as the Richmond witness also testified, Parsons was "married" to a free black barber in New Orleans. Louisiana law prohibited mixed-race marriages, however, so Parsons and the barber could have not been legally married. The district attorney quashed the case four months later.[27]

One month later Margaret A. Betts, a white woman, accused Julia Black, alias Anastasia Black, of having "grossly abused and insulted her on the gallery of her home," calling her "a huzzy [sic], an old whore and a bitch." A First District Court jury found Black guilty, and the judge sentenced her to pay a thirty-dollar fine and court costs of nine dollars. The following month, Louise Floran, a free woman of color, faced charges that she had insulted a white woman by calling her "a maquerelle which word translated into the English language is of the same meaning and signification as the English word pimp." The *Oxford English Dictionary* defines "maquerelle" as "one who ministers to sexual debauchery, a bawd, pimp, procurer or procuress; a panderer." The First District Court jury found Floran not guilty. Whether they decided that Floran's accusations were true, and that truth was its own defense, we cannot know. In 1848 Adelaide Dickinson, a free woman of color, stood accused of calling Margaret McKay an "Irish whore," and the following year a free woman of color named Catherine faced charges of calling a white woman "a thief and a whore." Neither case appears to have gone to trial.[28]

In 1850 a free woman of color and a prostitute, Brytania Washington, stood before the First District Court charged with insulting a white woman, Susan Fisher, by calling her a "whore" and alleging that she was not married to the man with whom she lived. At trial Washington's neighbor testified that although nothing but a thin, wooden wall divided their houses, she had never heard her "use insulting or degrading language toward Fisher or any other persons." Notwithstanding this testimony, the jury found Washington guilty of insulting, and the judge sentenced her to a fine of ten dollars, ordering her to remain in jail until she paid the fine. The same year a First District Court jury found another free woman of color, Julia Evans, guilty of insulting. The judge sentenced her to one week in the parish prison and to pay court costs and to remain in jail until she paid the costs. Before trial the judge had set bail for Evans at five hundred dollars. Marie Laveau, the famous "vodoo queen," provided the surety for the bail bond.[29]

In one instance the words of a group of four prostitutes caused police to jail a white woman as a free woman of color. Margaret Ford, Kate McCarty, Mary Lyons, and Julia Turpy brutally beat a woman named Jane Thomas in a house just off Gallatin Street. After they beat her, they had the police arrest her as a free woman of color in the state in contravention of the law. Louisiana law prohibited non-native-born free people of color from coming into the state to live. After spending the night in jail in a cell in which her roommate was a "negress," Thomas was able to prove that she was a white woman, and jailor released her. The *Picayune,* shocked by the incident, stated that "those who were guilty of so great an outrage against her person and status will be severely dealt with."[30]

Most altercations between public women tended to be physical rather than verbal. In 1846 Eliza Harris, a free woman of color, faced charges of assault of a white woman with a hatchet. The alleged victim, Ann Johnson, claimed that Harris had thrashed her with a hatchet and had stomped her feet on Johnson's face. Harris denied the accusations. At this point a white man, James M. Boazman, came before Recorder Bright and swore that Ann Johnson "is a common prostitute, that he would not [illegible word] her veracity and truth." He furthermore claimed that he saw the alleged incident and that it was Johnson who committed the assault and battery of Harris, not the other way around. The district attorney dropped the case with a nolle prosequi.[31]

The following year, a free woman of color, Celeste Marie Hernandez, came before the First District Court accused of assault and battery on a white woman, Maria Batistide, who claimed that Hernandez, from whom she rented a room, broke into her room and pushed her out into the street. The jury found Hernandez guilty but for some reason recommended her to the mercy of the court. Perhaps Batistide had not paid her rent. The judge sentenced Hernandez to forty-eight hours in jail and court costs.

The same month Elizabeth Parsons appeared once again before the First District Court, this time charged with the assault and battery of Sophia Helvring; Helvring also faced charges of assault and battery of Parsons. A jury found Helvring not guilty, and the case against Parsons never went to trial. Perhaps the district attorney realized that both women were at fault. [32]

Liddy Petit accused Caroline Smith of assaulting her and striking her on the head at the Globe Ballroom. Since the Globe served as a notorious place for public women to solicit customers, they were probably fighting over a prospective john. A few months later, Mary Lawrence claimed that Mary Seines assaulted her, "striking her with stones twice, and with a wash board & broom stick, also bit her hand, inflicting serious bodily injury." Neither of these cases ever went to trial. The next month Catherine O'Brien stood accused of assault and battery on Barbara Duinsbach, who testified that O'Brien was in the habit of drinking and that when she became intoxicated she was a nuisance to the whole neighborhood. On 7 July 1848 O'Brien assaulted and beat Cecilia Porter, another occupant of her brothel, and she also called Duinsbach a "German bitch." A First District Court jury found her not guilty, and the judge released her. [33]

In 1850 Elizabeth Kelly, a public woman, accused another prostitute, Ann Eliza Hopkins, of assaulting her and cutting her in the hand at the American Theater. The judge set bail at one thousand dollars. Phoebe Black, a free woman of color and a brothel owner, put up the surety bond for Hopkins's appearance, but the district attorney dropped the case with a nolle prosequi before it came to trial. The same year, at four o'clock in the morning on Phillippa Street, Phoebe Smith alleged that Sophia Montgomery, a brothel owner, assaulted and stabbed her, that Montgomery severely cut her "with a view and intent to kill." This case also did not go to trial. [34]

In another fight at the Globe Ballroom between prostitutes, Martha Brown walked up to Martha Johnson, called her a "slut," and attempted to strike her with a Colt handgun. Another violent incident in 1851 took the life of a public woman. Mary Roan, alias Mary Higham, beat Bridget Ahern severely enough to cause her death by peritonitis. Roan threw Ahern to the ground and proceeded to kick her in the head, breast, and abdomen, landing "several mortal strikes." The First District Court jury could not agree on a verdict in the first trial, and the judge declared a mistrial. Two weeks later a new jury heard the case and, incredibly, found Roan not guilty. No record of the trial exists, so we cannot know what facts influenced the jury. The same year, a free woman of color and a public woman named Nancy Davis knocked down and severely beat a white woman, Ellen Tourney, on Phillippa Street. Tourney's injuries were severe enough for her to be confined to Charity Hospital for more than a week. However, the district attorney dropped this case with a nolle prosequi before trial. [35]

In 1852 Eliza Boydel alleged that Margaret Hanna assaulted her by coming into her room and throwing the contents of a "filthy chamber pot" in her face. The district attorney dropped this case with a nolle prosequi. A few months later, Johanna Ford charged "Mrs. Clarke, Mrs. McDonald, and Mrs. Buckley, who live in that dissipated section of the city formerly known as Girod street," with assault. Ford alleged that she feared for her life and asked the recorder to arrest the three public women. No record exists of any proceedings against them. On the same day, Hannah Carey claimed that Mary Riley assaulted and battered her and broke all the windows in her house. Police brought Riley before the recorder, but as Carey did not appear to press charges, the recorder dropped the case and dismissed Riley. [36]

The following year, a free woman of color named Sarah Thayer faced charges of assaulting a white woman, Mary Ann Stewart, on Phillippa Street. Despite frequent searches, the constable could not find Thayer, and the case ended without proceeding to trial. In May 1853 Amelia Early charged Catherine McCann with assaulting and battering her with a hatchet, but the district attorney dropped the case with a nolle prosequi. The following November, a free woman of color named Clarisse assaulted and beat a white woman on her face with her fists and then with the handle of a gig whip. The justice of the peace found her guilty, but there is no record of her sentence. The same year, Catherine Dunn came before the First District Court charged with assault and battery and destroying property. According to witnesses, Dunn went to Julia McMahon's house and assaulted her with a chair. She then proceeded to break her plates and several lamps in her house. The jury found her guilty, and the judge sentenced her to one week in the parish prison and to pay court costs. One public woman faced charges of assault and battery and also charged a fellow prostitute with assaulting and battering her over a four-month period. Mary Wilson charged Julia Venere with attacking her. The district attorney dropped the case with a nolle prosequi. Three months later, Caroline Johnson accused Mary Wilson of assault and battery on Phillippa Street. The First District Court found her guilty, and the judge sentenced her to two months in the parish prison and court costs. [37]

In 1854 Charlotte, a free woman of color, came before the First District Court charged with assault and battery of a white woman, Bridget Mahoney, and with destroying property. Mahoney rented a room from Charlotte's sister. After Mahoney left her room for "une affair," Charlotte broke into her room and threw her mattresses out of the window and into the yard. When Mahoney returned, Charlotte assaulted her and struck her in the eye "without provocation and with violence." There is no explanation in the record as to why Charlotte acted the way that she did. Perhaps Mahoney had not paid her rent and was refusing to leave. The district attorney dropped the case with a nolle prosequi. In March 1854 three prostitutes, Ann Casssidy, Catherine Cassidy, and Ann Doyle, committed an assault and battery on Sophie Wischendoff, pulling a large hunk of hair from her head and beating her with ax handles. A First District Court found them guilty, and the judge sentenced Ann Doyle and Ann Cassidy to two weeks in the parish prison and Catherine Cassidy to two weeks and court costs. The following year, Catherine Cassidy invited "a quiet innocent looking girl, Ann Kelly," into her house and immediately "pitched into her guest and beat her and tore her hair in a most savage manner. She [Cassidy] is supposed to be actuated by some unfounded and unaccountable fit of jealousy." [38]

The next month Kate Hollingshade stood charged with assault and battery of a pregnant woman, Ann Dolan. A physician testified that Dolan kept to her bed for two weeks after the attack, after which she miscarried. In his opinion, Hollingshade's attack brought on the miscarriage. The case ended with several notations that the sheriff could not find her to bring her to court. However, Hollingshade had not left the city. Five weeks later Elizabeth Jones faced charges of having assaulted and battered Hollingshade on Phillippa Street. A First District Court jury found her guilty, and the judge sentenced her to pay the costs of prosecution. [39]

Two public women stabbed two other public women in 1854. Mary Ann Smith and Hester Ann Renau got into a fight "as to the relative superiority of their fancy men," and Smith stabbed Renau in the side. According to the *Picayune,* the wound was "severe" but "not a dangerous wound." In the other incident, Ellen Flemming, alias Judy Come Home with the Soap, stabbed Mary McManus in the face, "endangering her life." Neither case went to trial. [40]

The *Picayune* took notice of two other incidents between prostitutes in 1854. Two "abandoned women" assaulted a third named "Fatty." "As she was walking quietly along the street she was seized by one of them, named Biddy, while the other, known as Gallows Liz, daubed her all over with mud and filth gathered from the gutter, plastering her eyes, nose and mouth and nearly suffocating her." The recorder sent the two women to the workhouse for three months each as a punishment. The next month, two public women, Mary Poole, alias Sugar Mary, and Catherine Wearing, alias English Kate, "proceeded to the house of Mina Smith," where they broke her windows, threw tumblers at Smith's head, and abused her "most outrageously." They then turned to Frances Till, a woman of German extraction. They broke her windows, abused her, and denigrated her German ancestry. The recorder sent them to the First District Court to be tried, but there is no record of a subsequent trial. Two years later Sugar Mary utilized a tumbler once more in the commission of an assault and battery. This time she attempted "to beat in the breast of Ann Dorson with a tumbler."[41]

In 1855 Alice Williams and Isabella Goto faced charges of "disturbing the peace of the immaculate Phillippa street," being "lewd and abandoned," and for "using obscene language to officer Zeigler while in discharge of his duties." The following month, Caroline Hayder, "a Dauphine street syren [sic]," charged Mrs. Taylor with using obscene language toward her and Mr. Taylor with drawing a pistol and threatening to shoot her. The Taylors both were brothel owners.[42]

In 1856 Ann Horton, a public woman, faced Recorder Bright for leading a gang of "wild men and women" in entering the house of Ann Hymen and "breaking her doors, windows and furniture, beating her and blacking her eye." No record of a trial exists. Two months later a "nymph, known by the euphonious cognomen of Irish Kate," faced charges of severely beating Eliza Clansey and also tearing out her hair and stealing her headdress. The next month Mary Ann Mulder smashed a frying pan over the head of Elizabeth Jordan. Recorder Bright discharged Mulder "on the ground that the complainant deserved all that she got." The same month, Fanny Smith and a "nymph" named Lizzy got into a fight in which Fanny got the worst of it. The reporter for the *Picayune* noted: "When she commenced, she was all silk and satin. Her face like a picture book, was illustrated by cuts, and her hair was pulled out and scattered in a most reckless manner." In 1856 a woman whom the *Picayune* identified only as Mrs. McDonald went to Charity Hospital "covered with blood from her head to her heels." Bridget McGinn, another public woman, stood accused of cutting her with a knife and beating her with a blunt instrument. The reporter commented: "How a woman could beat another so, passes our comprehension."[43]

Glass tumblers often served as weapons of choice for public woman assaulting each other. Mahala Ann Hook, "a hooker," and her friend, Kate Wilson, went to the residence of Eliza Cook and beat Cook on the face with a tumbler "in a very severe and brutal manner." The same year Catherine Wilson beat Ellen Mulligan on her head with a tumbler with intent to kill, and the same day the *Picayune* reported that police arrested Eliza Wilson and

Ann Dawson for beating Kate Winters with a tumbler. Other items, however, were also used as weapons. In another violent act, Eliza Murray beat Mary Whitaker over the head with a hickory club. In a similar incident, Catherine Ryan and Mary Comerford stood accused of threatening to kill Bridget Connors with an ax. [44]

The year 1857 was an especially violent one for public women in New Orleans. Mary Stacy and Maria Gallagher faced charges before the First District Court of New Orleans for assault, battery, and mayhem on Ellen Quinn in two separate incidents on the same day. Mary Stacy threw brickbats at Quinn, which severely bruised her arm, and Gallagher struck Quinn in the head with a glass decanter, which cut her nose and left ear, maiming her. Gallagher also broke a crock over Quinn's head. There must have been some provocation because, although the jury found Stacy and Gallagher guilty, they recommended them to the mercy of the court. Each woman received a sentence to pay a fine of five dollars or spend five days in the parish prison. The next month, Recorder Stith ordered Mary Kelly to the workhouse for thirty days for "attempting to crack the crown of Catherine Foley with an iron poker." The *Picayune* observed that Kelly "was poked into the Workhouse for thirty days. Mary had a pair of frightfully black eyes in her head and a baby in her arms, and it was as much on account of her fondness for whiskey as for fighting that Mary was ordered to be confined." [45]

A few months later, "a Girod street female," Mrs. Moriarty, went to Charity Hospital "bleeding like a beef from a severe wound" that Elizabeth McManus allegedly inflicted on her with a heavy bottle, cracking her skull. McManus, whom the *Picayune* referred to as "a female thug," had an open knife in her possession when police arrested her. No record exists of a trial. Mary Hart, "a vigorous looking nymph," faced Recorder Stith charged with throwing a large pitcher of water over Fanny Smith and "threatening to break her head with a billet of wood." The same month, Kate Wilson faced charges once more, this time of severely injuring Elizabeth Haycraft by beating her on the head with an iron poker. Two other public women came before Stith charged with kicking and cruelly treating Maria Wilson in Corduroy Alley. The *Picayune* commented, "All the parties are alley nymphs." When the case came to trial, Wilson did not appear to press charges, so Stith discharged the two women. [46]

In 1858 Ann Stillman and Mary St. Clair, both public women residing at the same address, came before the First District Court charged with assault and battery of Emma Kirk. According to Kirk, the accused assaulted her "with bits of coal, billets of wood, also with an axe," and threatened

her life. They also "abused her by calling her a whore, [said] that she slept
with negroes and other epithets of an abusive nature and character." This
case never proceeded to trial. One year after the assault on Kirk, Stillman
turned on St. Clair, beating her severely with a curling tongue. The physician who attended St. Clair stated that she had several severe wounds on her
head, bruises and contusions on her arms, and a severe bite on one arm. He
believed that she had suffered a "concussion of the brain," and he could not
say with certainty what her long-term prognosis might be. Stillman admitted that she went to St. Clair's room with the intent to kill her. When St.
Clair cried out for the police, Stillman told her that she could kill her before
the authorities could come to her aid. She also told her that even if the police arrested her, she would get out on bail and come and kill St. Clair then.
Inexplicably, the case ended here with no resolution.[47]

In February 1858 Ellen McNabb, "the furious young female," faced Recorder Stith accused of having "violently entered" the house of Mary Ann
Coffey and "broke everything breakable, in the way of furniture, orna-
ments, looking glasses, etc.," and also threatened to take Coffey's life with
a dirk knife with "threats and jealousy." Although Stith sent the case to the
First District Court, there is no record of a trial. In May, Mary Ann Holt
made an assault on Kate Hollingshade with a knife, struck her with a billet of wood, bruised her on the breast with a brickbat, "and threatened to
kill her outright." And in July, the judge of the First District Court ordered
Mary Ann Fannan, alias Gallatin Mary, to post a two-hundred-dollar bond
to keep the peace toward Mrs. L. Larega, who had accused her of assaulting
and battering and insulting her on the gallery of her home.[48]

In 1859 Louann Hodges accused Kate Hughes, alias Irish Kate, of assaulting her; Hughes "dragged her down, tore off her bonnet, broke her parasol,
and beat her with a club." No record exists of a trial.[49] In a much more serious case, Ellen McNabb stabbed Jane Sullivan in her left eye "with intent
to kill" on 29 November 1859. Sullivan testified at a hearing before the recorder that she had gone with McNabb to have a drink at the Stockholm
coffeehouse. As Sullivan was leaving the coffeehouse, McNabb, who had
insulted her and challenged her to fight while they were drinking, came at
her with a knife and stabbed her in the eye, on the face, and on the hand.
Her injuries were serious enough to cause her to stay in Charity Hospital for
several days. The barkeeper of the Stockholm testified that he had witnessed
the incident and had taken the knife away from McNabb after she stabbed
Sullivan and gave it to the police. He identified the knife at the hearing.
The recorder sent the case to the First District Court, which charged Mc-

Nabb with assault with intent to murder. Although she pleaded not guilty, the testimony at trial substantiated the facts brought out at the hearing, and McNabb changed her plea to guilty of assault and battery. The judge sentenced her to six months in the parish prison and ordered her to pay the costs of prosecution. Finally, Mary O'Hara accused Johanna Collins of having bitten off her ear while they were engaged in a fight. For no reason that appears in the record, the district attorney dropped the case with a nolle prosequi. [50]

Court records and the New Orleans newspapers are filled with evidence that prostitutes lived extremely violent and dangerous lives. They faced injury, often severe, from their customers, their pimps, and especially from each other. No doubt competition for customers, jealousy, and alcohol fueled these fights. If a sisterhood among prostitutes existed, as some have suggested, it is difficult to see. In fact, the overwhelming weight of the evidence is to the contrary. At times prostitutes suffered the ultimate act of violence: murder. In these instances the murderers were never their fellow public women but their customers. The frequency of these homicides meant that prostitutes at times had to fear for their very lives.

7

THE MURDER OF A
"LEWD AND ABANDONED WOMAN"

State of Louisiana v. Abraham Parker

State of Louisiana v. Abraham Parker, a never officially reported appeal of an 1851 criminal prosecution for murder of a prostitute, provides an excellent illustration of the way historians can use court records to illuminate the workings of the law, courts, and attorneys. In addition, it exemplifies how one case can reveal antebellum attitudes about crime, law enforcement, the criminal justice system, gender, prostitution, and class status. This obscure case also demonstrates the richness and variety of legal history as it sheds light on the business of prostitution and the relationship between prostitution, gender, and slavery in New Orleans before the Civil War.[1]

As police lieutenant Michael Hughes walked his beat in the pre-dawn darkness of a mild but muggy New Orleans morning in May 1851, he heard the "quick footsteps" of a man "padding along in his stocking feet." Attracted by the sound, Hughes spotted a partially dressed man running headlong down Poydras Street. The policeman gave chase and finally caught the fleeing man, whom he recognized immediately as Abraham Parker, the pilot of the riverboat *C. E. Watkins.* Hughes asked Parker what difficulty had occurred to cause him to run down the street half dressed in the middle of night. Parker stated that he had done nothing, that he was only going to his boat on the river, and he asked Hughes to allow him to pass. After repeated questioning, Parker finally admitted—"with considerable embarrassment and hesitation"—that he had visited a woman in a house of ill fame somewhere on Basin or Bienville Street, that some people had attacked him and stolen his clothes, and that he had had to flee for his life. Hughes later testified that Parker "appeared very much excited," and Hughes, considering Parker's unusual appearance and the time of night, decided to take him to the watch house for further questioning.[2]

Not long after Parker arrived at the watch house with Lieutenant Hughes, several people burst in and reported the murder of a woman in a house of ill repute on Gravier Street between Circus and St. John streets, some distance from Basin or Bienville Street. Officers arriving at the scene had found a pair of boots, a hat, a coat, and a pistol in the adjoining yard. Muddy footprints tracked over the backyard fence, which had two pickets broken off at the top, as though a person had climbed over them in haste.[3]

Once inside the house, the officers found the bloody body of Eliza Phillips on the floor in the middle room, shot dead. When they returned to the watch house, Hughes asked Parker if the hat found at the murder scene belonged to him. Parker did not answer, but when Hughes handed him the hat, he placed it on his head. The police officer then conducted Parker to the Orleans Parish jail to await a hearing on the incident. After a postmortem examination, the coroner concluded that Eliza Phillips died of a gunshot wound "which passed through the chin of the deceased, came out through the neck, and again passed into the body," stopping finally at Phillips's third rib.[4]

City newspapers reported the case with headlines such as "Another Horrible Murder" and "A Woman Murdered in Gravier Street." One reporter described Phillips as being a "degraded woman . . . in the habit of living with some dissolute character who aided her in extorting money from her visitors." According to this journalist, if Phillips, a twenty-five-year-old English woman who had resided in the city only briefly, had not had the "bold aspect and visible depravity which characterize her class, she would be considered handsome." This writer described Parker as a man well known in New Orleans, about thirty-five years old, "middle sized and robust," a man "from whom better acts might be expected, than those for which he has become a criminal," an upstanding man who had a wife and children in Tennessee. The local press would continue to emphasize Phillips's status as a "degraded woman" and her murder as just "another of those frequent occurrences," while throughout the preliminary hearing and subsequent trial it portrayed Parker as a respectable husband and father.[5] As it turned out, the highest court in Louisiana would base its decision in this case on the same assumptions.

James Caldwell, the recorder of the Second Municipality, conducted the preliminary hearing on 12 May in front of a standing-room-only crowd. People who could not find space in the courtroom sat on the window sills within the chamber or tried to hear the proceedings from outside the building's open windows. Eugene Suchet, Phillips's "bedfellow" and almost certainly her pimp, testified first. With minor variations, all other testimony corroborated Suchet's description of the events of the night of 7 May and the early hours of 8 May. Toward the end of an evening of drinking on the town, Abraham Parker and an unidentified male friend decided to visit a brothel at 211 Gravier Street. The owner of the property, Sumpter Turner, a partner in the prosperous tobacco brokerage firm of Turner and Renshaw, entrusted the actual management of the brothel to his slave Eliza Turner, who also sold coffee and perhaps liquor in the front room of the house. Parker entered the house, put his arms around Phillips, whom he had obviously known previously, and "said he would like to go into a room with her, to which she consented." They walked together into a back room. Almost immediately Phillips emerged and showed the slave Eliza "a piece of money"; the slave gave her approval to "go ahead," and Phillips returned to the back room. After some time, Phillips came out of the room and walked out into the street. Parker went out into the front room dressed only "in his socks and drawers," sat down, and talked for some time with his friend. Phillips became angry when she returned to the coffee room and found Parker still there, undressed. "G——d d——d you, why don't you put on your clothes and go?" Phillips asked. Parker responded that she could "go to Hell," that it was none of her business, and he told her not to touch his clothes. Ignoring him, she went into the back room, retrieved his clothes, and threw them on a chair in the front room. As she did so, Parker's watch fell on the floor, shattering the crystal. Infuriated, Parker said, "D——d you, I told you not to touch my clothes."[6]

As he began to dress himself, the "partly drunk" Parker accused Phillips of stealing a Tennessee $10 bill from his vest pocket. Phillips called Parker a "damned liar" and denied taking the money. Parker drew a loaded pistol from his breast pocket and said to his friend that "the d——d bitch" had taken it. He then struck Eliza on the back of her neck with the back of his hand, a blow sufficiently powerful to propel her into the next room, saying, "Get it G——d d——d you, or I will shoot you . . . and everybody else in the house." Parker's friend tried to quiet him, suggesting that they leave the house. At this time Eugene Suchet entered the room and immediately tried to mollify the "somewhat intoxicated" Parker by assuring him that if Phillips had taken the money he would certainly "slap her face." When Phillips denied once more having the bill, Suchet told Parker that he did not believe she had stolen his money. Infuriated, Parker replied, "God damn you, you are taking up for the woman, I'll shoot you." Phillips continued to deny that she had the bill, and at his friend's suggestion, Parker took a candle and went into the bedroom to search for the money. When he did not find it, he took hold of Phillips and told her he knew she had the bill "and that he was bound to have it, that he had treated her well, and that she ought not to have robbed him." Phillips opened her purse to show that it contained only the $2.50 gold piece that Parker had given her for her services, a few other pieces of silver change, and a receipt for her weekly room rent of $9.00, signed by the slave Eliza. Once more, Phillips asked Parker to leave the house. At this, Parker cursed again, raised his pistol, put it to Phillips's neck, fired, and ran out the back door. Phillips "lingered a few minutes in dreadful agony, and then died." A thorough search of the dead woman's clothing and the house at 211 Gravier failed to produce the $10 bill.[7]

Local newspapers reported that Parker "appeared somewhat affected during the proceeding [the preliminary hearing] but heard evidence with perfect calmness." The crowd that packed the recorder's courtroom for the three-day hearing exhibited "the most lively interest in the proceedings." Randell Hunt, a well-known local attorney, served as counsel for the accused at the preliminary hearing. While Hunt did not deny that Parker had shot Phillips, he hinted that the gun had fired accidentally. His most strenuous defense of Parker lay in his insistence that Eugene Suchet's character was so depraved that no one could or should believe him, even on oath. Hunt called Suchet "an infamous scoundrel living upon an unfortunate woman . . . a dissolute and corrupt vagabond." Recorder James Caldwell agreed, stating publicly that if the case depended on the testimony of Suchet alone, he would immediately discharge the accused, "for, unsupported, he would not believe a word Suchet said . . . the manner in which he lived stamped him with infamy." Under cross-examination, Suchet claimed that he worked as a blacksmith when he could find work but that illness had prevented him from finding work for the past six months. He said he had known Phillips when she lived in a house on Perdido Street and that she had moved to the house at 211 Gravier two or three weeks before her death. Suchet admitted that he owned no property and had no income and that he had lodged with the deceased almost every night for the past six months. Although Caldwell professed disgust at Suchet's boasting that he had lived off Phillips, the recorder stated that he felt duty-bound to send the case to the First District

Court for a trial for murder. The grand jury found a true bill against Parker for murder on 30 May. Parker pleaded not guilty on 4 June, and the clerk of the First District Court set the case for trial on 17 June.[8]

Located in the Presbytere, one of the buildings flanking the St. Louis Cathedral on Jackson Square, the First District Court of New Orleans shared the rat-infested firetrap into which the building had degenerated with four other district courts and the Supreme Court of Louisiana. Just three weeks before the trial of *State v. Parker,* the grand jury complained that the constant noise of drays passing by the open first-floor windows of the First District Court interfered with jurors hearing important testimony at criminal trials. The building, ordinarily crowded by witnesses, attorneys, accused criminals, hangers-on, fruit vendors, spectators, civil litigants, and the clerks and judges of six separate courts, presented an unusually hectic scene on the first day of the trial of Abraham Parker: "It was crowded in every part by an anxiously expectant multitude, and hundreds who could not obtain admission crowded to the windows and every attainable spot from which sight or hearing of the proceedings could be obtained." Local newspapers noted that the reputation of the counsel for the defense, the "social position of the accused, and the awful crime with which he was charged" created an interest "seldom exceeded in criminal prosecutions."[9] Judge John Larue presided over the trial. A hardworking member of the bench who kept his docket up to date, Larue had made a reputation as a fair but tough jurist who handed down stiff sentences, "offering terrible prospect[s] to evildoers." The legal community considered Judge Larue "a man of rare natural abilities" who united "high legal attainment and a ready familiarity with the jurisprudence of Louisiana, and the principles and practice of criminal law."[10]

By the time the trial began, two attorneys had joined Randell Hunt on Parker's defense team: John Randolph Grymes and John Blount Robertson. Although Robertson, a young attorney just beginning his career, did not play a major public role in Parker's defense, Randell Hunt and John R. Grymes constituted a formidable legal pair. Grymes, one of the most flamboyant and best-known attorneys in New Orleans, had a reputation for an elegant lifestyle and a penchant for profanity as well as elocutionary eloquence and wit in the courtroom. Only a few days before the *Parker* trial, a New Orleans newspaper commented that Grymes, a member of a bar "not remarkable for its wit," sparked interest among courtroom spectators in a trial of another matter: "The cold unhesitating sophistry of Grymes, with his brief and pithy sentence [*sic*], wherein not always grammatical, every word is harmonious and appropriate." Once when Grymes attempted to postpone a case, he stretched out a speech to the time of the court's adjournment. The judge, "wearied out of all patience, cried out, 'Colonel Grymes, you must know the court has common sense at least.' 'May it please the court,' the colonel replied, '*I was not aware of that fact*'" (italics in original).[11]

The district attorney, Mortimer M. Reynolds, opened the trial by summing up the facts of the case and the applicable law. He then presented a series of witnesses who essentially restated the testimony given at the preliminary hearing. After Reynolds's questioning of Eugene Suchet, Randell Hunt cross-examined him and forced Suchet to admit that he had no income and that Eliza Phillips supported him. When Reynolds objected to this line of questioning, Hunt told the judge that he wished "to show the idle, dissolute, depraved character of the witness." Judge Larue sustained Reynolds's objection, stating that Hunt had taken "more latitude in denunciations of the witness than could be permitted." Hunt then proceeded to introduce witnesses to undermine Suchet's credibility; one witness testified that he would not believe Suchet under oath and that "he knew fifty people who would not believe him under oath either." This witness asserted that "Suchet had been in the habit of supporting himself by extorting money from persons who visited women of bad repute with whom he associated." Hunt then began a series of leading questions concerning the character of Suchet, such as "Is he not idle and vicious, etc.?" At this, Suchet asked for the protection of the court. Reynolds objected to the tone of Hunt's inquiry, and the judge, after considerable discussion among the attorneys, ruled that Hunt could introduce witnesses as related to Suchet's reputation for "truth and veracity" only. Judge Larue stated for the record that he based his ruling on the "Common Law of England."[12]

Grymes and Hunt then introduced witnesses to prove the good character of the defendant. One testified that he had known Parker for seventeen years on the river and that Parker had a wife and children in Tennessee: "He has always borne a good character." The captain of the *C. E. Watkins* also vouched for Parker's character, but on cross-examination he admitted that, after a fight in Cincinnati, authorities had charged Parker with manslaughter: "I heard that he was surrounded and cut his way out. I have seen him fight men. I heard that one man he cut in Cincinnati died . . . and again I heard he had not." Hunt and Grymes then introduced "a host of witnesses" who testified as to the "excellent character of the accused." When Reynolds objected, Judge Larue ruled that Hunt and Grymes had to restrict their character witnesses to testify only to the accused's general reputation for "peace and quietness."[13]

In a one-hour closing statement, which the *New Orleans Bee* described as one of his most "masterly efforts," Reynolds attempted to minimize the damage done to his principal witness by arguing that other witnesses had corroborated much of Suchet's testimony, including the fact that Parker had admitted that he had gotten into some difficulty with a woman on the night of the homicide. To witnesses who had alleged that Suchet's association with "lewd women" made it impossible to believe him, Reynolds posed this question, "Was it a greater offense for him to seek the association of such women—a single man without wife or children—than it was in the prisoner at the bar, who though husband and father, so cohabited with such women?" Reynolds warned the jury that the defense attorneys would play on their sympathy for Parker's wife and children but that the jury must remember that the defendant "ruthlessly sent a lonely and unprotected woman to her last account, without a moment's preparation, and though she was a fallen creature, though she led a life of shame, she was equally under the protection of the law as the chastest in the land." [14]

Randell Hunt captured the "undivided attention" of the large and excited crowd of spectators in his two-hour closing statement. "Mr. Hunt was particularly severe in the animadversions on the testimony of Eugene Suchet." In what one newspaper described as a "terrible excoriation," Hunt attempted to discredit Suchet's testimony as "wholly false and groundless." Although he had presented no evidence at trial to substantiate his charge, he closed his attack on Suchet with a cheap shot, accusing him of stealing the ten-dollar bill, thus causing Phillips's death. Hunt then characterized Parker as "a man brave and humane . . . when he visited this woman it was not with a feeling of enmity, but the very contrary." Although Hunt admitted that Parker had had sex with the deceased in what he characterized as "a moment of looseness and levity," he claimed that Parker had shot Phillips quite by accident. In closing, Hunt appealed to the sympathy of the jury, "which was a touching specimen of forensic eloquence." [15]

Much to the disappointment of the crowd, Grymes spoke for only ten minutes. As one of the newspapers observed, "Mr. Grymes speaks so rarely in a criminal case, and always with so much effect, that one of his arguments is a thing to be treasured up." In a "short, but telling" statement totally unsupported by the testimony, Grymes argued that "the homicide was excusable and accidentally committed" because Parker, anticipating an attack by Suchet, fired by accident. [16]

The district attorney had the final say. He argued that "the law presumed the homicide to be malicious by the fact that the prisoner carried about with him a loaded pistol, and used it fatally, without sufficient provocation" to commit "a cruel and unprovoked murder." [17]

Judge Larue then charged the jury, in "an impressive and impartial charge," warning them not to bow to outside influences such as "the excited crowd attending the trial" or the testimony of the friends or enemies of the accused or the deceased. The judge reminded the jury that the defense had conceded that "a woman has been murdered" and the jury had to decide whether her death resulted from accident or intentional act. "You must judge of this by common sense, by the rules that govern your judgment in every day transactions, your own heart and testimony. A better rule I cannot lay down for you." Judge Larue then explained the difference between murder and manslaughter to the jury, but he did not comment on the testimony. The jury left to deliberate at 1:40 in the afternoon. Unmoved by the defense's attempt to smear Suchet and sanctify Parker, the jury returned at 3:00 PM with a verdict of "guilty of manslaughter." On the following day, Judge Larue sentenced Parker to twenty years in the state penitentiary and a fine of one thousand dollars, not an unusually severe sentence for manslaughter. Parker's attorneys immediately applied for bail, which Larue set at fifteen thousand dollars. Parker posted bond the same day and left the courthouse, free on bail. He would never serve a day of his sentence. [18]

On 22 June, Judge Larue refused a petition for a new trial, and the defense attorneys appealed to the Supreme Court of Louisiana. Hunt and Grymes filed several bills of exceptions, asserting that Larue had violated the rules of evidence by restricting testimony concerning the character and misdeeds of Eugene Suchet. Specifically, the defense attorneys objected to not being allowed to introduce testimony to prove that Suchet "is a man of infamous character—notoriously guilty of *acting falsely* [italics in original] and fraudulently by extorting money by force . . . of living among lewd and abandoned women." Furthermore, the defense complained that Larue had not permitted them to prove that Suchet "had no means of support, and no means of obtaining money than those just set forth . . . and that from his Vices and General bad character . . . he is unworthy of credit [credibility]." Judge Larue answered this charge by saying simply that "he had felt bound to follow the rules of evidence set forth in the Common Law of England." The judge stated that although he had admitted proof concerning the general reputation of the witness "as to truth and veracity. . . [he] did not feel justified under the law in going further." [19]

A second bill of exceptions complained that Larue had restricted the defense attorneys from presenting evidence to prove anything about Parker's character beyond his reputation for "peace and quiet." Grymes and Hunt stated that Larue had erred by not allowing them to introduce witnesses who could testify that Parker "would be one of the last men on earth willingly to shed a woman's blood:—that he is a kind and affectionate husband and father—industrious & honest, of strict integrity & of pure morals." [20]

Isaac Johnson, the attorney general and a former governor of Louisiana, presented the state's case before the Supreme Court of Louisiana. Johnson denounced Grymes and Hunt's attempts to allow into evidence facts concerning the infamous character of Eugene Suchet: "The credit of a witness can only be impeached by general accounts of his character and reputation and not by particular crimes of which he was never convicted." Johnson defended Larue's determination "to rest his decision upon the rules of evidence . . . as it prevails at Common Law." He also defended Larue's restriction that witnesses could testify about Parker's character only to offer proof of his "general character . . . and not of particular acts." [21]

The Supreme Court rendered its decision on 23 February 1852. Ruling that Judge Larue had erred in restricting the defense to proof of Suchet's general reputation for "truth and veracity" alone, the high court held that the defense "should have been allowed to offer general evidence as to the general character of the witness impeached," to allow the state to inquire as to how the witnesses learned of his character. The justices made it clear that they approved of Larue's forbidding the defense to question witnesses who might testify about specific illegal or immoral acts committed by Suchet. After all, it was *not* Suchet who was on trial. Their approval may have been based on practical considerations rather than on their interpretation of the law, since they admitted that allowing witnesses' testimony concerning specific acts "might delay trials to a degree that might render the administration of justice impracticable." [22]

The ruling also faulted Larue for restricting the defense attorneys to proof of Parker's reputation for "peace and quietness . . . he should be permitted to show his character as to such particular moral qualities as have pertinence to the charge for which he is under trial." Citing Henry Roscoe's *Digest of the Law of Evidence in Criminal Cases* as authority, the justices sent the case back to the First District Court for a new trial, with instruction to Judge Larue to admit evidence of Suchet's bad character and testimony to prove Parker's high morals. A careful reading of Roscoe's treatise does not show unambiguous support for the justices' decision in *State v. Parker.* Roscoe stated that "the good character of the party accused, satisfactorily established by competent witnesses, is an ingredient which ought always to be submitted to the consideration of the jury . . . the nature of the charge and the evidence by which it is supported, will often render such ingredient of little or no avail . . . but the more correct course seems to be . . . to leave the jury to form their conclusion . . . whether an individual whose character was previously unblemished, has or has not committed the particular crime." However, Roscoe also stressed that if the jury entertained any doubt about the guilt of the accused, jurors could use evidence of good character to aid them in their deliberations. Therefore, as the defense admitted that Parker had shot Phillips, according to the Roscoe, admitting more extensive evidence of Parker's good character should not have played a part in determining the jury's verdict.[23]

Associate Justice Isaac Preston, under whose tutelage Larue had studied law, wrote a separate supporting opinion in *State v. Parker.* He defended the attempt of the defense attorneys to establish the bad character of Suchet, stating that they had only tried to prove that Suchet had "an infamous character, that he was addicted to crimes, which indicated a total disregard of truth without specifying a particular crime committed by him." Citing Roscoe, Justice Preston admitted that many English decisions supported the limitation on testimony imposed by Judge Larue. Still, using *Archbold's Summary of the Law Relating to Pleading and Evidence* as authority, Preston stated that Larue ought not to have limited the witnesses called to impeach Suchet only as to his general character for truth and veracity. Preston interpreted *Archbold* in Parker's favor, neglecting to mention that commentator's contention that if the facts stated by a witness very likely happened as the testimony indicated, "we may be induced to believe it, without very scrupulously inquiring into his character for integrity, veracity, etc." This reading of Archbold weakened Preston's argument, since other testimony corroborated Suchet's and made the establishment of Suchet's bad character irrelevant. Although Preston admitted that Larue based his rulings on the common law, he stated: "The ancient rules of evidence are . . . subject to *change* [italics his] where it is indispensable to truth and justice . . . the tendency of modern decisions is to relax the strict rules of evidence with a view to lay every thing [*sic*] before Courts and Juries which ought to have an influence upon the case before them." Preston used another and more liberal common-law commentator, Leonard MacNally, to justify his reasoning: "The ancient rules of the common law were much relaxed by statutes on this subject." This statement tellingly demonstrates not only the divergent paths of English common law and American law but also the willingness of American judges to ignore accepted common-law rules when it suited them. Therefore, Preston concluded, the trial court judge should have admitted evidence that Suchet "had notoriously the character of acting falsely & fraudulently, of extorting money by force and cheating from the unwary & feeble and of living among lewd and abandoned women." As no court had ever convicted Suchet of any of these acts, however, these charges constituted mere allegations. [24]

Preston used the same reasoning in defending Hunt and Grymes's objections to the limitations on testimony to establish Parker's good character: "The nature of his general character or good acts which the accused offers to prove should have a bearing upon the charges against him . . . and it appears to me so reasonable and humane that I cannot think it is inconsistent with the rules of evidence . . . it is but the just reward of many good actions that they should be of some avail to a man in his utmost need. " Preston again cited *MacNally's Rules of Evidence on the Pleas of the Crown* to support his decision. However, Preston selected those portions of MacNally's treatise that supported his reasoning. He cited an English case in which the judge allowed not only testimony as to the general good character of the accused but also a specific statement that the witness knew the defendant "to be a dutiful son, and that he supported a helpless parent by his industry." The judge in this case had ruled to admit this statement because he found "a humane reason for admitting such evidence"—and judges must temper justice with mercy. But MacNally also stressed that juries should give evidence of character more weight when only circumstantial evidence supported the prosecution's case. *State v. Parker* presented a case of conclusive evidence, as the defense conceded that Parker had shot Phillips. Concurring in the decision of the other justices, Preston sent the case back to Larue with instruction to admit the suppressed evidence in a new trial. [25]

A cursory reading of the supreme court's decision may appear fair, since the justices ruled that Larue's narrow rulings on the admissibility of character evidence for both Suchet and Parker constituted judicial error. But both parts of the supreme court's ruling ignored portions of the very authorities they cited in order to favor Abraham Parker. Criminal law in Louisiana and elsewhere was in a transitory stage of development in the 1850s. A new state constitution had granted jurisdiction over criminal appeals to the supreme court only in 1845. In the absence of much settled law, a justice who did not wish to credit the testimony of a pimp would find an authoritative voice on which to base his ruling. Thus *State v. Parker*, a ruling of expediency and circumstance, clearly favored a socially prominent man with skillful attorneys. Although no evidence exists to explain the rationale, the court reporter never published the decision in *State v. Parker*. Perhaps the justices preferred that no permanent record remain of the case so that no future attorneys could cite it as precedent, or perhaps Parker's well-known and skill-ful attorneys kept it from becoming published.[26]

The *New Orleans Daily True Delta* published an editorial criticizing the decision, noting that it "radically changes the ruling . . . in the law of evidence." The *New Orleans Daily Crescent* stated that the effect of the decision "will greatly prolong trials and make evidence rules uncertain." The ruling dismayed the staff of the First District Court. According to the *Delta,* "neither the Judge [Larue] nor the District Attorney [Reynolds] could conceal their dissatisfaction with the ruling of the higher tribunal." Prophetically, the *New Orleans Daily Picayune* observed on the same day that the decision to remand would result in dismissal of the case, since one of the principal witnesses had died and one had left for California.[27]

By the time Abraham Parker's new trial began, Judge Larue no longer presided over the criminal court. The Louisiana Constitution of 1852 made all positions on the formerly appointive state bench elective, including the judge of the First District Court of New Orleans. And although voters elected John Larue to that position in a landslide in May 1853, Larue announced in November of that year that he would resign his position on 1 January 1854 to resume private practice. One local newspaper reported that an act of the Louisiana legislature that restricted the First District Court exclusively to hearing criminal cases and a lowering of the annual salary of district court judges from $3,500 to $2,500 drove Larue to resign: "It is a painful and mortifying reflection that one of the most competent and useful judges who have ever sat upon the bench in Louisiana, has been forced to throw aside the ermine, and resume the active duties of his profession, from the inadequate compensation of his office . . . the false and dangerous economy of stinting the salaries of our judges." When the day arrived for Larue's resignation, the grand jury of the First District Court wrote a highly complimentary letter praising Larue's integrity and conscientious service on the bench. The attorney general attempted to place the letter in the record of the court and submit it to the local newspapers for publication, but Larue refused this commendation. He thanked the grand jury for their sentiments, "but as he had done nothing more than perform his duty, he could not permit the address of the Grand Jury to be put upon the records of the court." In an editorial, the *Picayune* stated: "It is a matter of regret that the judiciary of New Orleans has lost in the retirement of Judge Larue, one of its most able and faithful judges." John Blount Robertson, the third attorney on Abraham Parker's defense team, won the special election called to fill the position created by Larue's resignation.[28]

Three and a half years passed before the First District Court of New Orleans called Parker to stand trial again for the murder of Eliza Phillips. The long delay occurred because the prosecution, as the *Picayune* had foretold, could not find the necessary witnesses to retry the case. Although no record exists of the new trial, several New Orleans newspapers reported that it began and ended on 31 January 1855. The clerk called the names of the witnesses, but none appeared, and "it being apparent to the court that they could never appear," the district attorney entered a nolle prosequi, and the judge dismissed Parker. In neither trial did four significant eyewitnesses appear; nor were they called to testify. Abraham Parker's never identified male companion when he visited the brothel never testified in the case; in fact, his name never appeared in the record or in the newspaper accounts of the incident, no doubt to protect his reputation from the public knowledge that he had visited a house of prostitution, whether he used the services of one of the women or not. The two other prostitutes who lived in the house, the notorious Nancy Mayfield and Catherine Shay, never testified in either trial, although both were in the house at the time of the murder. Antebellum courts often discounted the testimony of prostitutes in felony trials on the basis that they were too depraved to be worthy of credibility. And of course, under Louisiana law, the slave Eliza Turner could not testify in court for or against any free person, black or white.[29] By the time of the new trial, Suchet had confirmed the accusations against his character. The *Picayune* reported in 1853 that Suchet faced a charge of stealing a gold watch worth forty-five dollars from a woman's house, and in 1854 he came before the recorder charged with assaulting and beating a woman. In reporting Parker's new trial, the *Delta* noted that Suchet "has become notoriously infamous, had several times been in the Work House, and is now a fugitive from justice on a charge of robbery." By 1855, Eliza Phillips was largely forgotten; two of the three newspapers that reported the case's dismissal gave her first name as Isabella and reported her address incorrectly, although still in the district in which many prostitutes resided. The *Delta,* echoing Grymes's false assertion in his closing statement, reported that Parker, fearing assault by a number of persons, had accidentally fired his gun.[30]

First District Court judge John Blount Robertson presided over the new trial and dismissal. Although the case did not proceed to trial, as a former member of Parker's defense team, Robertson should have recused himself. An act of the Louisiana legislature required judges to recuse themselves if they had any interest in the case, "having been employed, or consulted as advocate in the cause." Although Robertson played a minor role in Parker's defense at the first trial, and although he probably knew that the witnesses against Parker would in all likelihood not appear, he should have recused himself to remove any hint of impropriety. What would have happened had the case proceeded to trial?[31]

Abraham Parker never served a day for the killing of Eliza Phillips. It is not clear from the record whether he paid court costs. After his dismissal city directories continued to list him as a riverboat pilot who rented a succession of rooms in New Orleans until 1889, when his name disappeared from the directory.[32]

State v. Parker demonstrates the ability of court records to illumine the law and the workings of courts, attorneys, and judges and to reveal societal attitudes about crime, gender, and class status. An 1817 ordinance of the city of New Orleans made renting rooms or lodging to any woman "notoriously abandoned to lewdness" an offense punishable by a fine of fifteen dollars for each twenty-four hours the offender, after receiving notice from the mayor, continued to furnish housing to such women. The following year, the Louisiana legislature passed a law that prohibited keeping a brothel; violators faced a fine or imprisonment at the discretion of the court. State law did not make prostitution a crime, but the city ordinance made "any woman or girl notoriously abandoned to lewdness, who shall occasion scandal or disturb the tranquility of the neighborhood," subject to a fine of twenty-five dollars or one month in jail. An 1845 city ordinance made it illegal for such women to drink in cabarets or coffeehouses, with violators facing the same penalty. Eliza Phillips's living arrangements demonstrate that police, recorders, and judges enforced these laws sporadically, when they bothered to enforce them at all. Phillips rented a room in a building that housed several prostitutes. The owner of the building, a prominent white businessman, profited from this arrangement while his slave managed the brothel. Her arrest the morning after Phillips's death and subsequent appearance before Justice of the Peace Jacob Winter on a charge of keeping a brothel ended in a quick dismissal. Although no evidence exists that the slave manager sold liquor in the house, she did sell coffee to the public, further violating city ordinances. As no law specifically made selling sex a crime, most of the city's recorders charged so-called lewd women brought before them as vagrants, although they had residences and did not therefore fit the legal description of vagrants. A few days after Phillips's death the issue of whether recorders could charge prostitutes with vagrancy came before Recorder Caldwell's court: "There was quite a fluttering of silks and ribbons in Recorder Caldwell's court this morning, as the police last night made quite a haul in Perdido,

Phillippa, St. John, and Gravier streets; the consequences of which was that fifteen women, said to be lewd and abandoned, were arrested on a charge of vagrancy. . . .The women were not without legal counsel, who used much ingenuity and tact in explaining and twisting that much disputed law in relation to vagrants. After much argument, which wasted about an hour and a half, the Recorder fined the accused five dollars each." The attorney for the alleged vagrants argued successfully that the recorder could not charge the eighteen women brought before him with vagrancy because they had residences. However, the recorder could charge them with drinking in grog shops and fine them five dollars each. This police sweep of the Perdido-Phillippa–St. John–Gravier district came as a result of an outraged letter to the editor published by the *New Orleans Daily Crescent* one week after Phillips's death. The writer, who used the pen name "Decency," complained that the area had become "a depot for lewd and abandoned women . . . who appear to have wholly taken over that portion of the city . . . impossible to pass along without being insulted in the grossest manner . . . they mix with negroes both free and slave on terms of the most disgusting familiarity." A year following Eliza Phillips's death, Judge Larue sent a number of women charged with vagrancy back to the recorder's court, stating that "the [First District] court ought not to be troubled with such cases . . . Recorders should fine such offenders."[33]

A reading of Louisiana law prohibiting brothel keeping and acting as a "lewd and abandoned women" and even a cursory view of the enforcement of these state statutes and city ordinances make it clear that neither lawmakers nor the public sincerely wished to eradicate prostitution. Only a few dozen cases charging people with keeping a brothel came before the First District Court of New Orleans in the 1850s, and almost all these case records indicate that the prosecutor filed a nolle prosequi dismissing the case before the matter came to trial. The scarcity of these cases on the criminal docket contrasted sharply with local newspapers reports of dozens of arrests of so-called lewd women and operators of brothels each year. Unless prostitution caused a public nuisance or disturbed otherwise "respectable" neighborhoods, the authorities allowed the profession to exist and even flourish in antebellum New Orleans. A contemporary writer noted that men in New Orleans went quite openly to houses of prostitution. This writer estimated that prostitutes occupied at least three-fifths of the dwelling rooms in certain parts of the city and that an "immense number" of regularly established brothels operated quite openly: "It is not unusual to see the windows and doors of almost every house as far as the eye can recognize them, filled with these girls."[34]

State v. Parker also illuminates societal attitudes about prostitution and gender. Antebellum New Orleanians regarded prostitution as a women's offense, although obviously women could not commit this act alone. No evidence exists of prosecution of their customers or even newspaper accounts that reveal the names of such men. The *Parker* case record and the local newspapers demonstrate a notable lack of sympathy for prostitutes in general and Eliza Phillips in particular. Newspapers constantly referred to her as a "degraded woman" and could not even admit she that she appeared attractive without qualifying the statement by mentioning "the visible depravity that characterizes her class." Reports of arrests of prostitutes often referred to them sarcastically as "Nymphs de Pavé," literally nymphs of the pavement.[35]

The trial record in the *Parker* case also reflects the double standard that applied to men and women. Although many men in antebellum New Orleans supported wives who earned no wages, the defense attorneys used the fact that Suchet did not work and allowed Phillips to support him as one of the most damning pieces of evidence against his character. Newspapers described Parker as a socially prominent "robust" man without qualification and commented that "better acts might be expected of him." Although antebellum society characterized Phillips's status as "degraded" by her occupation, Parker's availing himself of her services only constituted "a moment of looseness and levity." Parker even bragged that "he had been good to her" when in reality he used her for his own gratification. The very fact that the defense attorneys successfully got their client off without punishment by using a defense stressing Parker's respectability and Phillips's degraded status reflects society's attitudes about men, women, and prostitution. Parker's status as husband and father by its very nature implied good character in antebellum New Orleans society. That the defense attorneys could unblushingly assert that Parker was a man of "pure morals" who would never hurt a woman even though he had spent an evening carrying a loaded, concealed weapon while drinking on the town, committed adultery by purchasing sex from a prostitute, and in a fit of drunken rage killed her speaks volumes about society's attitude. Only the judge and the district attorney mentioned at trial the plain fact that Parker had shot Phillips and that she deserved the protection of the law regardless of her occupation.

State v. Parker also opens a window on slavery in New Orleans. Louisiana law and city ordinances prohibited anyone from operating a brothel, but clearly the slave Eliza Turner managed the brothel at 211 Gravier Street. Phillips felt compelled to show the slave the gold piece Parker gave her before she had sex with him. Only after the slave woman told her to "go ahead" did Phillips enter the bedroom where Parker waited. Louisiana law forbade teaching slaves to read and write, but the rent receipt found in the dead woman's purse bore the slave woman's signature. And the slave woman's speedy dismissal on the charge of keeping a brothel indicated that her owner may have pressured the justice of the peace, or even bribed him, to release her. The facts of this case also demonstrate that the slave Eliza Turner violated several other state statutes and local ordinances. The *Black Code* prohibited slaves from selling "any commodity whatsoever," but Turner sold coffee and perhaps liquor in the front room of the brothel. Masters of slaves who sold goods could suffer penalties of a fine not less than fifty dollars and jail time of not less than one month. City ordinance also prohibited slaves from living away from their owners, but obviously Turner lived at 211 Gravier and her owner did not. Finally, the law did not allow white women "abandoned to lewdness" to live in the same house as women of color, or women of color to rent rooms to such white women.[36] In New Orleans, however, not only did slaves run brothels, but they sometimes worked in them as prostitutes. The *Picayune* reported that the slave Louisa kept a brothel, "the resort for slaves of an abandoned character." Police found two slaves there with passes from their owners and baskets of flowers "to hide their evil deeds." The slave women either convinced their owners that they sold flowers, or the owners knowingly allowed them to work as prostitutes and collected their wages. Six free women of color came before the Recorder Joseph Genois a week before Phillips's murder for keeping "disorderly houses which were frequented by lewd women." Obviously statutes and ordinances against these practices were ordinarily honored only in the breech.[37]

Finally, *State v. Parker* reveals something of the business of prostitution. Parker paid Phillips $2.50 for her services, a high price at a time when sailors earned $15 a month and female servants made between $8 and $12 a month, Phillips paid rent of $9 a week to the slave Eliza. At least two other prostitutes lived at 211 Gravier, as police found them in the house just after the murder. Even if only three prostitutes worked in the house, the owner of the property, Sumpter Turner, would have collected more than $100 a month from his slave manager, not counting any profit she may have made from the sale of coffee or liquor, if she sold liquor. A number of wealthy New Orleans businessmen profited from renting to prostitutes. The merchant John McDonogh made a practice of purchasing houses in fashionable neighborhoods and renting the premises to a brothel keeper. Recorder Caldwell himself rented property to brothel keepers. Sumpter Turner realized an above-average profit from the establishment at 211 Gravier Street. The *Picayune* estimated the average monthly rental for such establishments at $30.[38]

State v. Parker is but one illustration of the variety and vitality of legal history. The character in this drama about whom we know the least, Eliza Phillips, led a brief life that ended in a violent and untimely death. Nearly 150 years later, important historical lessons can still be learned from her death.

8

KEEPING A BROTHEL IN
ANTEBELLUM NEW ORLEANS

Efforts to suppress prostitution in antebellum New Orleans appear to have been feeble at best. Too many economic forces supported the "oldest profession": a huge influx of poor immigrants, low wages for women, merchants who profited from public women buying clothing and jewelry, corrupt politicians, and especially the wealthy landlords who rented their property to brothel managers. While prostitution flourished in many parts of the city, certain areas became known for their concentration of brothels and barrooms. Probably the most notorious was Gallatin Street, a two-block thoroughfare that bordered on the Mississippi River near Esplanade Street. An 1855 article in the *New Orleans Daily Picayune* stated, "But worst among the worst is Gallatin street . . . sons of fraud, treachery and blood meet there the daughters of the night, and with them hold high wassail and unhallowed revelry. There is no redeeming feature to this street of streets." The article mentions the arrest of Jacob Weber, who kept "a disorderly establishment where thieves and prostitutes unlawfully assemble." When police arrested Weber, they found a revolver, a Bowie knife, and a sheath knife under his counter. Another article mentioned that Gallatin Street was "a locality whose occupants are neither famous for their virtue nor sobriety." In 1855 the *Picayune* reported that "a number of the Knights of Gallatin and other distinguished thoroughfares, stand charged with having been engaged in orgies 'which e'en to name would be unlawful' in Black Sophie's house." Yet another article sarcastically referred to Gallatin Street as "that quiet, respectable thoroughfare." Following one of the almost nightly Gallatin Street brawls, this one involving brickbats and pistols and originating in an infamous dive named the California House, the *Picayune* editorialized: "It is time that Gallatin Street was cleaned up by the police. It is filled with low groggeries, and is the resort of the worst and most abandoned of both sexes. Thieves, murderers, prostitutes and drunkards, congregate there, and the sooner they are dispersed, the better for the community." Yet the police proved at times to be a part of the problem. The editorial continued: "A policeman named Phillips, who appears to be connected in some way with the gang, endeavored to prevent the arrest of the rowdies, and has been suspended to await the action of the Police Board."[1]

The New Orleans newspapers frequently reported mass arrests of brothel owners and public women. In 1847 sixteen "grandly dressed women" faced the recorder like the "twenty barbers all in a row." The reporter described them as "frail" (meaning their virtue, not their health) and made fun of them by stating that they could never have been accused of being "fair." Each received a fine of five dollars, and after they paid the fine, the newspaper reported that they "vamoosed." In 1853 the *Picayune* reported the arrest of two dozen brothel keepers on Dauphine Street and another thirty in the area of Customhouse and Burgundy streets. Recorder Ramos fined each twenty dollars, and those who could not pay had to go to the workhouse. Two years earlier the *Picayune* reported the arrests of one man for keeping a brothel and seven individual free women of color: John Wilson at 155 Conti Street, Cecelia Clay at 150 Conti Street, Adele Graval at 164 Conti Street, Fanny Palfrey at 89 Burgundy Street, Estelle Ravenel at 83 Burgundy Street, Herselin Davis at 81 Burgundy Street, Nancy, alias Josephine, at 75 and 77 Burgundy Street, and Felicita Vivrant at 60, 71, and 79 Burgundy Street.[2]

Notices of mass arrests of public women and brothel keepers appeared in the columns of the local newspapers with some regularity. Usually these numerous arrests resulted in low fines, which most of the women paid. As a result, they could be back on the street in a day or so. Such practices did little to suppress prostitution, although the fines helped to fill the city treasury and to pay for the recorders' salaries and court costs. Rounding up large numbers of public women and fining them amounted to an unofficial tax on sin and vice. For example, on one evening in 1850, police arrested twenty-two "lewd and abandoned women." The *Picayune* noted: "It was a sad sight to witness so many females, who might have been an ornament to society, and a delight to their friends, now as lost to shame and sunk to degradation . . . they had for some time past associated with the vile and depraved." The recorder fined them each five dollars. In 1851 a letter sent to the editor of the *New Orleans Daily Crescent* complained of the "insufferable nuisance" of Perdido Street between Baronne and Circus streets, which had become "a depot for lewd and abandoned women and thieves of the most desperate character." The writer complained of the impossibility of walking along that street "without being insulted in the grossest manner." He alleged that the public women congregated in the grog shops in the neighborhood, "where they mix with negroes both free and slave on terms of the most disgusting familiarity." The writer signed himself "Decency" and begged Recorder James Caldwell to do something to remedy the situation. Two days later police arrested sixteen women in the neighborhood. The *Picayune* described the scene in Recorder Caldwell's court room: "There was quite a fluttering of silks and ribbons in Recorder Caldwell's court this morning, as the police last night made quite a haul in Perdido, Phillippa, St. John and Gravier streets." The police arrested the women on the charge of vagrancy. They appeared with what the reporter characterized as "able legal counsel," who argued that vagrancy did not apply to the accused women as they all had places to live. Recorder Caldwell fined them each five dollars and dismissed them. Ten days later police arrested three men and three women and charged them with keeping a brothel on Girod Street, but there is no evidence of any further prosecution. Six months later, Caldwell fined a brothel keeper, Mary Hawking, twenty-five dollars and the four women in her house five dollars each.[3]

In July 1852 the *Picayune* reported the arrest of twenty-one women of Phillippa Street, a street notorious for its large number of brothels, on the charge of being "lewd and abandoned." According to the article, they came before the recorder "in platoons of six or eight at a time. They were a motley looking set, some being rather young and pretty, while others were shockingly old and ugly." The recorder ordered them to pay fines of five to ten dollars or go to the workhouse. The following year, police arrested twenty-five "nymphs de pavé [of] all ages, complexions and styles of beauty." The recorder ordered small fines or, if they could not pay, a trip to the workhouse. The *Picayune* recognized the futility of such actions. After the arrest of twenty-three women from the vicinity of Phillippa and Perdido streets resulted in the usual low fines or short terms in the workhouse, the newspaper reporter stated: "This wholesale grabbing up of women every now and then, and letting them go again, bears a strong similitude to the actions of that wonderful man we read of in ancient history, who 'marched up the hill and then marched down again.'"[4]

The *Picayune* noted the huge number of public women in the city and the inability or unwillingness of the understaffed police force to suppress the institution: "Ellen Crawly was arrested for being in a house of ill fame. If all persons in that predicament were taken up, the police officials would be obliged to commit suicide to avoid dying of fatigue and exhaustion." Five years later the newspaper editorialized: "The police are at present engaged in a crusade against the keepers of a disreputable class of houses who are constantly endeavoring to affix the stain of pollution on otherwise respectable neighborhoods. . . . The impunity with which such establishments have heretofore been kept open . . . has created no little of surprise among the thinking members."[5]

At the end of April 1852 police arrested numerous public women in "a number of miserable dens in the Third District . . . called Sanctity Row." Recorder Peter Seuzeneau sent them to the First District Court for trial on a charge of keeping a brothel. One week later police arrested more women from Sanctity Row and sent them to the parish prison to await trial. When the cases came to trial, Judge John Larue dismissed the women "with the remark that the court ought not to be troubled with such cases, and that the Recorders should fine such women." The next year police arrested eighteen men and women for either keeping or being in a brothel, one of a handful of cases in which men faced arrest for consorting with prostitutes.[6]

In 1854 the *Picayune* noted the arrest of forty or fifty public women in the Second District to await an appearance before the recorder. The reporter commented: "Most of them were young and pretty, and looked as if their original purity and innocence had never departed." Low fines and irregular attempts to get public women off of the streets failed to discourage prostitution. Under the headline "Arrest of Cyprians," the *Picayune* noted a "clean sweep" of Burgundy Street in August 1854 that netted nineteen "ladies of easy virtue and loose habits, whose indecent conduct scandalized the whole neighborhood." The police made another sweep on Phillippa and Gravier streets in September 1854. The *Picayune* noted that police cleared the streets "infested by lewd and abandoned women . . . a proceeding that rendered that usually noisy portion of the city perfectly quiet and decent. A number of the most abandoned women and riotous men were arrested and sent to the watch house." This report represents one of the few times that men faced arrests as well as women. At times the recorders tried to restrict brothels to less desirable parts of town. In 1855 "several of the lost females of Perdido street were up on charges of being disorderly inmates of disorderly houses. Most of them promised to move farther back towards the Swamp, and on that condition got off for the time being." Police arrested fifty-three "*nymphs de pavé*" in May 1855 from Customhouse, Bienville, and Burgundy streets. The reporter noted that these women "were more sinned against than sinning

[and] presented a woe-begone appearance aptly illustrative of their fallen fortunes." This comment represents a rare hint of sympathy for the plight of the public women. Near the end of 1855 the *Picayune* reported that the police "are at present engaged in a crusade against the keepers of a disreputable class of houses . . . police who have the moral courage to do their duty in the premises should be looked upon as public benefactors." The newspaper expressed shock that such establishments existed side by side with respectable residences. In 1856 police arrested a number of public women, "the originators of all kinds of scandal, from Dauphine, Burgundy and Conti streets. . . . The recorder fined them $10 each and sent them back to the streets." The same year, Charles Lahamon and Samuel Williams paid fines of $15 each for keeping a brothel, and the five women and seventeen men caught in the brothel all paid fine of $5 or their jail fees, one of the few instances in which men faced penalties for being with prostitutes.[7]

In 1857 police increased the number of arrests of public women, and some of them received slightly stiffer fines, although no evidence exists that prostitution declined. In February police descended on "the frail daughters of Gravier street" and arrested twenty-four public women. They faced Recorder Gerard Stith the next day charged with "leading lives of lewdness . . . the poor things represented all degrees of female degradation." Stith fined them each twenty dollars, and for those who could not pay, sixty days in the workhouse. More than half of them paid the fine, and Stith dismissed them. The next month police rounded up six more women "who were found walking in the way of wickedness." In August Recorder Stith sent "a large delegation of female frailties" of Perdido Street to the workhouse for three months. In September police arrested twenty more "Cyprians . . . for leading lewd and abandoned lives." In the same month police arrested "a score of frailties from Gravier, Rampart, and Perdido streets . . . to answer for their deeds of darkness. The array presented by them was far from being attractive. Some looked bloated, lustful and loathsome, while others . . . presented a bold, defiant front and appeared to glory in their shame." They appeared before Recorder Stith with their attorney (whom the newspaper did not name), who pleaded in their behalf. Stith dismissed most of them after they promised to leave the residences where they lived and practiced their profession. He actually fined only three of them, after which he released them. Finally, in December, police rounded up about fifty people, male and female, "in houses . . . which are alleged to be the resort of thieves and all manner of disreputable characters. Recorder Solomon fined the women ten dollars each and "the masculines were mulcted in smaller sums." Again, this is one of those very rare instances in which men faced arrest for patronizing public women. The fact that men paid a lower fine demonstrates the double standard that was applied. Eleven of the women could not pay the fine and went to the workhouse for three months. Three years earlier police had rounded up a number of brothel keepers and prostitutes, and also "a number of their pals and fancy men, who are charged with being dangerous and suspicious characters." This is another rare instance in which police arrested men as well as women. [8]

In 1858 the same pattern of numerous arrests of public women occurred, and the usual low fines or a brief confinement in the workhouse ensued. In April police arrested "a large lot of females, numbering somewhere between three and four dozen." The recorder dismissed some of them, and others received fines of between five and fifteen dollars. Some asked for their cases to be continued until they could be represented by an attorney. Probably wealthy landlords of the brothels paid the legal bills of attorneys who represented public women. Obviously, the women could not pay their rent if they ceased to work because they were in the workhouse or jail. If an attorney could expedite their release, they could return to work the sooner. The following month, police arrested eleven more public women. The recorder ordered them to leave their present residences and "carry their abandoned persons elsewhere. Whether they will obey the order remains to be seen." [9]

Occasionally outraged citizens made affidavits naming women in their neighborhood as prostitutes and demanding that the recorders have them arrested and punished. For example, in 1859 a Mr. Tappan alleged that "several frail nymphs, who rejoice in the euphronious names of Kate Tracy, Jenny Pleutin, Josephine Wall, Bobtail Joe and others are a perfect nuisance" in the neighborhood of Customhouse and Basin streets. Police sporadically arrested numbers of public women. In an article with the headline "War on the Women," the *Picayune* noted that "sixteen frail creatures, whose homes and behaviors are too disorderly to meet the sanction of their neighbors, were arrested by the Second District Police. They will appear before the Recorder today, a painful illustration of the same old tale—hunger, temptation, strong drink and vice." The next day, the newspaper reported the arrest of three brothel keepers of the houses from which the police arrested the sixteen women. Recorder Emile Wiltz fined the brothel keepers and the sixteen women fifteen dollars each or one month in the parish prison. Four of the women could not pay the fine and went to jail. Two days later police arrested six public women for violating city ordinances by standing in front of their doors or sitting on their steps. All paid the fifteen-dollar fine except one, who the newspaper reported "accepted lodgings in the P.P. [parish prison] Hotel." At the end of June police arrested nineteen "frail residents of certain streets." Once more Recorder Wiltz fined them fifteen dollars or a month in the workhouse. The newspaper article that reported the arrests noted that most paid their fine. In October 1859 seven free women of color successfully fought charges brought against them for being "lewd and abandoned. The Recorder found no basis for the charge of lewdness, and the women proved not to be abandoned, as they had quite a number of friends." The recorder dismissed their case.[10]

In 1860 a conscientious police officer and a recorder determined to suppress prostitution in the Second District (the French Quarter) made a concerted effort to get public women off the streets. In July 1860 Lieutenant Crevon and other officers arrested twenty women of Dauphine, Toulouse, and Burgundy streets and brought them before Recorder Anatole Blache. He sentenced each of them to pay a twenty-five-dollar fine or one month's imprisonment. Eight of the women paid the fine; the rest went to jail. The following month Lieutenant Crevon brought an additional thirty-six women of Gallatin Street before the same recorder. Blache told them "he was determined to rid his district of idle, vicious persons." He sent them all to the workhouse for six months and warned then that they would have to serve the full time, as "no influence could obtain their release." As the women climbed into the Black Maria (the paddy wagon), many "indulged in ribald jests and profane language of the most disgusting kind . . . whilst a few bowed their heads in shame." Apparently some of the men "who are the protectors and companions of these women were present . . . but none dared interfere." The *Picayune* editorialized: "We take pleasure in noticing the energy and impartial severity that have characterized Recorder Blache's course since his advent to the Recordership." The article also gave credit to the chief of police, who implemented the strategy of swooping down on several brothels at once, in such a manner that not one of the women escaped.[11]

Six weeks later the women of Gallatin Street sued for a writ of habeas corpus before the Fifth District Court, and Judge H. B. Eggleston granted the writ and released the women. An irregularity in Recorder Blache's affidavits formed the basis of his ruling. Although we cannot know what pressure the landlords brought to bear on the judge, he used a legal technicality to release the women. Undeterred, Recorder Blache ordered new arrests of the women and four brothel keepers: Mrs. Fitzsimmons, Laurens Seidler, Dan Rich, and George Kent, this time on a charge of disturbing the peace and committing scandal. No record exists of the sentences in these cases, but as the charges were for misdemeanors, the punishment must have been slight. The *Picayune* called for new legislation to discourage prostitution by a registry of the brothels and the listing of correct names of the prostitutes within: "We have known some to be arrested half a dozen times, under as many names. . . . In a word, establishments that shelter vice and crime . . . . where vagrants thieves and murderers congregate, ought to be 'houses of glass' always open to the vigilant eye of the well organized police." Finally in October Blache tried a new legal method to punish the women of Gallatin Street. He required eight of the women to give bail in the amount of one thousand dollars to keep the peace for six months. Only one could furnish the bail, and Blache sent the other seven to prison. Unless someone made bail for them, they would have to stay in jail for the six months. The *Picayune* observed smugly, "We will see how the degraded creatures will get over this." Finally toward the end of the month, Blache sent the four brothel keepers, Seidler, Fitzsimmons, Rich, and Kent, to the First District Court for trial. He set bail for each at five hundred dollars. However, no evidence exists that these cases ever appeared before the First District Court of New Orleans. George Kent had appeared before the First District Court in 1857 charged with keeping a brothel, but the district attorney dropped the case with a nolle prosequi. [12]

In 1860 "a great array . . . of the frail goddesses of the Second District" appeared before Recorder Louis Gastinel charged with being "lewd and abandoned." Three women received fines of twenty-five dollars, fourteen received fines of ten dollars, and the recorder released four because of insufficient evidence. The *Picayune* commented, "It is about this time of year annually, that the moral sensitivies of our police become suddenly alive to the immoral neighborhoods . . . of our city, and arrests are accordingly made to replenish the depleted treasury. It would be better for the morality of the city if the authorities would resort at once to direct taxation." Indeed, the violent and infamous Delia Swift, alias Bridget Fury, complained about the frequent fines levied on her "and coolly observed that it was but little use for them to make money if it were all extracted from them in the shape of fines." [13]

Seventy-five cases involving people charged with "keeping a brothel" or "keeping a disorderly brothel" came before the First District Court between 1846 and 1862. In nineteen of these cases men faced charges of keeping a brothel, and in five cases women faced charges jointly with men. The overwhelming majority of prosecutions for keeping a brothel involved women. None listed the name of the attorney for the brothel keepers. Whether their counsel did not want their names to appear in the record in such cases or whether the defendants did not hire an attorney cannot be ascertained. The first case heard by the First District Court of New Orleans provides an example of a typical case of this nature. Eliza Reynolds, a free woman of color, faced charges of keeping a brothel on Burgundy Street between Conti and Bienville streets. Described as a "griffe" woman (a term used to describe a person who appeared to be the offspring of a black and a mulatto), Reynolds, according to the record, "was in the habit of receiving disorderly persons both white and blacks [sic] slaves and free who are in the habit of committing scandals . . . and disturbing the peace and tranquility of the neighborhood." Reynolds must have either concealed herself or left town because the next and last notation in the case stated that the sheriff could not find her to summon her to trial. [14]

Almost all these cases either did not continue to trial, or the district attorney dropped the case with a nolle prosequi. In 1846 all three trials of people accused of "keeping a brothel" ended in nolle prosequi. Mrs. A. J. Collins faced charges of not only "keeping a disorderly brothel" but "keeping a disorderly tippling house." Her neighbor brought these charges against her, stating that she "did suffer persons of ill-fame and dishonest reputation to gather and misbehave themselves, to the great damage and scandal of the neighborhood." For unknown reasons, the neighbor withdrew his complaint on 29 August 1846, and the district attorney dropped the case with a nolle prosequi two days later. In the same month, Ferdinand Sanadet faced a charge of "keeping a brothel." The charge contained the same language as the *Collins* case but added that two white girls, age ten, were "brought to the house to sleep with men." This case also ended in a nolle prosequi. Finally, Nancy Dewett faced the charge of "keeping a disorderly brothel." After two months of inactivity following the charge, this case also ended with a nolle prosequi. [15]

The First District Court of New Orleans heard only one case of brothel keeping in 1847. Although the record of this trial has not survived, the docket book indicates that a trial did occur and ended in a hung jury, after which the district attorney dropped the case with a nolle prosequi. The same year one woman, Mathilda Raymond, alias Amelia Raymond, faced arrest three times for brothel keeping. Police first arrested four "light colored negro wenches" in August 1847 "for living in a house of ill fame . . . they are the slaves of Mathilda Raymond, kept in her house for the vilest of purposes." Police again arrested her in June 1848 at her residence at 188 Gravier Street (corner of Phillippa). At the time of her arrest, the record noted, she wore a gold watch and two diamond rings. On 22 July 1848, Judge John

McHenry sentenced her to a one-hundred-dollar fine for keeping a brothel. When she refused to pay, the sheriff had her arrested and confined in the parish prison. She sued under a writ of habeas corpus, and McHenry released her because the law under which the jury convicted her did not call for such a sentence. Subsequently this case ended in a nolle prosequi in January 1849. The third arrest occurred in July 1848 and ended in a nolle prosequi, also in January 1849. In this case a notorious slave trader, Elihu Cresswell, signed the appearance bond for Raymond, an indication of the connections between slavery and prostitution. [16]

Five more brothel-keeping cases, all involving brothels in the Phillippa-Gravier-Baronne neighborhood, came before the First District Court in 1848. The first two, the cases of Cynthia Moore, alias Turner, and Isabelle Jenkins, went to trial and resulted in convictions and sentences. The first case, in which the jury found Moore guilty but recommended her to the mercy of the court, resulted in a sentence of one month in the parish prison and court costs of $10.55. In the second conviction, Jenkins also received a sentence of one month and court costs of $8.15. In both cases a neighbor of Moore and Jenkins, Frank Young, brought the charges. Although both cases resulted in convictions, the light sentences did nothing to discourage prostitution. In the next two prosecutions, one against a woman and one against a man, the court reverted to its usual patterns; both cases ended in a nolle prosequi. The last case, against Amanda Williams, went to trial, and the jury found Williams not guilty, despite the testimony of a witness stating that he had seen men going in and out of the house at all hours of the day and night. [17]

At the end of 1848 the case of Eliza Fluhart came before the First District Court. She faced charges of running a "house of ill fame," and police officers testified that they had seen men going in and out of her house at all hours of the day and night. However, the jury could not agree on a verdict, and the case ended in mistrial. Fluhart, though, did not go quietly. She hired an attorney, J. M. Holland, and sued Recorder James Golding for ten thousand dollars for the treatment she received. She alleged that during a thirty-day period "she had been so much vexed harassed and distressed . . . almost to make her life insupportable." She claimed to have been twice seized during that period and thrown into prison "and made to undergo every kind of humiliation, degradation, bodily pain and distress of mind." She claimed that police took her "in her own home" and took her to the watch house, where they held her for three hours. After her release the police again seized her and took her to Recorder Golding's court, where the recorder placed her

in a "cage . . . which is generally used for the purpose of confining criminals." The recorder told her that her arrest was the result of her being "what
he was pleased to call a 'lewd and abandoned woman,' . . . which she be-
lieves is unknown to the laws of this state." She claimed that while she was
held in the dock she suffered from the "humiliating gaze of a great number
of persons . . . for five hours" without any charge or accusation being leveled
against her. Furthermore, although she told Golding that she could find a
person to post bond for her, he had her "forcibly conveyed to a prison called
the Workhouse" for thirty days at hard labor. At the workhouse, she alleged,
the staff "compelled her to divest herself of the decent apparel in which she
was dressed and compelled [her] . . . to dress herself in certain rough, coarse,
uncomfortable, degrading apparel." She also complained of the difficult and
humiliating work. After her release police again arrested her, this time for
being an "incorrigible vagabond." Once more Golding sent her to the workhouse, where the staff forced her to wear coarse clothes, perform hard labor,
and eat "coarse and unwholesome food." She filed for a writ of habeas corpus in the Fifth District Court, and Judge Alexander Buchanan released her,
stating that her imprisonment "was in violation of your petitioner's natural
rights and wholly unwarranted by law." Judge John McHenry of the First
District Court heard Fluhart's suit against the recorder for damages. In his
answer Golding stated that he had performed his duty "without malice."
One witness testified that Fluhart's reputation "is that of a woman of the
town." Another stated that "her general character is that of a lewd woman."
Horace Darling, who probably served as Fluhart's pimp, testified that he
had paid a portion of her rent and also her attorney's fees. The jury found in
Fluhart's favor but ordered Golding to pay Fluhart only twenty-five cents in
damages. Fluhart died soon after the decision, and Darling, who claimed to
have been appointed curator of her succession, appealed the decision to the
Supreme Court of Louisiana. J. H. Holland, Fluhart's attorney, wrote an elo-
quent brief to the supreme court in which he stated that when the first two
attempts to convict Fluhart for keeping a brothel failed, Golding resorted
to having her arrested for vagrancy. He especially complained of the policy
that allowed police to "*drag them* [public women] *from their home to a dungeon,
under the pretext that they have no home*. . . . Even if the Victim of their malice Should be a *poor weak and unprotected female* [italics in original] whom . . .
may at some time have strayed from the path of chastity? Freedom from such
treatment is secured to all white persons in this Country." In his brief he
also accused Golding of allowing testimony as to Fluhart's character, which
was not relevant to issue of vagrancy. He also argued that recorders did not

have the power to sentence people to hard labor. The supreme court ruled that Louisiana law had never made brothels illegal and that Golding treated Fluhart unjustly, arresting her twice in her home under false allegations of vagrancy. Although Fluhart died before the court rendered its decision, her case, in effect, kept prostitution alive for years. Although the court did not declare prostitution legal, the decision meant that it was explicitly not illegal. Fluhart's experiences demonstrate clearly the failure of the legal system to attempt to eradicate prostitution and also the amount of harassment public women could face. Incidentally, Theophilus Freeman signed the appearance bond in one of the brothel-keeping cases against Fluhart. An incredibly sleazy slave trader, Freeman sold Solomon Northup, a kidnapped free man of color from New York, into slavery up the Red River. He regularly represented slaves for sale as younger than their real ages to make more profit. He also sold young children away from their mothers, contrary to Louisiana law. Freeman owned a slave named Sarah Conner. When he fell deeply into debt, he freed her and transferred all his property to her to avoid it being seized by his creditors. He also reportedly hid slaves outside New Orleans to escape having them seized for his debts. Police arrested him several times in 1845 because his creditors feared he would flee the state. Freeman also rented houses to prostitutes, which may have been his connection to Fluhart.[18]

The First District Court heard two more brothel-keeping cases in 1849. James Ritchie faced charges that he kept a brothel on the corner of Casacalvo and Moreau streets called the Evening Star. The case went to the First District Court on 8 March 1849 and seemed to be proceeding to trial when the district attorney disposed of the case with a nolle prosequi on 4 May 1849. A note, dated on the same day, stated that the person bringing the charges, David Kemble, had withdrawn the charges. Whether Ritchie threatened or bribed him we cannot know. The second case involved a free woman of color, Charlotte Taylor. This case ended five months later when the sheriff reported to the court that Taylor could not be found and the signer of her appearance bond had left for California.[19]

Four cases of brothel keeping came before the First District Court of New Orleans in 1850. The first, *State v. Nougan,* resulted in a trial and a sentence of one month in the parish prison and a fine of one hundred dollars. The second, involving Frederick Wright and Sophia Montgomery, accused of keeping "a resort of lewd and abandoned women, negroes and other characters," never proceeded to trial. The third case charged Elizabeth Stone with keeping a house on Circus Street inhabited by "lewd and abandoned women." This case ended in a nolle prosequi. The fourth case, against three women for keeping a brothel on Spain Street that constituted a "perfect nuisance to the neighborhood," proceeded to trial, but the jury found the women not guilty.[20]

During these trials, Judge John Larue called for Recorder Peter Seuzeneau of the Third District to be removed from office because of his open protection of brothels in his district and because he had perjured himself before the First District Court by testifying under oath to the respectability and good character of several notorious public women. When people defending Seuzeneau protested, Larue stated that he would rather see a thousand men perish than see one of them corrupted. Peter Seuzeneau, nicknamed "Awful John," dispensed his form of justice in the "old, rickety, worm eaten, rat infested, spider infested, and mildewed" court room of the Third District. In these "sleazy surroundings, his attitude toward prostitutes who peddled their wares across the street from the court . . . was one of quiet and amused tolerance." Seuzeneau retaliated against Larue by sending him several brothel cases. Larue sent the first two cases, one against one Henry Durker and one against Christian Fink and Andrew Hayse, to the grand jury on charges of not only keeping a brothel but "keeping a disorderly tippling house." Durker, Fink, and Hayse kept an establishment called the Lion's Den. Both grand juries returned true bills against the three men, and both cases proceeded to trial. Both trial juries found the three men guilty. Larue, seeking to make an example of them, sentenced them to two months at hard labor, a fine of $250, and court costs. According to a newspaper article that appeared more than four months after Larue sent the men to jail because they could not pay the fine, the men owned no property and had no money. Their inability to pay the fine forced Larue to release them from prison.[21]

Seuzeneau then decided to test Larue by sending him a case against Salvador Viosca for brothel keeping. When Larue had tried Durker, Fink, and Hayse, he tried and sentenced three recent immigrants who had no political power, money, or connections. Viosca owned real estate assessed at twenty-five thousand dollars, and he operated two large ballrooms, the Globe and the Whitehall. Ordinarily police left Viosca alone, as the owner of the Globe ballroom sat on the New Orleans City Council. Viosca had strong ties to powerful political forces in the city. The Viosca case presented Larue with a dilemma. Larue had publicly condemned Viosca for permitting slaves and prostitutes to visit his ballrooms, and people who wished to see prostitution suppressed hoped for Viosca's conviction. However, Larue dismissed the charges with the lame excuse that he had no law for convicting brothel keepers. He could not justify his conviction of Durker, Fink, and Hayse, and he did not try. Larue had political ambitions, and he apparently sacrificed his integrity on the altar of political expediency.[22]

Larue heard six more brothel-keeping cases in 1851, all sent to him by Seuzeneau. This represented a clever way to embarrass Larue. Voters in the Third Municipality elected Seuzeneau, and when they objected to living among noisy and bawdy brothels, they complained to Seuzeneau. Wanting to satisfy his constituents but not to stifle prostitution, he passed the buck by sending the cases to Larue. He could explain to his constituents that he could not force Larue to take the cases to trial. Indeed, none ever went to trial, although three went to grand juries that declared the charges against them to be "a true bill." One of these involved James Ritchie, who had faced down similar charges in 1849, and one charged the infamous Archy Murphy, owner of the "Old House at Home" dance hall and brothel on Gallatin Street, with brothel keeping. Murphy also ran a brothel at 10 Frenchman Street. Another involved a brothel kept by Antoine Revel and a woman of color. One man, Moses Maier, testified that when he entered Revel's brothel, Revel offered him a choice of three young girls about ten or eleven years old. This case also did not proceed to trial, and the court dismissed Revel. One can only imagine Larue's discomfort at seeing the accused go free. After his action in the Viosca case, he could hardly reverse himself and begin trying brothel keepers once more.[23]

In 1852 seven brothel-keeping cases came before Larue and the First District Court, all against women. All ended in nolle prosequi. The first five came from Recorder Peter Seuzeneau's court. The wording in these cases changed slightly from the previous accusations. In four cases, the person bringing the charges was a Third Municipality policeman, C. O. Daubert. Perhaps the brothels quit paying him off, or perhaps he was making an honest effort to discourage prostitution. In each Daubert affirmed: "She is constantly calling Men to sleep with her . . . her house is the rowdy resort of robbers, Men and Women of bad character." The last two cases came from the Phillippa-Common-Gravier part of town. In *State v. McGiffin,* Marie McGiffin faced accusations that the women in her house "indecently expose their persons, appearing in open windows with the chemises on . . . stop[ping] men passing along and call[ing] them in." None of these cases went to trial. After the *Viosca* case, Larue could hardly make a real attempt to stanch prostitution.[24]

Six cases of brothel keeping, all from the Phillippa-Gravier-Perdido area, came to the First District Court of New Orleans in 1853. The first, *State v. Patton,* involved a woman named Lucinda Patton, whom the court charged with brothel keeping. Patton's landlord, John Brandy, had inserted a novel clause in her lease. The one-year lease called for payments of forty dollars a month for the first five months and sixty dollars for the last seven months of the year. Perhaps Brandy thought Patton would make more money as the year went on and therefore be able to pay more rent after she had become established at the address. The lease also contained this clause: "If the occupant has to move on account of complaints made by the police or city authorities . . . the said John Brandy will pay the occupant of the therein mentioned house the sum of $500 for damages for being obliged to remove from the said house." This clause constitutes the only known record of such a provision, but it may have been common in brothel leases. In May 1853 police had arrested Patton and charged her with keeping a brothel. The case went before the First District Court in June, and Brandy put up the appearance bond. The charge contained the usual language, including that the inhabitants of the house spent their time "drinking, tippling, whoring, and misbehaving themselves." The case never went to trial at this time, and Patton signed another lease with Brandy with an expiration date of May 1854. This new lease, however, did not contain the relocation clause. The court finally set a trial date for 9 July 1856. By this time Brandy had withdrawn his appearance bond, and one M. Massie had guaranteed Patton's appearance with a five-hundred-dollar bond. A note in the court record on 13 July 1856 stated that "after diligent search," the sheriff could not find either Massie or Patton. After receiving that news, the district attorney dropped the case with a nolle prosequi on 16 July 1856. The other five 1853 cases against women accused of brothel keeping either were discontinued indefinitely or ended in a nolle prosequi. All contained the usual language: "drinking, tippling, whoring, and misbehaving themselves." [25]

In 1853 Larue also heard a divorce case in which prostitution was the grounds for divorce. George Hester proved that his wife, Jane Wilson, alias Dunn, alias Moore, had committed adultery in their house on Frenchman Street with several men and subsequently moved to Basin Street to a "house of assignation . . . where she carries on the life of a woman lost to all sense of decency and virtue." A witness testified that Wilson lived at Suzanne's house, a brothel, and that "those who went there for anything were sure to get it." Judge Larue granted Moore a divorce on 22 June 1853. [26]

The year 1854 saw a change in the personnel of the First District Court. In 1852 the new Louisiana state constitution made all positions on the formerly appointive state bench elective, including the First District Court of New Orleans. Although voters elected John Larue to that position in a landslide in

May 1853, Larue announced in November that he would resign his position and resume private practice on 1 January 1854. One reason may have been that the Louisiana legislature reduced the annual salary of district judges from $3,500 to $2,500. Or perhaps the nuisance of the stream of brothel-keeping cases prompted Judge Larue's resignation. When he dismissed a number of these cases in 1852, he stated "that the court ought not to be troubled with such cases, and that the Recorders should fine such offenders." John Blount Robertson won the special election called to replace Larue.[27]

The first brothel-keeping case heard by Robertson, *State v. Stewart,* actually went to trial, but the jury seemed unimpressed by the case and found the defendant not guilty. They arrived at this verdict despite the evidence that the brothel, situated at 73 Phillippa Street, had ten young female residents. The case contained the usual language about "drinking, tippling, whoring, and misbehaving themselves" and also a statement about the brothel being a nuisance to the neighborhood. This case named the public women found in the brothel: Mary Taylor, Cora Winchester, Hetty Oakley, Delphine Payne, Jenny Glaser, Emma Franklin, Ellen Howard, Pauline Hébert, Ann Cotter, and Mary Webster. Six police officers testified in the case, including the chief of police, Stephen O. Leary. Despite their testimony and all evidence to the contrary, the jury inexplicably found Josephine Stewart not guilty.[28]

The other six cases that came before the First District Court in 1854 never went to trial. All were against women; the district attorney ended them all with a nolle prosequi. In two of the cases, both the defendant and the person who endorsed her appearance bond had disappeared, and the sheriff could not find them. In the other three cases, no explanation appears in the record for the case never going to trial. Apparently Robertson had little enthusiasm for discouraging prostitution.[29]

In 1855 only three cases involving brothel keeping came before the First District Court. The first, *State v. Downey,* contained a note from the district attorney telling the court "that there is no cause for the further prosecution of Mary Downey" and directed the clerk of court to enter a nolle prosequi. The case had begun in May 1855, when six of Downey's neighbors petitioned the court to have Downey and the other women in her house removed from the neighborhood. Perhaps Downey and the other women had relocated, and the neighbors withdrew the petition. The next case, *State v. Burns,* went to trial, and the jury convicted Henry Burns of brothel keeping. The record of this case has disappeared, so we cannot know the details of the case or the sentence. The third brothel-keeping case involved the infamous George Kent, who faced charges of "keeping a disorderly brothel" as well as "keeping a disorderly tippling house." Seuzeneau had sent this case to Robertson. Kent had impressive political connections, and his brothel and saloon, called the Stadt Amsterdam on Elysian Fields Avenue, was well known. Kent himself lived at another brothel and bar at 49 Gallatin Street. The charge in the case accused Kent of keeping a place where "lewd women and idle men do congregate, drink and whore together to the great scandal of the community." Despite these accusations the district attorney dropped the case with a nolle prosequi, but not until 20 March 1857. A delayed nolle prosequi could mean either that the district attorney could not find witnesses against the accused or that he did not think the case would go to trial because of insufficient evidence, or it could have been a way of threatening the accused.[30]

Brothel-keeping cases appeared before the First District Court of New Orleans five times in 1856. Robertson continued his policy of not attempting to suppress prostitution, as all six cases ended in nolle prosequi. In the first, *State v. McKinney*, a New Orleans policeman testified that he had arrested Mary McKinney numerous times for the same offense and that she kept a disorderly brothel that was often the scene of drunken arguments. Nevertheless, her case never went to trial. In another case neighbors complained that Andrew Costello kept a brothel and disorderly tippling house where he did "permit to congregate disorderly and idle men who . . . did sing obscene songs, boisterous and vulgar dances . . . [used] unruly and obscene language . . . and commit[ted] other indecencies . . . hallowing, shouting, drunken people." This case, like the others, never went to trial.[31]

Three brothel-keeping cases came before Judge Robertson in 1857, and as in the previous year, none went to trial. In one case, *State v. Brady*, Catherine Brady faced charges of keeping a brothel in which "disorderly and idle men and lewd women . . . did whore and commit other indecencies." The two police officers who testified in the case spoke of the great crowds of men and women "drinking and carousing . . . using obscene language both men and women." One officer told of "continual disturbances and drunken broils [sic] in the house . . . carousals and broils [sic] occur in the house nightly." Despite this testimony, the case ended in a nolle prosequi. In another case, *State v. Montgomery and Greene*, the names of the inhabitants of the house appear in the record: Ann Lee, Mathilda Donnely, Bridget Janaback, Caroline Shoester, and Ellen Greene. This case also never proceeded to trial. In 1857 Judge Robertson lost the next election, and Theodore G. Hunt took over as judge of the First District Court in April 1857.[32] No brothel-keeping cases appeared before Hunt in 1858 and 1859.

Three brothel-keeping cases came to the court in 1860, two against the same woman, Josephine Schneider. Both ended in a nolle prosequi on 12 December 1860. The other, State v. Arbuckle, did go to trial and resulted in a rare conviction for this offense. To understand this case, one has to know more about the defendant, a free woman of color named Julia Arbuckle. Arbuckle began life as a slave in Ray County, Missouri. Her owner, Samuel Arbuckle, owned thirty-eight slaves, twelve of whom he had freed before his death. In his will he freed the other twenty-six. However, shortly after her owner's death, Julia Arbuckle found herself in the hands of a slave trader, who sold her to Victorine Bouny, who owned a bakery in New Orleans. Despite her protestations that she was free, Bouny put her to work as a bread seller and showed no inclination to set her free. Arbuckle hired an attorney and sued for her freedom before the Fifth District Court of New Orleans, and she won. Bouny appealed to the Louisiana Supreme Court, which affirmed the decision that she was free. Despite this victory the slave trader and Bouny seized Arbuckle and held her as a virtual prisoner, beating her viciously. She escaped and hired another attorney to sue for damages of $400 for cruel treatment. Unfortunately, the second attorney she hired proved to be incompetent, and the case dragged on for years. Finally, after the Civil War, and after Arbuckle hired yet another attorney, the newly reconstituted Louisiana Supreme Court awarded her $240 in civil damages.[33]

Although witnesses at the trial of her suit for freedom had testified to Arbuckle's good character and industrious habits, the New Orleans newspapers and the records of the district courts provide clear evidence that after she gained her freedom she had become one of the Crescent City's more notorious "lewd and abandoned women." She had faced several charges of assault and battery, using "fowl [sic] and obscene language," as well as "keeping a disorderly brothel." Her accuser also testified that as Arbuckle was a Negro, under the law her color evoked the legal presumption that she was a slave. If she could be proved free, he testified, she would be in the state illegally and would have to leave. Her notoriety may have been the reason her case went to trial. The jury found her guilty in the brothel-keeping case, and the judge sentenced her to three months in the parish prison and court costs. In 1862 police arrested her for assault and battery because she "wantonly, unprovokedly, maliciously, threw a handful of salt" into the eyes of a five-month-old baby.[34]

Only two more cases involving charges of brothel keeping came before the First District Court in 1860—the last two cases before the court closed in 1862, the result of the fall of New Orleans to Union forces. Both contained the usual language, and both ended in nolle prosequi the following year.[35]

A survey of cases in which people, almost all women, faced charges of brothel keeping shows that judges and district attorneys made almost no effort to restrain prostitution in antebellum New Orleans. The overwhelming majority of cases did not proceed to trial, and the very few convictions resulted in trivial sentences. Judge John Larue proved the exception in giving stiff sentences in two cases. However, his efforts collapsed when he confronted a politically powerful person charged with brothel keeping. The First District Court failed to make any real effort to control or punish prostitution. It would be up to city leaders to attempt to legislate in order to regulate and make money for the city from prostitution. In doing so, they made no effort to inflict serious harm on the institution.

9

―――――∞∞∞――――――

"An Ordinance Concerning Lewd
and Abandoned Women"

The sex trade generated an enormous amount of money, estimated to be second in dollar value only to the Crescent City's port itself. In 1857 the New Orleans City Council decided to direct some of that revenue stream into the city's coffers. On 10 March it enacted "An Ordinance Concerning Lewd and Abandoned Women." The first attempt to contain and license prostitution in the United States, the law only minimally suppressed prostitution in some areas of the city; its real purpose was not to end the sex trade but to encourage the traffic to move away from the more respectable parts of town and to channel some of the profits into the city treasury. This act immediately became known in New Orleans as the Lorette law. "Lorette" referred to an area in Paris near the cathedral of Notre Dame de Lorette, a part of that city notorious for its numerous public women. The word "Lorette" became a slang expression for a prostitute. [1]

According to the first section of the act, public women were not to "occupy, inhabit, live or sleep in any one story house or building" or "any room or closet in the lower floor of any house or building" located in specified areas of the city. The forbidden area consisted of what present-day New Orleanians call the "sliver by the river," high, dry land close to the Mississippi River that had risen gradually over hundreds of years, the natural result of annual spring floods that deposited silt along the river's banks. This land, the most desirable and expensive in the city, was the first on which successive settlers built their dwellings and business places as the city spread upriver and downriver from the original settlement in the Vieux Carré. [2]

One purpose of this act, to drive prostitutes away from the most desirable locations in the city, offended the wealthy landlords who made great profits collecting high rents from brothels. But its intent was to make the streets of the "better" parts of town more respectable; women could not hang about on their porches or doorsteps to solicit customers. It also took aim at the landlords who constructed cheap, flimsy one-story hovels, referred to as "cribs," as these one-room huts were just large enough to contain a bed from which the lesser sort of prostitute operated. Violation of this section of the act resulted in a fine of twenty-five dollars for each offense and for each day a public woman plied her trade in a one-story dwelling in the specified districts. It was the duty of the New Orleans police to catch violators of the act and bring them to the recorder's courts, at which time they would pay a fine or, according to the ordinance, if they could not pay, "be imprisoned not less than sixty days." Lawmakers did not write a maximum time of incarceration into the law (such as "no less than sixty and no more than ninety days"); the law stated only that the period of incarceration was to be not be less than sixty days. If public women remained within the prohibited area, the next section of the act required them to pay a tax of $100 and receive a license to remain in the area, as long as the residence was not a one-story building. Anyone renting rooms to "lewd women" had to obtain a license at a price of $250 a year.[3]

The next section, designed to rid the streets of the presence of public women, forbade them from being on the sidewalk in front of their house, in the alley, in the doorway, or at the gate; it did not permit them to sit on the front steps "in an indecent posture." It also prohibited prostitutes from calling to or accosting or stopping people passing by, as well as outlawing them from walking up and down the sidewalks or "stroll[ing] about the streets of the city indecently attired." The fine for these behaviors was ten dollars for each offense or no less than fifteen days in jail. The ordinance also forbade public women from entering bars and coffee shops and drinking in these establishments, setting a fine of five dollars for each violation.[4]

To put a stop to the common practice of racially integrated brothels, the law required that white women and free women of color not live in the same houses and that brothels run by free women of color not allow white prostitutes to live within. Anyone renting to public women could be fined fifty dollars for each prostitute to whom the landlord or brothel manager rented. A minor revision of the ordinance stipulated that the act should become law on 1 April 1857, and the licenses were to run from the first of April for one year, after which the ordinance required that a new license be purchased for the following year.

Laws requiring licenses for many professions, occupations, and businesses were hardly new in the Crescent City, although prostitution and brothel keeping had never before been included. Before the Lorette law, all licensed professions and businesses had been legal; although practicing prostitution was not illegal, keeping a brothel had been against the law throughout the antebellum period. Therefore, the city council passed an ordinance taxing and licensing an illegal activity. City ordinances required approximately one hundred businesses and professions to pay annual license fees. Businesses such as wholesale and retail establishments, oyster stands, livery stables, billiard halls, ballrooms, slave pens, hotels, and even cock-fighting pits all paid license fees. The amount charged varied from year to year and from business to business. For example, groceries paid $100, coffeehouses (which also often sold liquor) $150. These taxes swelled the city's coffers. The total for license fees amounted to $965,519.41 in 1853 and $1,192,328.09 in 1854. Attorneys, physicians, surgeons, and dentists paid only $25.[5]

Within a short time, the New Orleans police began to enforce the Lorette law, although at first the courts seemed reluctant to try violators of the statute. In April, Recorder J. L. Fabre dismissed five free women of color accused of violating the Lorette law, stating that their cases "had not been sustained." The next day Fabre discharged Mary Jane Quinn, accused of violating the Lorette law by practicing her profession in the prohibited district, "on her promise to leave the premises." A few days later three free women of color came before Fabre charged with violating the Lorette law, "and for some reason they were dismissed." The *New Orleans Daily Picayune* noted that the courts were giving public women more time to move out of the restricted areas of the city. The *Picayune* also noted: "Quite a number of busy lawyers and interested landlords are trying to oppose the execution of the ordinance by which great numbers of abandoned women will be forced to remove from their present residences." The enforcement of the Lorette law meant that powerful landlords would be deprived of lucrative rents.[6]

In the middle of May the New Orleans police arrested thirty "frail daughters of Eve" for violating the Lorette law. Recorder Fabre fined each of them twenty-five dollars, but only two could pay the fine, and Fabre sent the rest to prison. After the sentence, Fabre had those who could not pay the fine placed "on board that four-wheel wanderer, the Red Maria [a horse-drawn paddy wagon], they favored the lookers on with yells, screeches and snatches of song and imprecations, which no masculine tongue, however depraved, would dare to utter." The *Picayune* noted that the women were "as fair as they are frail, and [they] were intended by nature to be the flowers of humanity." Five days later, in an article entitled "War on the Women," the

Picayune noted that the police had arrested sixty "daughters of frailty" on St. John, Phillippa, and Perdido streets to await a hearing in front of Recorder Gerard Stith.[7]

Three days later Recorder Stith heard a lengthy argument from the attorney defending the sixty women, stating that the Lorette law was in violation of the constitution of the state of Louisiana as well as the Constitution of the United States and the New Orleans City Charter. According to the women's counsel, never identified by the *Picayune,* it also violated the rights of citizens, impaired the obligation of contracts, and gave recorders powers that could only be given to a jury. He alleged that the impairment of the obligation of contract occurred under the Lorette law because the contract between the landlords and their "frail tenantry" required the tenants to relocate before the conditions of their leases had been fulfilled. The reporter for the *Picayune* stated: "It is time that a few of our public thoroughfares were purged of their vile tenantry, even if a certain class of landlords are to lose by it."[8]

Public women were not the only people arrested for violating the Lorette law. Two landlords, Jean Petrovich and Sam Wilson, came before Recorder Fabre charged with breaking the law. Petrovich faced charges of renting rooms to "notoriously abandoned white and colored women" and Wilson for renting rooms "for vile purposes" on Barracks Street (within the restricted district). Mrs. Spriggin, a brothel manager, had to pay a fifty-dollar fine for renting rooms in the prohibited area to "abandoned" women. A few days later Solomon and J. Remando faced charges of renting rooms to "abandoned" women on Dryades (Phillippa) Street.[9]

The usual fee for violating the Lorette law came to be a fine of twenty-five dollars or thirty days in jail. At the end of May 1857, Eliza Shadrick, Elizabeth Haycraft, Mary Swift, and the notorious duo Emeline Gibson and Delia Swift, alias Bridget Fury, faced Recorder Stith charged with practicing their profession within the area restricted by the Lorette law. Stith sentenced them to twenty-five dollars or thirty days in prison. The following day a Madame Randolph faced the same charges and received the same sentence. Just one day later Isole Darcole, Adolphe Lonis, Nicholas Robart, Azina Fields, and M. L. Saucier (the last two were both free women of color) appeared in front of Recorder Fabre. He sent them to prison for keeping a disorderly house "where slaves unlawfully congregate, and runaways are harbored and concealed in the restricted district."[10]

Apparently the landlords put pressure on Recorder Stith to stop enforcing the Lorette law. Under the headline "A Wise Choice," the *Picayune* reported that "the attempt to induce Recorder Stith to nullify one of the city's ordinances has been without avail." Stith contended that the "policy, constitutionality and legality" of city ordinances did not fall within the powers of recorders. He asserted that it was his responsibility to enforce city laws "as in enforcement of the ordinance concerning lewd and abandoned women." Stith stated that "his duty is clear, and he has determined to perform it." It is clear that the landlords waged a determined assault on the Lorette law. On the very same day that Stith's statement about his duty to enforce the Lorette law appeared in the *Picayune,* Adam Boek appeared before Recorder Fabre charged with renting rooms to "lewd and abandoned women" on Marais Street between Customhouse and Bienville in defiance of the Lorette law. His attorney argued that the recorder had no jurisdiction, that the Lorette law was "unconstitutional, illegal and against good morals"! Fabre disregarded this argument and fined Boek fifty dollars or thirty days in prison. On the same day Fabre fined Elizabeth Fuchs fifty dollars for renting rooms to "abandoned" women on Toulouse Street. [11]

Recorder Stith continued to enforce the Lorette law against landlords. In an atrocious pun the *Picayune* reported on 5 June that "Mrs. Ward will have to ward off charges of keeping a resort for the notoriously abandoned—of both genders—at the corner of Girod and Baronne streets." When J. Solzmon came before Stith charged with renting rooms to "lewd and abandoned" women in his residence at the corner of Perdido and Dryades (Phillippa) streets, Solomon's attorney "contested every stage of the prosecution at 'learned length.'" Eventually a witness testified that "she, as a public woman, had lived for nine months at the house of the accused, renting a room from him all the time." She testified that usually she paid him $2 a day, "which sum she was obliged to fork over every morning," but that recently, because times had become hard, he demanded only $1.50 every day. She further stated that she had left the house only two days before her appearance before Stith and that she was paid up when she left. Upon hearing this evidence, Stith fined Solzman $50. The defense attorney threatened to try to get the case up before one of the district courts, but no record exists that he succeeded. [12]

After the flurry of Lorette law cases that came before the city's recorders in May and June, no reports of accusations appear until the middle of August. The probable explanation for the absence of prosecution is that although the recorder's courts did not entirely suspend operations for the summer, all the district courts and the Louisiana Supreme Court closed. Thousands of people, including judges and recorders, left town during the yellow fever season. Recorder Stith was one of those who left, and Acting Recorder John E. Holland stood in for him.

In the middle of August, the infamous George Kent and six of the public women who lived in his brothel came before Acting Recorder Holland charged with "keeping an unlicensed brothel on Gallatin street." Holland allowed them to go free on bail, but the case never seems to have come up again. One day later, the infamous Delia Swift, alias Bridget Fury, and Alice Cunningham came before Holland charged with keeping a "house of ill fame" on Basin Street. As the summer ended, the recorder's courts became more active, and the number of arrests and fines for violating the Lorette law increased. In September Mrs. Price, Catherine Row, and Martha Whorley came before Recorder Stith for occupying a one-story house on Basin Street "for purposes not recognized as legal by existing ordinances." They each had to pay a fine of twenty-five dollars. The same charges and fine were leveled against Margaret Sauer, Louisa Johnson, and Ann Antoine in October. [13]

In the fall of 1857, resentment by the landlords regarding the Lorette law expressed itself in the district courts. William Rice, who owned a string of tenements on 243, 245, 247, 251, 253, and 257 Gravier Street known as "Rice's Row," hired well-known trial attorney, A. P. Field, to contest the Lorette law before the Fourth District Court. Although the public women who lived in Rice's Row had paid the license under the Lorette law, the neighbors went before the mayor of New Orleans, M. Waterman, to state that the inhabitants of Rice's Row were a nuisance to the whole neighborhood and that the citizens wanted them removed and relocated. Recorder Stith had ordered the women to be expelled from Rice's Row for being nuisances, and Field appeared in court on their behalf and that of Rice's. The judge of the Fourth District Court, J. W. Price, ordered Stith "to desist in molesting and disturbing them," in effect allowing them to remain in Rice's dwellings. Field presented the injunction to Stith, and he stated in no uncertain terms that he would not obey it. Stith said he was obliged to enforce the laws of the city and that he would accept the consequences of his actions. Stith furthermore reminded Field that he had promised to have the women leave their rooms and that only on this promise had Stith not fined them as vagrants and nuisances. Field then asked for copies of the original documents in the case, and Stith refused, saying he knew that Field was trying to "interrupt the course of justice and the execution of the city ordinances." The following day, Field appealed to the judge of the Third District Court to order Stith to show in writing why he should not be granted an appeal. Field's argument rested on the assumed right of the district courts to reverse the rulings of the recorders. The judge of the Third District Court rejected this argument, stating that "it would be impolitic, if not illegal to interfere with the recorders in the regular discharge of their duties as criminal and committing magistrates." Finally, on 10 December, A. P. Field obtained a writ of habeas corpus to free the public women whom Stith had sent to the workhouse when they could not pay the twenty-five-dollar fine, and the judge of the Third District Court released them to return to Rice's Row.[14]

There is a strange footnote to this incident. On the same day that Field won the release of the women, he received a summons from Stith concerning an alleged trespass. It seems that one of the women who lived in one of Rice's hovels, who had paid her rent in advance to the end of the month, found that she could not occupy her room. The room was on the second floor, accessible only by an outside stairway. For reasons unknown, Rice tore down the stairway, preventing her from going to her room, or from leaving if she got in. Stith sent Rice to face trial before the First District Court on charges of committing a trespass, but there is no record that a trial in that court took place.[15]

Many public women were just as outraged about the Lorette law as were the landlords, and at least three of them paid the licensing fee under protest but then sued the city, claiming that the Lorette law was illegal and unconstitutional. In suits filed in April and May, Caroline Harley and Mrs. A. Bell brought suit against the city before the Fourth District Court. Harley sued to recover the $250 she had paid for the license. She alleged that the ordinance was "illegal, opposed to the constitution of this State, is unequal, oppressive and unjust to the common right." On Christmas Eve 1857, the judge of the Fourth District Court rendered a judgment in her favor and ordered the city to pay her the $250 with legal interest from 30 April 1857 and mandated that the city pay court costs. On the same day he rendered a similar decision against the city, including costs and interest, in the case of Mrs. Bell. As the reporter for the *Picayune* noted: "The judge takes the broad ground, that the ordinance is illegal, unconstitutional, and null and void. A fine new prospect now opens for reclamations against the city on the part of all who have paid the license taxes under the ordinance approved 10th March 1857."[16]

In May 1857 the city of New Orleans filed suit against Eliza Castello in the Second District Court for operating a brothel in the restricted section of the city without paying the $250 licensing fee. Castello had refused to pay the $250 or the fine of $10 a day for each of the occupants of her establishment, or to relocate to the "free streets in the rear portion of the city." Through her able attorneys, L. Madison Day and M. M. Reynolds, she declared the "tax was illegal, and the penalties tyrannical" and "unreasonable in restraint of trade and common right." The city demanded the $250 plus a $2.50 railroad tax (levied on all city licenses), plus an additional 5 percent interest and 10 percent for attorney's fees. Both this suit and the *Harley* and *Bell* suits should have been filed in the First District Court, the criminal court. The Fourth District Court was primarily concerned with general civil litigation, and the Second District Court was a probate court. Although no evidence appears in the records, the judge of the First District Court must have recused himself. Since 1852, judges of the district courts were elected, not appointed, and the judge of the First District Court may not have wanted to be involved in these controversial cases.[17]

On 5 November, the judge of the Second District Court, P. H. Morgan, rendered a decision in *City of New Orleans v. Castello* in favor of Eliza Castello. In his judgment, Morgan focused on the fourth section of the Lorette law, which fined violators one hundred dollars or, if they could not pay, imprisonment for not less than thirty days. In his decision, Morgan questioned whether this provision meant the recorders could sentence the offenders to thirty years or to life in prison. Observing that there were no maximum limits to the incarceration, he ruled that provision illegal. He went on: "The final result of her not paying is imprisonment for an indefinite period. A sum of money for a license is nothing more than a debt. If the ordinance stands, the Common [city] Council can imprison for debt—this has long been abolished in this state. The common council could make non payment a cause for hanging." He observed that the Common Council "has overstepped their legislative bounds." Noting that if any part of an ordinance was illegal, all of the ordinance was illegal, Morgan declared the entire Lorette law void and dismissed the city's suit with costs.[18]

The city appealed Morgan's decision to the Supreme Court of Louisiana. The attorneys for the city argued that taxes from occupational licenses were necessary to secure funds needed to provide city services and that no profession should be exempt from them. They argued that public women constituted "the most bothersome class of occupation and the least entitled to public credit." They contended that brothels cost the city huge sums of money as these "establishments [were] an enormous source of expenditures to the city. . . [because] they [were] places of disturbances of every kind." Not that the city attorneys called for an abolition of all brothels. Indeed, in their argument before Louisiana's highest court, they admitted that brothels were what they termed "necessary evils," and they argued that they were as much of a business as any other and therefore should not be exempt from taxation. This allowed the city to self-righteously condemn the sex trade while profiting from it at the same time.

In their brief to the supreme court, Castello's attorneys contended that the

Lorette law was unconstitutional. The Louisiana Supreme Court rendered a judgment on the *Castello* appeal on 18 January 1859. The justices based their decision on aspects of the Lorette law that were never even mentioned in any of the attorney's briefs. The Louisiana Constitution stipulated that all licenses were to run from 1 January to 31 December of each year. As the Lorette ordinance required public women and brothel keepers to obtain a license on 1 April, Chief Justice Edwin Merrick ruled the entire ordinance illegal and void. We can never know the pressures put on the Louisiana Supreme Court by the wealthy landlords of New Orleans. The fact that the court overturned the entire ordinance on such a flimsy technicality suggests that the justices, all prominent and wealthy white men, were sympathetic to the interests of others of their status. Some of the justices may also have themselves been landlords. Unfortunately the tax records for this period are not complete enough to prove this allegation, but it is certainly possible. One historian has suggested that the decision was influenced by a corrupt underworld that controlled prostitution and gambling in New Orleans. Regardless, the court struck down the entire ordinance in what is arguably a fraudulent decision.[19]

For the next forty years, until the creation of the famous Storyville district in 1897, city leaders passed eight new versions of the Lorette law, all of which attempted unsuccessfully to control, regulate, or just make money on prostitution through a number of methods. Finally in 1897, New Orleans city leaders gave in to their belief that sin and vice were inevitable, and in creating the Storyville district in which the sex trade was legal, as one historian has said, they "looked Satan in the eye, cut a deal and gave him his own address."[20]

Clearly the *Castello* decision was a great triumph not only for the landlords but also for the public women and the brothel keepers, and they celebrated with a huge and naughty parade of horse-drawn carriages carrying hundreds of joyously cheering, scantily clad women. The entourage rolled down Canal Street and into the French Quarter, the busiest part of town. One historian called the procession "one of the lewdest spectacles in American history. . . . It was made of hundreds of bawds, carriage borne, driving through the city streets, variously costumed, a great many nude." Some of those wearing suggestive clothing were costumed as Egyptian dancers or as sailors in skin-tight trousers who "wiggled insultingly as New Orleans ladies drew aside their skirts." Some wore figure-revealing tights and rode "with a leg lolling over the side of the carriages to wave at the respectable citizens." These "painted, buxom women . . . shouted obscenities . . . and snatched male bystanders with whom they improvised erotic displays." We can only imagine the exact details of the vulgar "exotic displays" and the horrors and disgust of the respectable spectators, yet these jubilant women were not to be denied their exultant and bawdy celebration. This outrageous display left little doubt that the sin industry had won an extraordinary victory.[21]

CONCLUSION

The regular prostitutes come in at the opening of business in the fall, and return to the North in the spring as business closes. . . . The prostitutes of this migratory class form the great mass of the inmates of the regular kept brothels, of which there is an immense number in the city. These houses are easily recognized, as the girls who occupy them are constantly seen at the doors or windows, inviting men as they pass by to come in. And in some of the principal streets of the city, just at evening, it is not unusual to see the windows and doors of almost every house as far as the eye can recognize them, filled with these girls. The municipal regulations are such that these creatures are prohibited from promenading the streets; hence they are obliged to resort to other measures to make themselves known.

—A RESIDENT, IN *New Orleans As It Is* (1849)

Evidence abounds in the New Orleans newspapers and court records that prostitution in the city flourished virtually unchecked throughout the antebellum period. While the sex trade existed in other southern cities, one is struck by the large numbers of public women in New Orleans. One historian has identified 180 public women in Civil War–time Richmond, a city with 40,000 more people than New Orleans, while in the Crescent City well over a thousand engaged in the trade. There is evidence that some of these women came to the city during the "business season," from October to May, and then moved on, but arrest records indicate that many were in residence year round. So the sheer volume of the trade in the city surpassed that in other southern cities.

One reason for the scale of the sex trade in New Orleans was the enthusiastic, if covert, support that the wealthiest and most prominent white land-lords and merchants gave to the city's sex workers. Unlike the situation in antebellum New York and postbellum St. Paul, the public women of New Orleans usually did not own the land or the buildings that housed their brothels. Landlords charged public women inflated rents, but frequent arrests and stints in the workhouse eroded their ability to meet their obligations. This prompted the landlords to hire the best criminal attorneys in town to get them out of the parish prison or the workhouse and back to work as soon as possible in order to enable them to satisfy the conditions of their leases. We get a glimpse of how this system worked when we see the wealthy to-bacco merchant Sumpter Turner, owner of the brothel where Eliza Phillips met her untimely death, get the charges dropped against his slave Eliza, who ran the brothel at 211 Gravier for him. It was the wealthy landlords, such as Turner, who made the real money from the sex trade, not the women themselves. Merchants who supplied the women with glamorous apparel and flashy accessories also made huge profits.

Not only did the individual public women not enjoy the lion's share of the profits, but court records show that many led unhappy and violent lives. Evidence of self-medication with alcohol and laudanum, a form of opium, appears often in newspaper accounts and court records, and suicide among public women was not an uncommon occurrence. And unlike the find-ings of other historians about prostitutes forming some kind of sisterhood, the overwhelming evidence in antebellum New Orleans is that these were women who lived by their wits and whose main consideration was their own well-being, not that of their fellow sex workers. Working for the "man," the landlord and merchant, mitigated against the formation of strong bonds of support and sisterhood among public women. This lack of support is seen most clearly in court records that show them stealing from one another, es-pecially money, jewelry, and fancy clothing; incidents of savage violence among prostitutes; and episodes of jealous rage. Competition among public women was evidently fierce and prevented bonds of friendship from grow-ing between them. The need to successfully compete with their fellow pros-titutes drove out sisterhood. The "scarlet sisterhood" existed in name only.

Prostitution in New Orleans was also unique among southern cities be-cause of the degree of sex across the color line in the houses of assigna-tion. It was not unusual for the staff of a brothel to be composed of white women and black women, slave and free, nor for a brothel to be staffed by white women but managed by a slave, such as Sumpter Turner's brothel, which was staffed by three white public women and managed by the slave

Eliza. Moreover, slaves and free women of color often ran brothels staffed by slave women, whose owners collected their earnings. Although Louisiana law prohibited slaves from owning anything or having money, slaves were often accepted as customers at brothels and had money to purchase the sexual services of women, white and black, free and slave. Often free men of color, white men, and slaves all patronized the same brothels on any given night. This amount of racial integration in brothels was unknown in other southern cities.

The very act of selling their bodies exposed public women to the possibility of violence. On at least some level, these women were victims of exploitation and subject to degradation, even if they were willing participants in the exchange. Selling the most intimate form of human contact reduced them to commodities to be bought and sold, used and then discarded. When Abraham Parker paid Eliza Phillips $2.50 to have sex with him in "a moment of looseness and levity," she paid for it with her life. Equally disturbing and sad is the overwhelming evidence of the all-too-frequent sexual exploitation of very young women and girls. Although one historian has found this trend in antebellum New York, it seems to have been more of a pattern in pre–Civil War New Orleans than in other southern cities.

Politicians and judges, such as Peter Seuzeneau, were deeply involved with prostitution, and even usually upstanding judges, such as John Larue, sometimes became ensnared in prostitution cases for political reasons. In 1857, responding to citizens' complaints, politicians on the New Orleans City Council passed an ordinance designed to confine public women to certain, less respectable parts of town and most of all to make prostitution fill the city coffers with steep licensing fees. The Lorette law's purpose was not intended to discourage the oldest profession but to give the city a cut of the high profits that the trade engendered. Landlords, fearing that the public women would comply with the ordinance and move away from their properties, depriving them of the benefit of their inflated rents, complained of the unfairness of the Lorette law and pressured the Louisiana Supreme Court, which was staffed by men of the same social and economic class as the landlords, to void the law. The high court ignored the arguments of the city's attorneys at the appeal and declared the entire law null and void on a minor technicality—that the licenses began on 1 April, not 1 January as required by the state constitution. The court could have voided just that portion of the law containing the date, but it chose to support the interests of the landlords by declaring the entire ordinance unconstitutional. The supreme court ruling meant that public women were now free to reside and ply their trade unrestricted in any part of town they chose. The decision of the high court also relieved them of the yearly obligation of purchasing an expensive license to practice their profession. Likewise, brothel owners did not have to pay an exorbitant licensing fee each year to operate their establishments. Although the prostitutes' response to the court's decision resulted in an outrageous, jubilant, and bawdy parade in celebration of what they perceived as their victory, the real winners when the dust settled were the merchants and especially the wealthy white property owners of New Orleans who rented to the prostitutes.

NOTES

INTRODUCTION

1. Quoted in Herbert Asbury, *The French Quarter: An Informal History of the New Orleans Underground* (New York: Alfred A. Knopf, 1936), 4; Phil Johnson, "Good Time Town," in *The Past as Prelude: New Orleans, 1718–1968,* ed. Hodding Carter (New Orleans: Pelican Publishing Co., 1968), 234–35; letter quoted in Mother St. Therese Wolfe, *The Ursulines in New Orleans and Our Lady of Prompt Succor* (New York: P. J. Kennedy and Sons, 1925), 230; Marie-Madeleine Hachard, *De Rouen à la Louisiane: Voyage d'une Ursuline en 1727* (Rouen, France: Publications de l'Université de Rouen, 1988), 79. Thanks to Dr. Emily Clark of Tulane University for this citation. Dr. Clark pointed out that the whipping would have not taken place within the convent enclosure, as men were not allowed to enter. Official quoted in Hachard, *De Rouen à la Louisiane,* 79. Mathé Allain, *"Not Worth a Straw": French Colonial Policy and the Early Years of Louisiana* (Lafayette: Center for Louisiana Studies, 1988), 83–87. I am not going to refer to public women as strumpets, whores, harlots, tarts, *nymphs de pavé,* ladies of the evening, or Cyprians unless these derogatory terms are contained in contemporary quotations.

2. Asbury, *French Quarter,* 3; statistics from Dennis C. Rousey, *Policing the Southern City: New Orleans, 1805–1889* (Baton Rouge: Louisiana State University Press, 1996), 58; Frederick Law Olmsted, *The Cotton Kingdom: A Traveller's Observations on Cotton and Slavery in the American Slave States,* ed. Arthur M. Schlesinger Sr. (New York: Random House, 1984), 235; Benjamin H. Latrobe, *Impressions Respecting New Orleans: Dairy and Sketches, 1818–1820,* ed. Samuel Wilson (New York: Columbia University Press, 1951), 18.

3. *New Orleans As It Is, by a Resident* (anonymous pamphlet) (Ithaca, N.Y.: De Witt C. Grove, 1849), 46–49, 52. Almost every issue of the *New Orleans Daily Picayune* carried advertisements for costumed and masked balls. See, for example, *New Orleans Daily Picayune,* 24, 25 December 1855. Henry Kmen, "Singing and Dancing in New

Orleans: A Social History of the Birth and Growth of Balls and Opera, 1791–1841"
(Ph.D. diss., Tulane University, 1961), 53. One ballroom owner unsuccessfully sued
the city of New Orleans and the mayor, John L. Lewis, for closing his ballroom because he did not have a license or permission from the mayor to operate the facil-
ity. *Valory v. City of New Orleans and Lewis,* no. 10,788, Fifth District Court of New
Orleans, 14 February 1856; *New Orleans Daily Picayune,* 6 October 1855. Terpsichore was the Greek muse of dancing. New Orleans's naughty image persists to this
day. I recently overheard a conversation between two well-dressed businessmen on
a flight bound for the city. It was early in the morning, but both men ordered cock-
tails. One said to the other, "We're going to New Orleans, so we might as well start
drinking now."

4. Johnson, "Good Time Town," 236. Johnson's characterization of New Orleans
as the "prostitution capital of all America" may be overstated. A New York newspaper
stated that three-quarters of the sexual relations in that city were "venal, licentious,
and adulterous." Quoted in Timothy J. Gilfoyle, *City of Eros: New York City, Prostitution, and the Commercialization of Sex* (New York: W. W. Norton and Co., 1992),
105. See also Marilyn Wood Hill, *Their Sisters' Keepers: Prostitution in New York City,
1830–1870* (Berkeley: University of California Press, 1993). *New Orleans As It Is,* 37;
Report of the Orleans Parish Grand Jury, 14 July 1845, 30 June 1855, in Records of
the First District Court of New Orleans; *New Orleans Daily Picayune,* 21 May 1850,
13 July 1852; Rousey, *Policing the Southern City,* 67, 73, 80. A visit to the Museum of
Sex in New York convinced me that prostitution was much more organized in the
antebellum period in New York than it was in New Orleans. The New York sex
trade during this period had directories of prostitutes and advertisements touting the
charms of individual women. One ad claimed that in its brothel there were women
who performed the "French Treatment," a term meaning oral sex. Antebellum New
Orleans had neither directories nor advertisements. *How New York City Transformed
Sex in America* (New York: Scala Publishers, 2002); www.museumofsex.org.

5. *Louisiana Courier,* 5 August 1851 (Dr. James), 5 August 1860 (Dr. Hunter); *New
Orleans Daily Picayune,* 27 March 1852 (Watson, Mullen, Thompson).

6. *New Orleans Daily Picayune,* 25 December 1852, 17 August 1855, 4 April 1856,
12 December 1850, 2 January 1860; *New Orleans Daily True Delta,* 25 December 1859;
Asbury, *French Quarter,* 316.

7. *New Orleans Daily Picayune,* 27 November 1855, 13 January, 2 February 1857,
2 July 1852, 30 June 1854, 10, 16, 18, 20 August 1854.

8. Judith Kelleher Schafer, *Becoming Free, Remaining Free: Manumission and Enslavement in New Orleans, 1846–1862* (Baton Rouge: Louisiana State University Press,
2003). No book-length scholarly study exists on public women in New Orleans in
the antebellum period, and there is only one article, which is twenty-eight years old:
Richard Tansey, "Prostitution and Politics in Antebellum New Orleans," *Southern
Studies* 18 (Winter 1979); *New Orleans Daily Picayune,* 2 December 1857, 15 June 1854.

9. Jack D. L. Holmes, "Do It! Don't Do It! Spanish Laws on Sex and Marriage,"

in *Louisiana's Legal Heritage,* ed. Edward F. Haas (Pensacola: Perdido Bay Press, 1983), 20–21; "An Act for the Punishment of Crimes and Misdemeanors," Act of 4 May 1805, *Orleans Territory Acts, 1805,* sec. 2, p. 416; Lewis Kerr, *An Exposition of the Criminal Laws of the Territory of Orleans* (1806; repr., New Orleans: William W. Gaunt and Sons, 1986), 42.

10. *New Orleans Daily Picayune,* 28 March, 23 July 1851, 3, 7, 10 November 1858, 10, 13 November 1855, 7 October 1856, 17 July 1860.

11. Ibid., 7 June, 20 November 1855, 22 April 1852, 10 July 1856, 7 December 1858, 19 March 1847, 27 April 1850, 24 February 1859, 29 June, 1850.

12. *Desban v. Pickett,* no. 12,088, Third District Court of New Orleans, 11 February 1858; *Desban v. Pickett,* no. 5,973, Supreme Court of Louisiana (unreported), 12 January 1860; *State v. Thompson, Brunel, and Doane,* no. 13,612, First District Court of New Orleans, 3 June 1858. Theophilius Freeman was the slave dealer who sold the kidnapped Solomon Northup to a planter in the Red River region; Solomon Northup, *Twelve Years a Slave,* ed. Sue Eakin and Joseph Logsdon (1853; repr., Baton Rouge: Louisiana State University Press, 1968). *New Orleans Daily Picayune,* 24 April 1858; *State v. Parker,* no. 6,505, First District Court of New Orleans, 17 June 1851; *State v. Parker,* no. 2,392, Supreme Court of Louisiana (unreported) (February 1852). Ann, the slave of Mr. L. Genart, kept a brothel on Rampart Street. *New Orleans Daily Picayune,* 4 August 1853.

13. Tansey, "Prostitution and Politics." Tansey is the only historian to look at the First District Court's case records. However, he looked at prosecutions only for brothel keeping, not for larceny, assault and battery, and other types of prosecutions. Gilfoyle, *City of Eros;* Joel Best, *Controlling Vice: Regulating Brothel Prostitution in St. Paul, 1865–1883* (Columbus: Ohio State University Press, 1998); *New Orleans Daily Picayune,* 25 July 1852.

14. Tansey, "Prostitution and Politics," 452.

15. Christine Stansell, *City of Women: Sex and Class in New York, 1789–1860* (Urbana: University of Illinois Press, 1987), 172, 176; Nickie Roberts, *Whores in History: Prostitution in Western Society* (London: HarperCollins, 1992), 231.

16. Earl F. Niehaus, *The Irish in New Orleans, 1800–1860* (1965; repr., North Stratford, N.H.: Ayer Publishers, 1998), 66, 137–38; *New Orleans Daily Picayune,* 27 June 1852, 6 July 1854; *New Orleans Daily Crescent,* 26 May 1851.

17. William W. Sanger, M.D., *The History of Prostitution: Its Extent, Causes and Effects throughout the World* (1858; repr., New York: Medical Publishing Co., 1897), 450–51, 488, 675–76.

18. Ibid., 612. Tawnya Dudash, "Peepshow Feminism," in *Whores and Other Feminists,* ed. Jill Nagle (New York: Routledge, 1997), 104.

19. *New Orleans Daily Picayune,* 18 August, 23 October 1860, 22 June, 2 September 1854, 3 June 1855, 3 March 1859, 13 February 1852.

20. Ruth Rosen, *The Lost Sisterhood: Prostitution in America, 1900–1918* (Baltimore: Johns Hopkins University Press, 1982), xvii.

1. SELLING SEX AND THE LAW

1. Gerald L. Newman, "Anomalous Zones," *Stanford Law Review* 48 (1996): 1208; Ann M. Lucas, "Race, Class, Gender, and Deviation: The Criminalization of Prostitution," *Berkeley Women Law Journal* 10 (1995): 47, 50; "An Act to Amend the Penal Laws of This State," Act of 12 March 1818, *Louisiana Acts, 1818,* sec. 7, p. 168; "An Act Relative to Crimes," Act of 14 March 1855, *Louisiana Acts, 1855,* sec. 92, p. 145; Henry J. Leovy, *The Laws and General Ordinances of the City of New Orleans* (New Orleans: E. C. Wharton, 1857), Ordinance of 20 May 1817, no. 403, art. 3, p. 14.

2. For the duties and rules of the recorder's courts, see Leovy, *Ordinances,* nos. 638–44, pp. 224–26.

3. *Municipality no. 1 v. Wilson,* no. 8,478, Fourth Justice of the Peace Court, 21 August 1850; *Municipality no. 1 v. Wilson,* no. 1,925, Supreme Court of Louisiana, 5 La. Ann. 747 (1850); Mary R. Ryan, *Women in Public: Between Banners and Ballots, 1825–1880* (Baltimore: Johns Hopkins University Press, 1990), 98. A later decision of the Louisiana Supreme Court clarified this decision. In *Lyman v. Townsend,* the Louisiana Supreme Court held that "the prohibition here expressed is not against the keeping of houses of the kind mentioned, but against keeping disorderly houses of the character specified. . . . It seems then that no law of this State prohibits the disreputable calling or occupation . . . on the condition that it be prosecuted in an orderly manner." *Lyman v. Townsend,* no. 2,631, Supreme Court of Louisiana, 24 La. Ann. 625 (1872).

4. *New Orleans Daily Picayune,* 25, 26 July, 27 January 1854, 14 October 1853; Report of the Orleans Parish Grand Jury, First District Court of New Orleans, 30 June 1855, 4 January 1856, in Records of the First District Court of New Orleans.

5. Leovy, *Ordinances,* Ordinance of 20 May 1817, no. 403, p. 142; Ordinance of 17 February 1845, nos. 404–5, p. 142; Ordinance of 2 December 1856, no. 519, p. 175; *New Orleans Daily Picayune,* 31 July 1854, 4 August 1853, 14 July 1852, 29 July 1851, 24 September 1852.

6. *New Orleans Daily Picayune,* 27 June, 7 July, 4, 11 August, 21 September 1854, 7 June, 29, 11 September 1856, 26 August, 7, 8, 21 October 1857. For other women's arrests for indecent exposure, see ibid., 12 June 1855, 13 July 1856, 1 September, 21 August 1855, 20 June 1854.

7. Ibid., 8 August 1854, 6 January 1858, 19 September 1854, 20 May 1857, 2 June 1854, 23 May 1853, 14 August 1853. For other men arrested for indecent exposure, see ibid., 16 July 1856, 20 August 1855.

8. "An Act to Regulate Inns and other Houses of Entertainment," Act of 21 May 1806, *Louisiana Acts, 1806,* sec. 7, p. 42; Leovy, *Ordinances,* Ordinance of 2 December 1856, no. 502, p. 173; *New Orleans Daily Picayune,* 21 February 1859, 14, 15 August 1856, 17 December, 5 October 1857, 18 October 1861, 13 July 1857, 19 September 1854. For other arrests of women using obscene language, see *New Orleans Daily Picayune,* 1, 11 June 1853, 11, 15 October 1854, 21 August 1855, 13 September 1856,

27 November 1856, 8, 25 September 1857, 31 March 1858, 1 September, 8 October 1859. Occasionally men faced recorders for using obscene language. See, for example, *New Orleans Daily Picayune,* 26 September 1857, 4 August 1854. Police arrested one bookstore keeper for selling "indecent, vulgar, and debasing books, prints, engravings, [and] statues." *State v. Keller,* no. 7,199, First District Court of New Orleans, 15 January 1852.

9. *New Orleans Daily Picayune,* 6 July 1851, 11, 23 February 1853, 16 May 1854, 1 March, 10 May 1855, 7 February 1856. For cross-dressing generally, see Marjorie Garber, *Vested Interests: Cross-Dressing and Cultural Anxiety* (New York: Routledge, 1992).

10. Reid Mitchell, *All on a Mardi Gras Day: Episodes in the History of New Orleans Carnival* (Cambridge: Harvard University Press, 1995), 135–36.

11. *New Orleans Daily Picayune,* 3, 8, 9 November 1855, 28 August 1856, 22 October 1853.

12. Ibid., 16 July 1856, 23 October 1860, 23 May 1857.

13. Ibid., 15 February 1856.

14. Ibid., 11 July 1856.

15. Ibid., 13 January, 21 October 1854, 10 March 1859, 27 September 1861.

16. Ibid., 1 May 1857, 25 September 1856, 23 February, 22 April 1857, 11 July 1846, 11 July, 20 August 1855. For other reports of women wearing men's clothes, see ibid., 29 December 1853, 25 March 1854, 8 February 1855.

17. "An Act Prescribing the Rules and Conduct to Be Observed with Respect to Negroes and Other Slaves of This Territory," Act of 7 June 1806, *Orleans Territory Acts, 1806,* sec. 40, pp. 188–90 (hereafter referred to as the *Black Code); State v. Florian, f.w.c.,* no. 1,301, First District Court of New Orleans, 19 November 1847; *State v. Boyard, f.w.c.,* no. 8,463, First District Court of New Orleans, 26 August 1852; *State v. Eubanks, f.w.c.,* no. 8,462, First District Court of New Orleans, 18 April 1852; *State v. Palfrey, f.w.c.,* no. 8,464, First District Court of New Orleans, 23 April 1853; *State v. Gobet, f.w.c.,* no. 2,612, First District Court of New Orleans, 27 November 1850; *State v. Love, f.w.c.,* no. 10,291, First District Court of New Orleans, 13 May 1855. The initials "f.w.c." and "f.m.c." stand for "free woman of color" and "free man of color," respectively. The law required free people of color to use these initials after their names in all legal proceedings. "An Act to Prescribe Certain Formalities Respecting Free Persons of Color," Act of 31 March 1808, *Orleans Territory Acts, 1808,* 138–40.

18. Leovy, *Ordinances,* Ordinance of 14 March 1855, sec. 120, p. 181; *State v. Rose and Blunk,* no. 552, First District Court of New Orleans, 10 December 1846.

19. *New Orleans Daily Picayune,* 16, 17 May, 30 September 1859; 23 May 1854, 22 March 1852.

20. Tansey, "Prostitution and Politics," 449, 462, 476; *Louisiana Courier,* 5 August 1860. For reasons unknown, A. P. Field grabbed another man by the throat, pulled

a knife on him, and struck him several blows with a stick in the alley next to the courthouse. The case never proceeded to trial, apparently dropped by the prosecutor. *State v. Field*, no. 7,579, First District Court of New Orleans, 29 April 1852; Glenn R. Conrad, ed. *Dictionary of Louisiana Biography* (Lafayette: Center for Louisiana Studies, 1988), 1:301; *New Orleans Times Picayune*, 22 August 1876.

21. *New Orleans Daily True Delta*, 30 May 1851; *New Orleans Daily Crescent*, 30 May 1851; *State of Louisiana in rel. Yerger, Harper and Lambert*, no. 14,185, Third District Court of New Orleans, 7 December 1859; *New Orleans Daily Picayune*, 11 January 1860.

22. *Johnson, praying for a writ of habeas corpus*, no. 2,312, First District Court of New Orleans, 20 May 1848; *New Orleans Daily Picayune*, 14 June, 14 July 1853, 11 February 1855, 23 December 1855, 5 August 1860.

23. *Norman, praying for a writ of habeas corpus*, no. 10,498, First District Court of New Orleans, 25 July 1855.

24. *New Orleans Daily Picayune*, 16 March 1853, 16 November 1856, 10 March, 18 April, 25 July, 26, 29 August 1857. For some other reports of public women arrested for vagrancy, see ibid., 11 July 1853, 19 October, 26 December 1856, 1, 6 April, 27 May, 2 September, 10 October, 13 November, 1 December 1857.

2. "DISGUSTING DEPRAVITY"

1. Martha Hodes, *White Women, Black Men: Illicit Sex in the Nineteenth-Century South* (New Haven: Yale University Press, 1997), 144–45, 12. The word *miscegenation* did not come into wide usage until after the war, when emancipation engendered white fears of race mixing. *Civil Code of the State of Louisiana* (New Orleans: J. C. De St. Romes, 1825), art. 95, p. 17. On plaçage, see Caryn Cossé Bell, *Revolution, Romanticism and the Afro-Creole Protest Tradition in Louisiana, 1718–1868* (Baton Rouge: Louisiana State University Press, 1997), 112–13. *New Orleans Daily Picayune*, 26 March 1856.

2. *New Orleans Daily Picayune*, 10 October 1854; *State v. Miller*, no. 9,810, First District Court of New Orleans, 1854 (missing record); *Civil Code of the State of Louisiana*, art. 74, p. 17.

3. *New Orleans Daily Picayune*, 12 November 1854; *State v. Thompson alias Robinson and Baer*, no. 13,539, First District Court of New Orleans, 5 June 1858; *State v. Thompson alias Robinson and Baer*, no. 5,799, Supreme Court of Louisiana, 13 La. Ann. 515 (1858).

4. *New Orleans Daily Picayune*, 24 August 1855, 4 September 1858.

5. Ibid., 24 August 1855.

6. Ibid., 20 December, 15 April 1852, 17 February, 18 November 1853, 16 October 1854, 10 April 1858, 8 February, 13 September 1859.

7. Ibid., 23 July 1854.

8. Ibid., 11 August, 15, 2 December, 1857, 15 October 1852, 18 September 1854, 27 March 1858; *New Orleans Daily Delta,* 1 May 1860.

9. *New Orleans Daily Picayune,* 21 July 1855, 18 October 1854, 2 September 1858, 18, 19 January 1859.

10. Ibid., 22 April 1855, 13 May 1852, 2 March 1858, 3 February, 13, 3 March, 3 September 1859.

11. Ibid., 24 July, 18 October 1852.

12. Ibid., 25 July 1852.

13. Ibid., 9 December 1852, 18 November 1858.

14. Ibid., 27 August 1855.

15. Ibid., 31 May 1853, 18 May, 19 January 1855.

16. Ibid., 5 August 1858, 23 August 1855. See also 4 September 1858.

17. Ibid., 26, 27 January 1855.

18. Ibid., 14, 15, 16 August, 2, 3, 21 September 1855. Louisiana law required slaves accused of crimes to be tried in special slave tribunals made up of six slaveholders and a justice of the peace. By law, the verdicts of these tribunals could not be appealed because of any error of form. *Black Code,* "Crimes and Offences," sec. 7, p. 198.

19. *New Orleans Daily Picayune* 15, 27 September 1854, 13, 17 July 1855.

20. *New Orleans Bee,* 29 March 1849; *New Orleans Daily Picayune,* 13 May 1851; *State v. Parker,* no. 6,505, First District Court of New Orleans, 17 June 1851; *State v. Parker,* no. 2,392, Supreme Court of Louisiana (unreported) (February 1852); *New Orleans Daily Picayune,* 21 July, 18 November 1852, 2 October 1855, 5 July, 7 August 1855, 24 June, 28 December 1856, 30 June, 17, 31 August, 2 September 1857.

21. *State v. Raymond,* nos. 2,495, 2,868, First District Court of New Orleans, 17 June, 14 November 1848; *New Orleans Daily Picayune,* 13 August 1847.

22. *New Orleans Daily Picayune,* 29 July 1851, 30 April 1851; H. E. Sterkx, *The Free Negro in Antebellum Louisiana* (Cranberry, N.J.: Associated University Presses, 1972), 230–31; *State v. Richardson,* nos. 8,491, 8,504, First District Court of New Orleans, 26 April 1853; *New Orleans Daily Picayune,* 7 August 1855, 17 April, 15 July, 14 August 1857, 20 May 1859.

23. Hans W. Baade, "The Law of Slavery in Spanish Louisiana, 1769–1803," in *The Past as Prelude,* ed. Carter, 43–86; Sterkx, *Free Negro,* 38. *New Orleans Daily Picayune,* 11 January, 17 October 1857, 4 March 1859; *Carmelite, f.w.c., v. Lacaze,* no. 2,506, Supreme Court of Louisiana, 7 La. Ann. 629 (1852).

24. *Carmelite, f.w.c., v. Lacaze,* no. 2,506, Supreme Court of Louisiana, 7 La. Ann. 629 (1852).

25. *State v. Reynolds,* no. 203, First District Court of New Orleans, 24 November 1846.

26. *State v. Sanadet,* no. 205, First District Court of New Orleans, 9 September 1846.

27. *New Orleans Daily Picayune,* 18 June 1852.

28. Ibid., 23 June 1853, 10 January, 1 June 1855.

29. Ibid., 10 October 1855, 19, 10 March 1856, 3 November 1859.

30. Ibid., 6 December, 5 June, 18, 21 August 1857.

31. *State v. Scott, slave of Stewart,* no. 10,830, First District Court of New Orleans, 4 February 1856. *New Orleans Daily Picayune,* 27 July, 4, 16 August 1855; Hodes, *White Women, Black Men.* 61–62.

32. *In the matter of Alice Darthenay alias Constance LaFabre praying for a writ of habeas corpus,* no. 10,501, First District Court of New Orleans, 4 August 1855. *New Orleans Daily Picayune,* 27, 28 July, 3, 4, 16, 22 August 1855.

3. THE SEXUAL EXPLOITATION OF CHILDREN

1. Gilfoyle, *City of Eros,* 63–64; Stansell, *City of Women,* 206–7; Hill, *Their Sisters' Keepers,* 51–52.

2. *Civil Code of the State of Louisiana,* art. 41, p. 9, art. 99, p. 17; Kerr, *Exposition of the Criminal Laws,* 36; *State v. David, slave of Drake,* no. 312, Supreme Court of Louisiana (unreported) (1862).

3. *New Orleans Daily Picayune,* 26 August, 23 July 1854, 20 September, 19 January 1853, 7 May 1854.

4. Ibid., 11, 16, 18 June 1853.

5. Ibid., 16 August, 3 May 1856, 26 August 1859.

6. Ibid., 10 November 1855, 16 March 1854.

7. Ibid., 24 November 1855, 7 February 1856, 31 August 1854.

8. Ibid., 11 June 1852, 9, 14 May, 4 June, 15 September, 5, 26 October 1854, 1 April, 27 June, 24 July, 1 August 1855, 20 March, 13 April, 26 July, 21 December 1856, 3 April, 27 May 1857, 2 January, 21 March, 10 April, 12 May, 3 August 1858, 27 April 1859, 8 July 1861.

9. Ibid., 2 September, 29 November 1857, 21, 22, 24 July, 13 August 1858.

10. Ibid., 8, 21 November 1849; *State v. Sanadet,* no. 205, First District Court of New Orleans, 9 September 1846; *New Orleans Daily Picayune,* 24 August 1849, 24 December 1856, 23 January 1857, 21 July 1856, 11 October 1851. For other cases involving young girls in brothels, see *New Orleans Daily Picayune,* 23 March 1855, 18 September 1856, 12 August 1857, 22 March, 19 May, 14 August 1858.

11. *New Orleans Daily Picayune,* 12 April, 28, 29 March, 12, 30 April, 18 June, 11 May 1856; *State v. Fields, f.m.c.,* no. 12,193, First District Court of New Orleans, 17 June 1856.

12. *New Orleans Daily Picayune,* 17 August 1857, 17 April, 10 July 1856.

13. Ibid., 28 March, 5 April 1856, 13, 14, 15 August, 11 October 1855. For other cases of enticing a young woman to become a prostitute, see ibid., 24 February, 9, 14 September 1854, 14 January, 25 February, 13 May, 10 June, 1 September 1855, 16 April 1856.

14. Ibid., 15 May, 3 September 1853, 10 January, 7 June 1853, 3 December 1857.

15. Stansell, *City of Women*, 175–208; Schafer, *Becoming Free, Remaining Free*, xvii–xviii; Roberts, *Whores in History*, 231.

16. Gilfolye, *City of Eros*, 69.

17. Al Rose, *Storyville, New Orleans: Being an Authentic, Illustrated Account of the Notorious Red-Light District* (Tuscaloosa: University of Alabama Press, 1979), 15.

18. *State v. Viosca*, no. 5,931, First District Court of New Orleans, 29 May 1851; Tansey, "Prostitution and Politics," 454–55; *New Orleans Bee*, 14 July 1853; *State v. Quintera*, no. 9,052, First District Court of New Orleans, 18 July 1853.

19. Ibid., 29, 30 April, 2, 7, 19 May, 3 October 1854, 9 November 1855, 1 January 1856, 27, 28 August 1853, 15, 18, 20, 27, 29, 30 August 1861.

20. Ibid., 23 August 1849, 12 December 1850.

21. Ibid., 6 May 1852; *Louisiana Courier*, 13 June 1852; *State v. Bonnand, f.m.c.*, no. 7,644, First District Court of New Orleans, 17 April 1852.

22. *New Orleans Daily Picayune*, 12, 13 July 1852; *State v. Dalbaret and Monk*, no. 8,151, First District Court of New Orleans, 13 January 1853.

23. *New Orleans Daily Picayune*, 17 May, 16 July, 9, 10 August 1856, 17 August 1858.

24. *State v. Vorygrumbler*, no. 9,824, First District Court of New Orleans, 19 March 1855. I thank Herman Freudenberger, Ph.D., for translating this document.

25. *New Orleans Daily Picayune*, 1, 2 September 1854, *Louisiana Courier*, 3 September 1854.

26. *New Orleans Daily Picayune*, 20 April 1855; City of New Orleans, Tax Registers, no. 10,103, folio 258, square 92 (1855), 579; no. 11,115, folio 192, square 92 (1856), 563.

4. INFAMOUS PUBLIC WOMEN

1. *State v. Golden alias Hoozier Mary*, no. 33, First District Court of New Orleans, 23 July 1846; *State v. Reels alias Charleston Pet*, no. 15, 441, First District Court of New Orleans, 25 October 1861; *State v. Lattimore and Johnson alias Cincinnati Mary*, no. 8,630, First District Court of New Orleans, 19 April 1853; *New Orleans Daily Picayune*, 21, 25 October 1852, 16 September 1858, 11 February 1857, 16 January 1857, 22 June 1854, 10 June 1853, 5 August 1856, 19 November 1853, 29 September 1859, 11 September 1856, 19 May 1854, 7 January 1857; *Louisiana Courier*, 24 April 1855.

2. *New Orleans Daily Picayune*, 19 July 1856; Rose, *Storyville, New Orleans*, 15; Gary Potter, *The Antecedents of Southern Organized Crime* at www.policestudies.eku .edu/POTTER/International/Southhistory.htm, 14 (accessed July 2004); *New Orleans Daily Picayune*, 19 July 1856.

3. *New Orleans Daily Picayune*, 2, 18 February 1857.

4. *New Orleans Daily Picayune*, 12, 20 May 1857.

5. Ibid., 21 June, 1 July 1857.

6. Ibid., 17 August 1857.

7. Ibid., 5 November 1857.

8. Ibid., 16, 20 June, 25 August 1858.

9. Ibid., 4, 12, 13, 17 September, 5 November 1858; *State v. Swift alias Fury,* no. 13,778, First District Court of New Orleans, 16 May 1859; *New Orleans Daily Crescent,* 14 September 1858.

10. *State v. Swift alias Fury,* no. 6,318, Supreme Court of Louisiana, 14 La. Ann. 827 (1859); Asbury, *French Quarter,* 344; Potter, "Antecedents of Southern Organized Crime," 14; Asbury, *French Quarter,* 344–45.

11. *Black Code,* sec. 40, pp. 188–90.

12. *State v. Gibson, f.w.c.,* no. 5,136, First District Court of New Orleans, 29 June 1850; *New Orleans Daily Picayune,* 31 May 1850.

13. *State v. Gibson, f.w.c.,* no. 8,562, First District Court of New Orleans, 3 January 1853; *New Orleans Daily Picayune,* 6, 23 July 1853.

14. Gilfoyle, *City of Eros,* 77–79; Hill, *Their Sisters' Keepers,* 167.

15. *New Orleans Daily Picayune,* 22 August, 7 September 1854; *State v. Duprat, Reeves et al.,* no. 9,814, First District Court of New Orleans, 16 June 1855.

16. *New Orleans Daily Picayune,* 4 September, 23 October, 7 November 1854.

17. Ibid., 10 October 1855.

18. Ibid., 8, 19 March, 16 April, 15 May 1856; *State v. Gibson, f.w.c.,* no. 12,398, First District Court of New Orleans, 10 June 1857.

19. *New Orleans Daily Picayune,* 17 May 1856.

20. Ibid., 29 October 1856; 11 December 1857.

21. Ibid., 12 February 1856.

22. Ibid., 5, 8 June 1856.

23. Ibid., 14, 18, 31 May, 16 June 1858.

24. Ibid., 16 June 1859, 23 June 1860; *State v. Gibson, f.w.c.,* no. 14,634, First District Court of New Orleans, 4 July 1860.

25. *State v. Mayfield,* no. 3,910, First District Court of New Orleans, 20 May 1849; *State v. Mayfield,* no. 5,258, First District Court of New Orleans, 23 December 1850.

26. *State v. Mayfield,* no. 2,799, First District Court of New Orleans, 11 November 1848.

27. *State v. Mayfield and Kenner,* no. 7,074, First District Court of New Orleans, 2 February 1852; *New Orleans Daily Picayune,* 13 February 1852, 2 August 1853.

28. *State v. Mayfield,* no. 9,759, First District Court of New Orleans, 26 October 1854; *State v. Mayfield,* no. 9,431, First District Court of New Orleans, 14 June 1854; *State v. Mayfield,* no. 9,432, First District Court of New Orleans, 14 June 1854; *State v. Mayfield,* no. 9,433, First District Court of New Orleans, 14 June 1854; *New Orleans Daily Picayune,* 24 March 1854.

29. *State v. Mayfield,* no. 9,946, First District Court of New Orleans, 15 May 1855; *New Orleans Daily Picayune,* 25, 27 December 1854.

30. *New Orleans Daily Picayune,* 8 January, 4 August 1855.

31. Ibid., 22, 26 April 1856; *State v. Feenan*, no. 12,221, First District Court of New Orleans, 15 May 1856. One month later, the *Picayune* reported that Mayfield had dropped charges against Bob Johnston for an assault and battery on her. *New Orleans Daily Picayune*, 6 May 1856.

32. *New Orleans Daily Picayune*, 28 March, 18 April 1857; *State v. Golding*, no. 12,810, First District Court of New Orleans, 11 April 1857.

33. *New Orleans Daily Picayune*, 14, 16 April, 15 November 1858.

34. Ibid., 6, 10, 15 August, 1, 5 December 1858.

35. Ibid., 27 September, 16, 21 October 1858, 28 September 1860.

36. Ibid., 9 February 1859, 18 September 1860.

37. *State v. Eubanks, f.w.c.*, no. 8,031, First District Court of New Orleans, 11 November 1852; *State v. Eubanks, f.w.c.*, no. 8,462, First District Court of New Orleans, 18 April 1853, 21 February 1856.

38. *State v. Emily and Elisabeth Eubanks, f.w.c.*, no. 15,017, First District Court of New Orleans, 6 March 1861.

39. *State v. Emily and Elisabeth Eubanks, f.w.c.*, no. 15,176, First District Court of New Orleans, 7 November 1861.

40. *New Orleans Daily Picayune*, 3, 24, 29 August, 28 September 1857.

41. Ibid., 4 May, 7 August, 9, 12 November 1858.

42. Ibid., 14 February, 19, 26 August 1859.

43. Ibid., 11 July 1860. A virago is an old word for a woman who was scolding, ill tempered, or quarrelsome. "A la Heenan" is a reference of unknown origin.

44. Hill, *Their Sisters' Keepers*, 293–94.

5. LARCENY AND ROBBERY AMONG PROSTITUTES

1. Kerr, *Exposition of the Criminal Laws*, 54. For instances in which public women stole money from each other, see *State v. Coyle*, no. 2,401, First District Court of New Orleans, 23 June 1848; *State v. Marrah*, no. 8,281, First District Court of New Orleans, 20 January 1853; *New Orleans Daily Picayune*, 22 June 1854, 24, 27 February, 16 December 1855; *State v. Leinahan*, no. 14,302, First District Court of New Orleans, 18 November 1859.

2. *State v. McGlove*, no. 9,948, First District Court of New Orleans, 11 December 1856; *State v. Mr. and Mrs. McGlove*, no. 9,951, First District Court of New Orleans, 24 March 1855.

3. *State v. Cox*, no. 5,860, First District Court of New Orleans, 15 January 1851; *New Orleans Daily Picayune*, 15 March 1856.

4. *New Orleans Daily Picayune*, 25 November 1854, 14, 24 October 1857, 6 November, 24 December 1857. See also 22, 23 December 1854, 1, 20 May 1857.

5. *State v. Dorman*, no. 5,788, First District Court of New Orleans, 21 January 1851; *State v. Osnaburg*, no. 7,771, First District Court of New Orleans, 26 May 1852;

New Orleans Daily Picayune, 1 December 1855; *State v. Kearns*, no. 9,874, First District Court of New Orleans, 10 January 1855; *New Orleans Daily Picayune*, 17 June, 22 December 1856, 17 January, 8 September, 17 December 1857, 13 November 1858; *State v. Conley*, no. 3,532, First District Court of New Orleans, 18 April 1849. For other cases in which prostitutes stole clothes or money from each other, see *New Orleans Daily Picayune*, 22 January, 17 June 1856, 17 January, 17 December 1857, 3 November 1858; *State v. Pickett*, no. 1,578, First District Court of New Orleans, 26 November 1847; *State v. Hartigan alias McLigh alias Calleday*, no. 9,131, First District Court of New Orleans, 20 June 1849; *State v. Brown*, no. 8,947, First District Court of New Orleans, 22 May 1853; *State v. McElroy*, no. 9,323, First District Court of New Orleans, 19 December 1853; *State v. Bonsigneur, f.w.c.*, no. 9,486, First District Court of New Orleans, 13 May 1854; *State v. Walsh alias Connolly alias Brian*, no. 9,720, First District Court of New Orleans, 27 November 1854; *State v. Brown*, no. 9,859, First District Court of New Orleans, 14 December 1854; *New Orleans Daily Picayune*, 25 February, 16 September 1855.

6. *New Orleans Daily Picayune*, 8 September 1857.

7. Ibid., 1 December 1855.

8. Ibid., 4 October 1857, 3, 31 July 1858; *State v. Parker, f.w.c.*, no. 13,610, First District Court of New Orleans, 21 May 1858.

9. *State v. Myers*, no. 453, First District Court of New Orleans, 30 November 1846; *State v. Montgomery*, no. 3,652, First District Court of New Orleans, 7 May 1849; *State v. Wood*, no. 5,981, First District Court of New Orleans, 14 February 1851.

10. *State v. Hubbard*, no. 34, First District Court of New Orleans, 28 July 1846; *State v. Golden alias Hoozier Mary*, no. 33, First District Court of New Orleans, 23 July 1846. For similar cases in 1846, see *State v. Taylor*, no. 84, First District Court of New Orleans, 27 July 1846; *State v. Jones*, no. 340, First District Court of New Orleans, 16 November 1846.

11. *State v. Butterwick, f.w.c., Taylor and Perry*, no. 640, First District Court of New Orleans, 15 February 1847; *State v. Reid*, no. 940, First District Court of New Orleans, 27 May 1847; *State v. Sloan*, no. 1,311, First District Court of New Orleans, 15 November 1847. For a similar 1847 case, see *State. v. Wilson*, no. 583, First District Court of New Orleans, 8 February 1847.

12. *State v. Moran and McDonald*, no. 3,177, First District Court of New Orleans, 22 November 1848. For similar cases, see *State v. Love, f.w.c.*, no. 2,567, First District Court of New Orleans, 17 July 1848; *State v. Davis*, no. 4,216, First District Court of New Orleans, 27 August 1849.

13. *State v. McLaughlin alias Doris*, no. 4,697, First District Court of New Orleans, 22 January 1850. For two similar cases, see *State v. Green*, no. 4,578, First District Court of New Orleans, 6 January 1850; *State v. Davis*, no. 4,681, First District Court of New Orleans, 20 February 1850.

14. *State v. Royal, Jackson, and Wilson*, no. 7,230, First District Court of New Or-

leans, 19 December 1851; *New Orleans Daily Picayune,* 28 December 1851; *State v. Royal,* no. 7,571, First District Court of New Orleans, 18 May 1852. For more on Seuzeneau and cases involving "keeping a disorderly brothel," see chapter 8.

15. *State v. Blaise and Matus,* no. 6,129, First District Court of New Orleans, 27 March 1851.

16. *State v. Williams,* no. 7,643. First District Court of New Orleans, 15 April 1852; *State v. West,* no. 7,642, First District Court of New Orleans, 25 April 1852. See also *State v. Lowrie,* no. 7,671, First District Court of New Orleans, 3 May 1852.

17. *State v. Horn,* no. 8,046, First District Court of New Orleans, 23 October 1852; *State v. Lucy,* no. 8,391, First District Court of New Orleans, 31 December 1852; *State v. Wilson,* no. 7,623, First District Court of New Orleans, 16 October 1852.

18. *State v. Jones,* no. 8,441, First District Court of New Orleans, 1 January 1853; *State v. Hulsey,* no. 8,542, First District Court of New Orleans, 14 April 1853; *State v. Lattimore and Johnson alias Cincinnati Mary,* no. 8,630, First District Court of New Orleans, 19 April 1853.

19. *State v. Kelly and Kearny,* no. 9,119, First District Court of New Orleans, 17 November 1853.

20. *New Orleans Daily Picayune,* 1 November, 29 December 1854. See also 19 May, 26 October, 7, 10, 27 December 1854.

21. Ibid., 1 May, 4, 23 August 1855. See also 17 January 1855.

22. Ibid., 9 January, 4 September, 6 October 1855.

23. Ibid., 20, 22 October, 3 November, 11, 22, 25 December 1855. See also *State v. Reid,* no. 10,648, First District Court of New Orleans, 24 October 1855.

24. *New Orleans Daily Picayune,* 8, 9 January, 6, 20 February, 22 March, 3 May, 19 July, 16 September 1856. See also 22 January, 18, 23 February, 10 March, 8 May 1856.

25. Ibid., 9, 12 June 1856. See also 22 June 1856.

26. Ibid., 22 June, 9, 24 July 1856.

27. Ibid., 27 December 1856. See also 10 June, 8 July, 17 December 1856, 14 January 1857, 22 January 1860.

28. Ibid., 22 March, 2 April 1857; *State v. Godfrey and O'Neill,* no. 12,844, First District Court of New Orleans, 16 June 1857.

29. *State v. Miller,* no. 12,784, First District Court of New Orleans, 4 May 1857; *New Orleans Daily Picayune,* 11, 17 February 1857.

30. *New Orleans Daily Picayune,* 10, 11, 18 July 1857.

31. Ibid., 6, 9 October 1857. For another case of larceny on the same day, see 6 October 1857. There were a large number of larceny cases involving public women in 1857. They include the cases reported ibid., 5, 16, 23, 31 January 1857; *State v. Sullivan,* no. 12,690, First District Court of New Orleans, 21 February 1857; *State v. Purdy,* no. 12,651, First District Court of New Orleans, 5 May 1857; *New Orleans Daily Picayune,* 23 May, 2, 10, 17, 18, 23, 26 June, 1 July, 1, 2, 24 August, 22, 25, 27 October, 8, 19, 22, 24 November 1857; *State v. O'Marah,* no. 13,249. First District

Court of New Orleans, 9 December 1857; *New Orleans Daily Picayune,* 12, 16, 17, 22, 27 December 1857.

32. *New Orleans Daily Picayune,* 21 March 1858, There were a number of cases that involved public women and larceny in 1858: *State v. Kane,* no. 13,349, First District Court of New Orleans, 15 January 1858; *New Orleans Daily Picayune,* 19, 20 January 1858; *State v. Holmes,* no. 13,374, First District Court of New Orleans, 28 January 1858; *State v. Burk,* no. 13,394, First District Court of New Orleans, 5 February 1858; *New Orleans Daily Picayune,* 20 February, 21, 30 April 1858; *State v. Boyle, Smith and Williams,* no. 13,578, First District Court of New Orleans, 11 May 1858; *New Orleans Daily Picayune,* 2, 11, 24 June, 10, 18 July, 9, 27 August, 16, 27 September, 26 November, 16 December 1858.

33. *New Orleans Daily Picayune,* 14, 15 March 1859; *State v. Collins et al.,* no. 13,993, First District Court of New Orleans, 31 March 1859.

34. *New Orleans Daily Picayune,* 24 March, 11 May 1859. For other incidents involving larceny and public women, see 3 March, 5 November 1859; *State v. Holmes,* no. 14,159, First District Court of New Orleans, 14 November 1859.

35. *New Orleans Daily Picayune* 26 July, 8 September 1861; *State v. Giggons, f.w.c.,* no. 15,493, First District Court of New Orleans, 25 October 1861. See also *State v. Bertrand,* no. 14,720, First District Court of New Orleans, 2 November 1860; *State v. Reels alias Charleston Pet,* no. 15,441, First District Court of New Orleans, 25 October 1861; *State v. Hines,* no. 15,479, First District Court of New Orleans, 18 October 1861; *State v. Jones and Lewis,* no. 15,580, First District Court of New Orleans, 18 December 1861; *State v. Gallagher and Snaffer,* no. 15,113, First District Court of New Orleans, 13 May 1861; *State v. Smith,* no. 15,229, First District Court of New Orleans, 17 October 1861; *New Orleans Daily Picayune,* 23 March 1862.

6. VIOLENT LIVES

1. *New Orleans Daily Picayune,* 6 July, 1, 12 October 1855.

2. Ibid., 8, 31 May 1856.

3. Ibid., 7 October 1861.

4. Ibid., 22 January 1858, 23 July 1858, 27, 28, 29 September 1859, 21 October 1861.

5. Ibid., 19 November 1853, *Louisiana Courier,* 24 April 1855; *New Orleans Daily Picayune,* 4 September 1856, 10 February, 12 May 1857.

6. *New Orleans Daily Picayune,* 12, 25 April 1858, 6 November 1859, 9 November 1862.

7. Ibid., 25 May 1852.

8. Ibid., 18 November, 11 June 1856, 4, 27 March 1858.

9. Ibid., 1, 3, 6, 14 July 1858.

10. Ibid., 8, 9 July 1861, 3 January 1860.

11. Ibid., 9 January 1856, 4, 6 December 1857, 15 January, 17 February 1858.

12. Ibid., 9, 19, 23, 28 June 1857.

13. Ibid., 15 July 1857; *State v. Brunetto,* no. 13,009, First District Court of New Orleans, 15 July 1857; *State v. Brunetto,* no. 5,376, Supreme Court of Louisiana, 13 La. Ann. 45 (1858).

14. *New Orleans Daily Picayune,* 18, 26, 28 July 1857, 28 January 1858.

15. *State v. Kent,* no. 8,825, First District Court of New Orleans, 5 March 1853; *New Orleans Daily Picayune,* 6 September 1855, 7 March, 30 November 1856, 4 December 1856; *State v. Kent,* no. 12,631, First District Court of New Orleans, 5 May 1857; *New Orleans Daily Picayune,* 6 December 1857, 4 August 1859; *State v. Hickey, Dutch Kitty and McNaff,* no. 14,218, First District Court of New Orleans, 24 October 1859; *New Orleans Daily Picayune,* 10 December 1861.

16. *State v. Murphy and Rowan,* no. 3,165, First District Court of New Orleans, 22 November 1848; *State v. Murphy,* no. 6,943. First District Court of New Orleans, 25 October 1851; *New Orleans Daily Picayune,* 27 August 1855; *State v. Murphy,* no. 9,274, First District Court of New Orleans, 31 October 1856; *State v. Murphy,* no. 10,871, First District Court of New Orleans, 7 February 1857.

17. *New Orleans Daily Picayune,* 11, 26 August 1855.

18. Ibid., 5, 19, 23 January 1856.

19. Ibid., 28, 29 June 1856.

20. Ibid., 30 October 1857.

21. Ibid., 26 March 1858, 10 April 1859.

22. Ibid., 3 January, 22, 26 August, 27, 28 September 1855, 2 January 1851, 23 January 1858. Eugene Suchet was the pimp of a prostitute named Eliza Phillips, who was murdered in New Orleans in 1851. See chapter 7.

23. Ibid., 30, 31 January, 2 February 1855.

24. Ibid., 3 February, 3, 24 April, 16 August 1856.

25. Ibid., 26 January, 6 June, 12 November, 1, 4, 5 December 1857.

26. *Black Code,* sec. 40, pp. 188–90; Leovy, *Ordinances,* no. 757, p. 259.

27. *State v. Parsons, f.w.c.,* no. 680, First District Court of New Orleans, 19 May 1847.

28. *State v. Black, f.w.c.,* no. 1,095, First District Court of New Orleans, 3 July 1847; *State v. Florian, f.w.c.,* no. 1,301, First District Court of New Orleans, 19 November 1847; *State v. Dickinson, f.w.c.,* no. 2,811, First District Court of New Orleans, 11 October 1848; *State v. Catherine, f.w.c.* (docket number illegible), First District Court of New Orleans, 20 December 1849.

29. *State v. Washington, f.w.c.,* no. 5,123. First District Court of New Orleans, 15 June 1850; *State v. Evans, f.w.c.,* no. 5,410, First District Court of New Orleans, 22 November 1850. For another case of insulting, see *State. v. Hubbard, f.w.c.,* no. 9,856, First District Court of New Orleans, 13 April 1855.

30. *New Orleans Daily Picayune,* 1 February 1857; "An Act to Prevent Free Persons of Color from Entering This State and for Other Purposes," Act of 16 March 1830, *Louisiana Acts, 1830,* pp. 90–96.

31. *State v. Harris, f.w.c.,* no. 148, First District Court of New Orleans, 27 August 1846.

32. *State v. Hernandez, f.w.c.,* no. 323, First District Court of New Orleans, 6 March 1847; *State v. Parsons,* no. 1,284, First District Court of New Orleans, 8 November 1847; *State v. Helvring,* no. 1,246, First District Court of New Orleans, (date illegible) 1847.

33. *State v. Smith,* no. 1,936, First District Court of New Orleans, 18 March 1848; *State v. Seines,* no. 2,444, First District Court of New Orleans, 2 June 1848; *State v. O'Brien,* no. 2,553, First District Court of New Orleans, 13 June 1848. See also *State v. Smith alias Carrollton,* no. 2,418, First District Court of New Orleans, 27 June 1848; *State v. Cassidy,* no. 2,467, First District Court of New Orleans, 28 June 1848.

34. *State v. Hopkins,* no. 4,550, First District Court of New Orleans, 14 February 1850. See also *State v. Davis,* no. 4,878, First District Court of New Orleans, 20 May 1850; *State v. Montgomery,* no. 4,998, First District Court of New Orleans, 22 May 1850. See also *State v. Bolon,* no. 5,092, First District Court of New Orleans, 25 May 1850; *State v. Hill,* no. 5,080, First District Court of New Orleans, 29 May 1850.

35. *State v. Brown,* no. 5,893, First District Court of New Orleans, 15 January 1851; *State v. Roan alias Higham,* no. 5,635, First District Court of New Orleans, 9 March 1851; *State v. Davis, f.w.c.,* no. 6,503, First District Court of New Orleans, 10 June 1851; *New Orleans Daily Picayune,* 15 May 1851; *New Orleans Bee,* 15 May 1851; *New Orleans Daily True Delta,* 15 May 1851. See also *New Orleans Daily True Delta,* 12 February 1851; *State v. Jet, f.w.c.,* no. 6,172, First District Court of New Orleans, 11 March 1851.

36. *State v. Hanna,* no. 7,507, First District Court of New Orleans, 13 May 1852; *New Orleans Daily Picayune,* 12 August 1853.

37. *State v. Thayer, f.w.c.,* no. 9,350, First District Court of New Orleans, 10 May 1854; *State v. McCann,* no. 8,928, First District Court of New Orleans, 27 January 1857; *State v. Clarisse, f.w.c.,* no. 9,439, First District Court of New Orleans, 13 February 1854; *State v. Dunn, f.w.c.,* no. 9,078, First District Court of New Orleans, 5 November 1853; *State v. Venere,* no. 9,231, First District Court of New Orleans, 24 February 1854; *State v. Wilson,* no. 9,172, First District Court of New Orleans, 31 January 1854.

38. *State v. Charlotte, f.w.c.,* no. 9,485, First District Court of New Orleans, 30 October 1836; *State v. Cassidy, Cassidy and Doyle,* no. 9,541, First District Court of New Orleans, 14 June 1854; *New Orleans Daily Picayune,* 25 November 1855.

39. *State v. Hollingshade,* no. 9,237, First District Court of New Orleans, 19 April 1854; *State v. Jones,* no. 9,661, First District Court of New Orleans, 31 October 1854.

40. *New Orleans Daily Picayune,* 28 April, 17 August 1854.

41. Ibid., 31 August, 15, 18 September 1854, 17 June 1856.

42. Ibid., 28 June, 27 July 1855. See also *New Orleans Bee,* 18 August 1855; *New Orleans Daily Picayune,* 30 August, 2 September 1855.

43. *New Orleans Daily Picayune,* 15 March, 6 May, 11, 14 June, 22, 29 July 1856. See

also *State v. Sweany alias Big Anna,* no. 10, 883, First District Court of New Orleans, 20 September 1856; *New Orleans Daily Picayune,* 29 May, 9 July, 19 August 1856.

44. *New Orleans Daily Picayune,* 22, 29 June, 27 February, 25 October 1856. See also 28 June, 11 October 1856.

45. *State v. Stacey and Gallagher,* no. 12,666, First District Court of New Orleans, 29 June 1857; *New Orleans Daily Picayune,* 7 February 1857.

46. *New Orleans Daily Picayune,* 1, 3, 7 April, 23 March, 8 April, 21, 30 July 1857. For other assaults and batteries in 1857, see 6 January, 15, 21, 30 April 1857; *State v. Johnson alias Layton,* no. 12,826, First District Court of New Orleans, 30 May 1857; *New Orleans Daily Picayune,* 30, 31 July, 4 August, 18 September 1857.

47. *State v. Stillman and St. Clair,* no. 13,394, First District Court of New Orleans, 10 January 1858; *State v. Stillman,* no. 14,114, First District Court of New Orleans, 22 June 1859.

48. *New Orleans Daily Picayune,* 19, 29 February, 1 May 1858; *State v. Fannin alias Gallatin Mary,* no. 13,682. First District Court of New Orleans, 26 November 1858.

49. *New Orleans Daily Picayune,* 8 July 1859.

50. Ibid., 8 July, 8 December 1859; *State v. McNabb,* no.14,321, First District Court of New Orleans, 17 January 1960; *New Orleans Daily Picayune,* 21 January 1860. See also 13 January, 14, 30 April, 10 May, 2, 16 August, 27, 30 September, 8 October 1859; *State v. Handly,* no. 13,878, First District Court of New Orleans, 12 November 1858; *State v. Collins,* no. 14,776, First District Court of New Orleans, 28 January 1861; *New Orleans Daily Picayune,* 19, 25 July, 7, 29, 30 August, 13 September, 16, 22 October 1861; *State v. Williams,* no. 15,410, First District Court of New Orleans, 16 November 1861.

7. THE MURDER OF A "LEWD AND ABANDONED WOMAN"

1. *State v. Parker,* no. 6,505, First District Court of New Orleans, 17 June 1851; *State v. Parker,* no. 2,392, Supreme Court of Louisiana (unreported) (February 1852).

2. *New Orleans Daily True Delta,* 18 June 1851; *New Orleans Daily Crescent,* 13 May 1851, 10 May 1951; *New Orleans Daily True Delta,* 13 May 1851. The *C. E. Watkins,* a side-wheel packet boat, had a regular route between New Orleans and Memphis. Frederick Way Jr., comp., *Way's Packet Directory, 1848–1983: Passenger Steamboats of the Mississippi River System since the Advent of Photography in Mid-Continent America* (Columbus: Ohio State University Press, 1983), 65. *New Orleans Daily Picayune,* 18 May 1851.

3. *New Orleans Daily Picayune,* 18 June 1851. Preliminary hearing, *State v. Parker,* no. 6,505, First District Court of New Orleans, 17 June 1851.

4. Preliminary hearing, *State v. Parker,* no. 6,505. Although the records of the recorder's courts no longer exist, the coroner's report and the record of the preliminary hearing before the recorder exist in the case file. *New Orleans Daily Picayune,* 18 June 1851.

5. Preliminary hearing, *State v. Parker,* no. 6,505; *New Orleans Bee,* 9 May 1851; *New Orleans Daily Crescent,* 9 May 1851; *New Orleans Daily True Delta,* May 9, 13 May 1851.

6. *New Orleans Daily True Delta,* 13 May 1851; *New Orleans Daily Crescent,* 14 May 1851; *New Orleans Daily Picayune,* 13 May 1851. James Caldwell pursued several careers during his lifetime: actor, theater manager, businessman, recorder of the Second Municipality, councilman, alderman, and state legislator. During the same month as the preliminary hearing, one of the New Orleans newspapers called him an "imbecile dotard," a corrupt and incompetent official who sided with police, and accused him of leniency with vagrants and prostitutes because he himself owned houses of ill fame. A reporter blamed Caldwell for an increase of crime in the Second Municipality: "Crime is allowed to stalk through the streets." *New Orleans Daily Crescent,* 29 May 1851; *New Orleans Bee,* 18 June 1851. Conrad, *Dictionary of Louisiana Biography,* 1:145. *New Orleans Daily True Delta,* 9 May, 13 May, 1851. The slave Eliza appeared before Justice of the Peace Jacob Winter and was charged with "keeping a disorderly brothel." The records of the justices courts no longer exist, but the newspapers indicate that Winter dismissed the case, probably at Turner's request. *New Orleans Bee,* 13 May 1851.

7. *New Orleans Daily True Delta,* 13 May 1851; *New Orleans Daily Picayune,* 13 May, 18 June 1851; *New Orleans Daily Crescent,* 9 May 1851. Police testimony at the preliminary hearing indicated that two other prostitutes, Nancy Mayfield and Catherine Shay, lived at 211 Gravier at the time of Phillips's death. For more information on Nancy Mayfield, see chapter 4.

8. *New Orleans Daily Crescent,* 14 May 1851; *New Orleans Bee,* 14 May 1851; *New Orleans Daily True Delta,* 14 May 1851. Randell Hunt had the reputation of being one of the most able attorneys in New Orleans. Originally an attorney in South Carolina, Hunt had opposed nullification and left South Carolina as a result. He served as a Louisiana legislator and a delegate to the 1852 Louisiana constitutional convention. Although he opposed secession in 1861, he remained loyal to his adopted state. A professor of law at the University of Louisiana (later Tulane University), he taught commercial law, the law of evidence, and constitutional law. He served as the university's president from 1867 to 1884. Conrad, *Dictionary of Louisiana Biography,* 1:418. *New Orleans Bee,* 31 May 1851. The center of the red-light district in the Second Municipality formed a rough horseshoe around the Second Municipality's City Hall (now Gallier Hall) and included Gravier and Perdido streets, as well as Circus (Rampart), Phillippa (O'Keefe), St. John (Loyola), and Girod. During the interval between the preliminary hearing and the trial of the *Parker* case, police arrested fifteen "lewd and abandoned women" in a one-night sweep of Perdido, Phillippa, St. John, and Gravier streets. They each received fines of five dollars, and the recorder discharged them after payment. *New Orleans Daily Picayune,* 29 May 1851.

9. *New Orleans Daily Picayune*, 20, 24 May 1851; 10 August 1851. See also 25 November 1849, 19 June 1851; *New Orleans Bee*, 18 June 1851, for descriptions of the court building.

10. *New Orleans Daily Picayune*, 7 September 1852, 13 November, 1 May 1853.

11. *New Orleans Daily Crescent*, 18 June 1851; *New Orleans Daily True Delta*, 29 May 1851.

12. *New Orleans Daily Picayune*, 18 June 1851; *New Orleans Daily True Delta*, 18 June 1851. In restricting himself to the "Common Law of England," Larue followed the criminal law of Louisiana as stated in the Crimes Act of 1805. This act stipulated that the method of trial and rules of evidence should conform to the common law of England, "changing what ought to be changed." "An Act for the Punishment of Crimes and Misdemeanors," Act of 4 May 1805, *Orleans Territory Acts, 1805*, sec. 33, p. 441.

13. *New Orleans Daily True Delta*, 18 June 1851; *New Orleans Bee*, 18, 19 June 1851.

14. *New Orleans Daily True Delta*, 19 June 1851; *New Orleans Daily Crescent*, 19 June 1851.

15. *New Orleans Daily Picayune*, 19 June 1851; *New Orleans Bee*, 19 June 1851; *New Orleans Daily Crescent*, 19 June 1851.

16. *New Orleans Daily Crescent*, 19 June 1851.

17. Ibid.

18. *New Orleans Daily True Delta*, *New Orleans Daily Picayune*, *New Orleans Bee*, *New Orleans Daily Crescent*, 19 June 1851. Charge to jury, *State v. Parker*, no. 6,505. On one day in 1853, Larue sentenced four men convicted of manslaughter to twenty years in the state penitentiary and one thousand dollars in fines. On the same day, he also sentenced a man convicted of murder to hang. The newspaper that reported the sentences commented on the uselessness of recommending a criminal to the mercy of Larue's court: "I'd as soon think of recommending a small rabbit to a boa-constrictor." However, the reporter went on to applaud Larue's actions: "Now and then a vigorous exercise of the severities of justice is needed in this city. . . . Judge Larue has the energy and will to put down such assaults on the peace of society, and with a proper jury to second his efforts, the lawless will soon find out that the law does not always slumber in New Orleans—the sword will drop sometimes, offering a terrible prospect to evildoers." *New Orleans Daily Picayune*, 1 May 1853. The *Code of Practice* instructed judges to limit themselves "to giving the jury a knowledge of the laws applicable to the cause submitted them, and he shall abstain from saying anything about the facts, or even recapitulating them, so as not to exercise any influence on their decision." James O. Faqua, ed. *Code of Practice in Civil Cases for the State of Louisiana with the Statutory Amendments from 1825 to 1866 Inclusive* (New Orleans: Bloomfield Steele, 1867), art. 516, p. 240. In 1853 the Louisiana legislature passed a law reiterating the restriction in the *Code of Practice*. "An Act to Restrict the Charge

of the Judge in Every Criminal Case to an Opinion on the Law," Act of 29 April 1853, *Louisiana Acts, 1853,* 249–50. In an editorial, the *New Orleans Daily Picayune* denounced this act, stating that the act meant that "juries are practically deprived of all assistance from the bench in making up their verdicts—a deprivation which, in our opinion, is very injurious to the public weal." *New Orleans Daily Picayune,* 17 November 1853.

19. Bill of exceptions, *State v. Parker,* no. 6,505.

20. Ibid.

21. Attorney general's argument, *State v. Parker,* no. 2,392 Supreme Court of Louisiana (unreported) (February 1852). Isaac Johnson served his native state as state legislator (1833–39), state judge (1839–45), governor (1846–50), and attorney general (1850–52). He died of a heart attack in 1853 at the age of fifty. Carolyn E. DeLatte, "Isaac Johnson," in *The Louisiana Governors: From Iberville to Edwards,* ed. Joseph G. Dawson III (Baton Rouge: Louisiana State University Press, 1990), 122–26.

22. Decision of the Supreme Court of Louisiana, *State v. Parker,* no. 2,392. Three justices signed the majority decision of the court: Chief Justice George Eustis and Associate Justices Pierre Adolph Rost and Thomas Slidell. Eustis served the state as attorney general (1830–32), secretary of state (1832–34), associate judge of the Supreme Court of Louisiana (1838–39), delegate to the 1845 state constitutional convention, and chief justice (1846–52). Conrad, *Dictionary of Louisiana Biography,* 1:290. Rost studied law under Joseph E. Davis (brother of Jefferson Davis) and served as state senator (1826–30) and associate judge and justice of the Supreme Court of Louisiana (1839, 1846–53). During the Civil War, he served the Confederate States of America as minister to Spain. Conrad, *Dictionary of Louisiana Biography,* 2:697. Governor Isaac Johnson appointed Thomas Slidell associate justice of the Supreme Court of Louisiana. He served from 1845 to 1852, when voters elected him chief justice of the court, in which position he served until 1855. Conrad, *Dictionary of Louisiana Biography,* 2:747.

23. Decision of the Supreme Court of Louisiana, *State v. Parker,* no. 2,392; Henry Roscoe, *A Digest of the Law of Evidence in Criminal Cases* (London: Stevens, Sweeny and Maxwell, 1835), 72.

24. *New Orleans Commercial Bulletin,* 17 November 1856; John Frederick Archbold, *Archbold's Summary of the Law Relating to Pleading and Evidence in Criminal Cases* (New York: Gould, Banks, 1846), 43; Leonard MacNally, *MacNally's Rules of Evidence on the Pleas of the Crown* (Dublin: J. Cook, 1802), 285; Justice Preston's decision, *State v. Parker,* no. 2,392. Isaac Preston served on the court from 1850 to 1852. He died in a steamboat accident on the Fourth of July in 1852. Warren M. Billings, ed., *The Historic Rules of the Supreme Court of Louisiana, 1813–1879* (Lafayette: Center for Louisiana Studies, 1985), 48.

25. Decision of the Supreme Court of Louisiana, *State v. Parker,* no. 2,392; MacNally, *Rules of Evidence,* 322–23.

26. Historians have no way of knowing the legal texts to which the court had access. No record exists of the holdings of the supreme court library or of any of the justices in the 1850s. Henry Bullard's succession inventory listed Simon Greenleaf, *A Treatise on the Law of Evidence*, 2 vols. (Boston: Little, Brown, 1842–46), among his possessions that fell under an auctioneer's hammer after his death in 1851, but we do not know if the supreme court had access to Greenleaf. Robert Feikema Karachuk, "A Workman's Tools: The Law Library of Henry Bullard" (master's thesis, University of New Orleans, 1996), 10, 38. Modern attorneys refer to the practice of the supreme court of not reporting certain cases as "deep-sixing" the case.

27. *New Orleans Daily True Delta, New Orleans Daily Crescent, New Orleans Daily Picayune*, 25 February 1852.

28. *Constitution of the State of Louisiana, 1852* (New Orleans: E. LaSere, 1852), art. 64, p. 81; Wayne M. Everard, "Louisiana's 'Whig' Constitution Revisited: The Constitution of 1852," in *In Search of Fundamental Law: Louisiana's Constitutions, 1812–1974*, ed. Warren M. Billings and Edward F. Haas (Lafayette: Center for Louisiana Studies, 1993), 47–48; *New Orleans Daily Picayune*, 17 May 1853, 13 November 1853; "An Act to Organize District Courts for the Parish and City of New Orleans," Act of 28 April 1853, *Louisiana Acts, 1853*, secs. 2, 6, pp. 190–91; Report of the Committee on Retrenchment in *Journal of the House of Representatives of the State of Louisiana, 1852* (New Orleans: E. LaSere, 1852), 10. The Committee on Retrenchment also recommended lowering the governor's annual salary from $6,000 to $4,000, eliminating one of the associate justices of the supreme court, and lowering the chief justice's salary from $6,000 to $4,000 and the salaries of the remaining associate justices from $5,500 to $3,500. Recorders' salaries fell from $2,400 to $2,000. *New Orleans Daily Picayune*, 16, 17 April, 14, 22 May 1852; *New Orleans Daily Picayune*, 1 January 1854. Larue died very suddenly of "congestion of the chest" in 1856. *New Orleans Commercial Bulletin*, 17 November 1856.

29. Patricia Cline Cohen, *The Murder of Helen Jewett: The Life and Death of a Prostitute in Nineteenth-Century New York* (New York: Alfred A. Knopf, 1998), 312–14. After Judge Robertson issued a citation for contempt of court for one of the sheriff's deputies "in a tone unnecessarily harsh and intemperate," the deputy demanded an apology and, receiving none, attacked Robertson with a sword cane near the courthouse. In the struggle, Robertson produced two concealed weapons, a pistol and a dagger, but his assailant prevented him from using either. A jury later acquitted the judge of a charge of carrying concealed weapons. The judge claimed in his defense that he needed the weapons for self-defense. *New Orleans Daily Picayune*, 3 April 1856 and 30 November 1856. In March 1857, Robertson announced that he would not seek reelection, and Theodore Hunt won election as judge of the First District Court the following month. One of Hunt's first actions as judge was to clear hundreds of old cases from the docket that had been left by his predecessor by either trying or dismissing them. *New Orleans Daily Picayune*, 7 April and 26, 28, 29 May 1857. A

July 1857 grand jury noted that Judge Hunt reduced the docket from 857 cases to 171 cases in just four months. Report of Orleans Parish Grand Jury, *New Orleans Daily Picayune*, 7 July 1857.

30. *New Orleans Daily True Delta, New Orleans Daily Crescent, New Orleans Daily Picayune*, 1 February 1855. Only the *Picayune* reported Phillips's first name and address correctly. Suchet's arrests appear in *New Orleans Daily Picayune*, 6 March 1853; *New Orleans Bee*, 3 June 1854.

31. "An Act to Organize District Courts for the Parish and City of New Orleans," 190. The *Code of Practice* required recusal of judges in civil matters for the same reasons. Faqua, *Code of Practice*, art. 338, p. 193.

32. Parker never appeared in the Louisiana censuses. He probably maintained his residence in Tennessee and rented rooms in New Orleans for the times when his boat docked in the city. He appeared in the newspaper following the case's dismissal twice: when the rooms he rented burned in a fire and when he found a lost child. *New Orleans Daily Picayune*, 23 November 1857, 4 December 1857.

33. Leovy, *Ordinances*, Ordinances of 20 May 1817, no. 403, and 17 February 1845, nos. 404–5, 142; "An Act to Amend the Penal Laws of This State," Act of 12 March 1818, *Louisiana Acts, 1818*, sec. 7, p. 168. *New Orleans Bee*, 13 May 1851; *New Orleans Daily True Delta*, 30 May 1851; *New Orleans Daily Crescent*, 30 May 1851; *New Orleans Daily Picayune*, 29 May 1851, 19 May 1852.

34. Examples of cases dismissed without trial by the First District Court of New Orleans for keeping a brothel include *State v. Raymond*, no. 2,495, 17 June 1848; *State v. Robinson, Riley, and Massit*, no. 7,421, 13 May 1852; *State v. Fanning*, no. 7,572, 19 May 1852; *State v. Mayfield*, no. 7,959, 31 October 1854; *State v. Black*, no. 9,761, 3 January 1855; *State v. Taylor*, no. 9,762, 3 January 1855; *State v. Murray*, no. 9,763, 30 October 1854. Recorders sent approximately six cases of people accused of keeping a brothel each year to the First District Court of New Orleans between 1846 and 1862. The court sentenced one of the few people convicted of this offense to two months in jail and a fine of $250. *State v. H. Durker*, no. 5,929, 15 March 1851; *New Orleans As It Was*, 36–37. See chapter 8.

35. Arrests and prosecutions of men accused of prostitution do not exist in the New Orleans court records or the newspapers. Much of the scholarship on prostitution in the United States centers on the Gilded Age and Progressive period. The standard work on the law of prostitution is Thomas Mackay's "Red Lights Out: A Legal History of Prostitution, Disorderly Houses, and Vice Districts, 1870–1917" (Ph.D. diss., Rice University, 1984). One of the first studies of prostitution is Sanger, *History of Prostitution*. Other general works on prostitution include John C. Burnham, *Bad Habits: Drinking, Smoking, Taking Drugs, Gambling, Sexual Misbehavior, and Swearing in American History* (New York: New York University Press, 1993), and Rosen, *Lost Sisterhood*. Scholarship on prostitution in New Orleans is largely confined to the late nineteenth and early twentieth centuries. See, for example, Alecia P. Long,

The Great Southern Babylon: Sex, Race, and Respectability in New Orleans, 1865–1920 (Baton Rouge: Louisiana State University Press, 2004); Bergen Brooke, *Storyville: A Hidden Mirror* (Wakefield, R.I.: Moyer Bell, 1994); Rose, *Storyville, New Orleans;* Russell Levy, "Of Bards and Bawds: New Orleans Sporting Life before and during the Storyville Era, 1897–1917" (Ph.D. diss., Tulane University, 1967); and Stephen Longstreet, *Sportin' House: A History of the New Orleans Sinners and the Birth of Jazz* (Los Angeles: Sherbourne Press, 1965). Newer work on the subject in the antebellum period includes E. Susan Barber, "Depraved and Abandoned Women: Prostitution in Richmond, Virginia, across the Civil War," in *Neither Lady nor Slave: Working Women of the Old South,* ed. Susanna Delfino and Michele Gillespie (Chapel Hill: University of North Carolina Press, 2002); Stansell, *City of Women,* 171–92; and Cohen, *Murder of Helen Jewett.* Jane H. Pease and William H. Pease, *Ladies, Women and Wenches: Choice and Constraint in Antebellum Charleston and Boston* (Chapel Hill: University of North Carolina Press, 1990). Dell Upton, ed., *Madaline: Love and Survival in Antebellum New Orleans* (Athens: University of Georgia Press, 1996), is a collection of the writings of a kept woman in New Orleans. An examination of the political and financial underpinnings of prostitution appears in Tansey, "Prostitution and Politics." Tansey had only limited use of the records of the First District Court of New Orleans. A new postbellum book on prostitution is Best, *Controlling Vice.*

36. Conviction for teaching a slave to read or write merited a sentence of not less than one month nor more than twelve months. "An Act to Punish the Crimes Therein Mentioned, and for Other Purposes," Act of 16 March 1830, *Louisiana Acts, 1830,* sec. 3, p. 96; *Black Code,* sec. 38, pp. 182–84. Leovy, *Ordinances,* art. 750, p. 257; art. 1091, p. 378.

37. *New Orleans Daily Picayune,* 18 November 1852, 2 July 1852, 30 April 1851.

38. Tansey, "Prostitution and Politics," 450–51; *New Orleans Daily Picayune,* 26 July 1852.

8. KEEPING A BROTHEL IN ANTEBELLUM NEW ORLEANS

1. *New Orleans Daily Picayune,* 1, 29 December 1855, 19 October 1852, 27 November 1857, 10 August 1854.

2. Ibid., 9 July 1853, 30 April 1851.

3. Ibid., 23 November 1850; *New Orleans Daily Crescent,* 27, 29 May 1851; *New Orleans Daily Picayune,* 29 May, 10 June, 16 December 1851.

4. *New Orleans Daily Picayune,* 28 July 1852, 9 June 1853, 12 May 1848.

5. Ibid., 4 April 1850, 7 December 1855.

6. Ibid., 30 April, 7, 19 May 1852, 8 July 1853.

7. Ibid., 28 May, 25 September 1854, 18 May, 17 December 1855, 10, 16 August, 15 November 1856.

8. Ibid., 14, 15 February, 2 March, 5 August, 30 September, 4 October, 10, 11

December 1857. A "Cyprian" is an old word for a prostitute. Ibid., 19 May 1854.

9. Ibid., 27 April, 22 May, 12 July, 24 August, 13 September, 2, 7 December 1858.

10. Ibid., 17 February, 26, 27, 29, 31 March, 2 April, 29 June, 1 October 1859.

11. Ibid., 23 July, 1, 2, 4 August 1860.

12. Ibid., 19 September, 4, 28 October 1859; *State v. Kent*, no. 10,535, First District Court of New Orleans, 20 May 1857. Police arrested Dan Rich in 1854 for keeping a brothel "which is the resort of abandoned women," but no record of a prosecution exists. *New Orleans Daily Picayune*, 23 May 1857. In August 1857 a recorder ordered George Kent and Dan Rich to pay fines of fifty dollars each for keeping a brothel. *New Orleans Daily Picayune*, 16 August 1857. Seidler sued for a writ of habeas corpus before the First District Court of New Orleans in December 1857. Judge Hunt released him from the custody of the recorder but committed him to the parish prison until discharged by due course of law, a "leap out of the frying pan into the fire." *New Orleans Daily Picayune*, 18 December 1857.

13. *New Orleans Daily Picayune*, 13 July 1860, 17 August 1857.

14. *State v. Reynolds, f.w.c.*, no. 203, First District Court of New Orleans, 24 November 1846.

15. *State v. Collins*, no. 203, First District Court of New Orleans, 31 August 1846; *State v. Sanadet*, no. 204, First District Court of New Orleans, 9 September 1846; *State v. Dewett*, no. 206, First District Court of New Orleans, 18 November 1846.

16. *State v. Cox*, no. 502, First District Court of New Orleans, 9 January 1847; *State v. Raymond*, no. 2,495, First District Court of New Orleans, 19 January 1849; *State v. Raymond*, no. 2,868, First District Court of New Orleans, 24 January 1849; *New Orleans Daily Picayune*, 13 August 1847, 22, 25 July 1848. Cresswell faced several lawsuits for selling slaves as healthy when in fact they were diseased. When he died, he left a will freeing all the slaves he owned at the time of his death and ordered his executor to take them to a free state. *Coulter v. Cresswell*, no. 2,734, Supreme Court of Louisiana, 7 La. Ann. 367 (1852); *Succession of Cresswell*, no. 2,423, Supreme Court of Louisiana, 8 La. Ann. 122 (1853).

17. *State v. Moore alias Turner*, no. 2,546, First District Court of New Orleans, 14 November 1848; *State v. Jenkins*, no. 2,547, First District Court of New Orleans, 16 December 1846; *State v. Stubblefield*, no. 2,901, First District Court of New Orleans, 14 December 1848; *State v. Willey*, no. 2,902, First District Court of New Orleans, 29 November 1848; *State v. Williams*, no. 2,903, First District Court of New Orleans, 20 December 1848.

18. *State v. Fluhart*, no. 2,904, First District Court of New Orleans, 24 January 1949; *Fluhart v. Golding*, no. 1,930, Supreme Court of Louisiana, 7 La. Ann. 233 (April 1852); *Succession of Fluhart*, no. 3,549, Fourth District Court of New Orleans, 5 April 1852. Conrad, *Dictionary of Louisiana Biography*, 1:323; Northup, *Twelve Years a Slave*, 51–60. For a case showing Freeman's renting a house to a brothel, see *State v. Freeman*, no. 14,020, First District Court of New Orleans, 1 April 1856. In this

case Sarah Ann Garrett charged Theophilius Freeman with trespass when he tried to evict her from his property for nonpayment of rent. Freeman and Connor both faced charges of perjury and subornation of perjury in 1852 cases because they falsely accused one Charles Commenger of slave stealing. One witness testified that Freeman offered him fifty dollars to testify against Commenger. *State v. Freeman*, no. 7,159, First District Court of New Orleans, 19 January 1852; *State v. Connor*, no. 7,158, First District Court of New Orleans, 30 June 1852. In 1858 three public women faced charged of assault and battery for entering Freeman's house, breaking Freeman's windows, furniture, and crockery, and drawing a knife on him. The nature of their quarrel with him is unknown, but the case ended in a nolle prosequi. *State v. Thompson, Brunel, and Doane*, no. 13,612, First District Court of New Orleans, 3 June 1858.

19. *State v. Ritchie*, no. 3,583, First District Court of New Orleans, 4 May 1849; *State v. Taylor*, no. 4,752, First District Court of New Orleans, 6 February 1850.

20. *State v. Nougan*, no. 4,752, First District Court of New Orleans, 23 March 1850; *State v. Wright and Montgomery*, no. 4,587, First District Court of New Orleans, 26 January 1850; *State v. Stone*, no. 5,111, First District Court of New Orleans, 14 June 1850; *State v. McGiff, Foley, and McDonald*, no. 5,184, First District Court of New Orleans, 26 June 1850.

21. Robert C. Reinders, *End of an Era: New Orleans, 1850–1860* (New Orleans: Pelican Publishing Co., 1964), 73; *State v. Durker*, no. 5,929. First District Court of New Orleans, 15 March 1851; *State v. Fink and Hayes*, no. 5.930, First District Court of New Orleans, 20 March 1851; Tansey, "Prostitution and Politics," 463–64, 468; *New Orleans Daily Picayune*, 13 September 1852.

22. Tansey, "Prostitution and Politics," 454, 468–69; *State v. Viosca*, no. 5,932, First District Court of New Orleans, 30 January 1851.

23. *State v. Lopez*, no. 5,973, First District Court of New Orleans, 1 March 1851; *State v. Tarride and Schnexnayder*, no. 5,975, First District Court of New Orleans, 8 April 1851; *State v. Desmouideaux*, no. 6,013, First District Court of New Orleans, 5 April 1851; *State v. Ritchie*, no. 6,107, First District Court of New Orleans, 11 March 1851; *State. v. Ravel*, no. 7,010, First District Court of New Orleans, 26 August 1851; *State v. Murphy*, no. 6,108, First District Court of New Orleans, 11 March 1851. Archy Murphy "operated a major prostitution syndicate on Gallatin street." www .policestudies.eku.edu/POTTER/InternationalSouthhistory.htm, 15 (accessed July 2004).

24. *State v. Robinson, Riley, and Massit*, no. 7,421, First District Court of New Orleans, 13 May 1852; *State v. Royal alias McMahon*, no. 7,571, First District Court of New Orleans, 19 May 1852; *State v. Fanning*, no. 7,572, First District Court of New Orleans, 19 May 1852; *State v. Allen alias Wallace*, no. 7,573, First District Court of New Orleans, 17 May 1852; *State v. Harris*, no. 7,574, First District Court of New Orleans, 19 May 1852; *State v. McGriffin*, no. 8,247, First District Court of New Or-

leans, 13 July 1852; *State v. Greene*, no. 8,315, First District Court of New Orleans, 3 November 1852.

25. *State v. Patton*, no. 8,444, First District Court of New Orleans, 16 July 1856; Tansey, "Politics and Prostitution," 452; *State v. Burke alias McGundy*, no. 8,527, First District Court of New Orleans, 27 May 1857; *State v. Montreville*, no. 8,955, First District Court of New Orleans, 1 May 1853; *New Orleans Daily Picayune*, 7 July 1853; *State v. Cruet*, no. 9,045, First District Court of New Orleans, 27 June 1853; *State v. Davis*, no. 9,047, First District Court of New Orleans, 27 June 1853; *State v. Stewart*, no. 9,046, First District Court of New Orleans, 6 June 1853; *New Orleans Daily Picayune*, 11 June 1853.

26. *Moore v. Wilson, his wife*, no. 7,078, First District Court of New Orleans, 22 June 1853.

27. *Constitution of the State of Louisiana, 1852*, art. 64, 81; *New Orleans Daily Picayune*, 17 May, 13 November 1853; "An Act to Organize District Courts for the Parish and City of New Orleans," Act of 28 April 1853, *Louisiana Acts, 1853*, secs. 2, 6, pp. 190–91. Report of the Committee of Retrenchment, *Journal of the House of Representatives of the State of Louisiana, 1852*, 10.

28. *State v. Stewart*, no. 9,351, First District Court of New Orleans, 11 May 1854.

29. *State v. Taylor*, no. 9,762, First District Court of New Orleans, 3 January 1855; *State v. Black*, no. 9,761, First District Court of New Orleans, 31 October 1854; *State v. Murray*, no. 9,763, First District Court of New Orleans, 30 October 1854; *State v. Nolan*, no. 9,764, First District Court of New Orleans, 6 May 1854; *State v. Mayfield*, no. 9,759, First District Court of New Orleans, 31 October 1854; *State v. O'Brien*, no. 9,765, First District Court of New Orleans, 13 May 1854 (missing record).

30. *State v. Downey*, no. 10,471, First District Court of New Orleans, 26 June 1855; *State v. Burns*, no. 10,534, First District Court of New Orleans, 19 November 1855 (missing record); *State v. Kent*, no. 10,535, First District Court of New Orleans, 20 May 1857.

31. *State v. Wilson and Leblanc*, no. 12,119, First District Court of New Orleans, 15 May 1857; *State v. McKinney*, no. 12,094, First District Court of New Orleans, 4 April 1857; *State v. Fields, f.m.c.*, no. 12,193, First District Court of New Orleans, 17 June 1856; *State v. Costello*, no. 12,316, First District Court of New Orleans, 20 March 1857; *State v. Clarisse, f.w.c.*, no. 12,417, First District Court of New Orleans, 27 May 1857. The last case was heard by a new judge of the First District Court, Theodore Hunt.

32. *State v. Brady*, no. 12,712, First District Court of New Orleans, 23 February 1857; *State v. Montgomery and Greene*, no. 12,848, First District Court of New Orleans, 18 March 1857; *State v. Mr. and Mrs. Reims*, no. 12,676, First District Court of New Orleans, 26 June 1857; *New Orleans Daily Picayune*, 31 July 1856.

33. *State v. Schneider*, no. 14,737, 14,848, First District Court of New Orleans, 12

December 1860; *State v. Arbuckle, f.w.c.,* no. 14,740, First District Court of New Orleans, 7 December 1860; *Arbuckle, f.w.c., v. Bouny and Talbot,* no. 1,570, Fifth District Court of New Orleans, 11 October 1848; *Arbuckle, f.w.c., v. Bouny and Talbot,* no. 1,380, Supreme Court of Louisiana (unreported) (1849); *Arbuckle, f.w.c., v. Bouny and Talbot,* no. 2,523, Fifth District Court of New Orleans, 4 June 1849; 22 July 1865; *Arbuckle, f.w.c., v. Bouny and Talbot,* no. 1,632, 5 La. Ann. 699 (1850).

34. *State v. Arbuckle, f.w.c.,* no. 14,740, First District Court of New Orleans, 7 December 1860; Schafer, *Becoming Free, Remaining Free,* 120–21.

35. *State v. Knight, f.w.c.,* no. 14,826, First District Court of New Orleans, 27 February 1861; *State v. Seligman,* no. 15,250, 10 November 1861.

9. "AN ORDINANCE CONCERNING LEWD
AND ABANDONED WOMEN"

1. Johnson, "Good Time Town," 236. "An Ordinance Concerning Lewd and Abandoned Women," in Leovy, *Ordinances,* nos. 1,084–99, pp. 376–79; Rose, *Storyville, New Orleans,* 9. Long, *Great Southern Babylon,* 3. Claude Augé and Paul Augé, *Nouveau Petit Larousse* (Paris: Librairie Larousse, 1958), 589. The author wishes to gratefully acknowledge the contributions of Kathryn Fernandez to this chapter.

2. "Ordinance Concerning Lewd and Abandoned Women," no. 1,084, p. 376; Pierce F. Lewis, *New Orleans: The Making of an Urban Landscape* (Santa Fe, N.M., and Charlottesville, Va.: Center for American Places in association with the University of Virginia Press, 2003), 27.

3. "Ordinance Concerning Lewd and Abandoned Women," nos. 1,085–87, pp. 376–77.

4. Ibid., nos. 1,095, 1,090, p. 377.

5. *New Orleans Daily Picayune,* 23 November 1854, 10 February 1855, 2 February 1853, 17 November 1858.

6. Ibid., 25, 26 April, 3 May 1857.

7. Ibid., 14, 21 May 1857.

8. Ibid., 24 May 1857.

9. Ibid., 22, 26, 28 May 1857.

10. Ibid., 27, 28, 29 May 1857.

11. Ibid., 30 May 1857.

12. Ibid., 5, 14 June 1857.

13. Ibid., 15 August 1857, 16 September 1857, 10 October 1857. For other violations of the Lorette law, see 25 March, 12, 15, 16, 20 May, 12, 17, 21 June, 15, 17, 18, 20 August, 27 October 1857.

14. Ibid., 9, 10, 14 October, 10 December 1857.

15. Ibid., 10, 21 December 1857.

16. Ibid., 24 December 1857.

17. *City of New Orleans v. Castello*, no. 11,925, Second District Court of New Orleans, 5 November 1857; *New Orleans Daily Picayune*, 6 November 1857; *Constitution of Louisiana, 1852*, sec. 78. Al Rose mistakenly identified the public woman in the suit by the city as Emma Pickett, not Eliza Castello. He also said that Pickett had paid the licensing fee and then sued the city to recover it; Castello refused to pay the city, and the city sued her for the fee. Rose, *Storyville, New Orleans*, 8. The only lawsuit that involved Emma Pickett indicated that she ran a brothel on Basin, renting the property from James Desban. She fell behind on her rent and sold her furniture to a furniture dealer, after which she left New Orleans. Under Louisiana law, the landlord was entitled to a lien on any furniture abandoned after a tenant skipped out on the lease. Desban sued Pickett for the furniture, since she was behind on her rent when she left town. There is an extensive inventory of the brothel's furniture, including a number of gilt-framed mirrors, Brussels carpets, rosewood tables, mahogany and walnut armoires, eight bedsteads, and twenty mattresses. *Desban v. Pickett*, no. 5,973, Supreme Court of Louisiana, 16 La. Ann. 350 (1861).

18. *City of New Orleans v. Castello*, reported in *New Orleans Daily Picayune*, 6 November 1857.

19. *City of New Orleans v. Castello*, no. 5,408, Supreme Court of Louisiana, 14 La. Ann. 37 (1859); Levy, "Of Bards and Bawds," 19–20.

20. Long, *Great Southern Babylon*, 106–7.

21. Robert Tallant, *Romantic New Orleanians* (New York: Dutton, 1950), 129; Johnson, "Good Time Town," 236–37; Rose, *Storyville, New Orleans*, 9.

BIBLIOGRAPHY

CASES

First District Court of New Orleans

In the matter of Alice Darthenay alias Constance LaFabre praying for a writ of habeas corpus,
  no. 10,501, 4 August 1855
Johnson, praying for a writ of habeas corpus, no. 2,312, 20 May 1848
Moore v. Wilson, his wife, no. 7,078, 22 June 1853
Norman, praying for a writ of habeas corpus, no. 10,498, 25 July 1855
State v. Allen alias Wallace, no. 7,573, 17 May 1852
State v. Arbuckle, f.w.c., no. 14,740, 7 December 1860
State v. Bertrand, no. 14,720, 2 November 1860
State v. Black, no. 9,761, 31 October 1854
State v. Black, f.w.c., no. 1,095, 3 July 1847
State v. Blaise and Matus, no. 6,129, 27 March 1851
State v. Bolon, no. 5,092, 25 May 1850
State v. Bonnand, f.m.c., no. 7,644, 17 April 1852
State v. Bonsigneur, f.w.c., no. 9,486, 13 May 1854
State v. Boyard, f.w.c., no. 8,463, 26 August 1852
State v. Boyle, Smith and Williams, no. 13,578, 11 May 1858
State v. Brady, no. 12,712, 23 February 1857
State v. Brown, no. 5,893, 15 February 1851
State v. Brown, no. 8,947, 22 May 1853
State v. Brown, no. 9,859, 14 December 1854
State v. Brunetto, no. 13,009, 15 July 1857
State v. Burke, no. 13,394, 5 February 1858

State v. Burke alia McGundy, no. 8,527, 27 May 1857

State v. Burns, no. 10,534, 19 November 1855 (missing record)

State v. Butterwick, f.w.c., Taylor and Perry, no. 640, 15 February 1847

State v. Cassidy, no. 2,467, 28 June 1848

State v. Cassidy, Cassidy and Doyle, no. 9,541, 14 June 1854

State v. Catherine, f.w.c. (docket number illegible), 20 December 1849

State v. Charlotte, no. 9,485, 30 October 1836

State v. Clarisse, f.w.c., no. 9,439, 13 February 1854

State v. Clarisse, f.w.c., no. 12,417, 27 May 1857

State v. Collins, no. 203, 31 August 1846

State v. Collins, no. 14,776, 28 January 1861

State v. Collins et al., no. 13,993, 31 March 1859

State v. Conley, no. 3,532, 18 April 1849

State v. Conner, no. 7,158, 30 June 1852

State v. Costello, no. 12,316, 20 March 1857

State v. Cox, no. 502, 9 January 1847

State v. Cox, no. 5,860, 15 January 1851

State v. Coyle, no. 2,401, 23 June 1848

State v. Cruet, no. 9,045, 27 June 1853

State v. Dalbaret and Monk, no. 8,151, 13 January 1853

State v. Davis, no. 4,216, 27 August 1849

State v. Davis, no. 4,681, 20 February 1850

State v. Davis, no. 4,878, 20 May 1850

State v. Davis, no. 9,047, 27 June 1853

State v. Davis, f.w.c., no. 6,503, 10 June 1851

State v. Desmouideaux, no. 6,013, 5 April 1851

State v. Dewett, no. 206, 18 November 1846

State v. Dickinson, f.w.c., no. 2,811, 11 October 1848

State v. Dorman, no. 5,788, 21 January 1851

State v. Downey, no. 10,471, 26 June 1855

State v. Dunn, f.w.c., no. 9,078. 5 November 1853

State v. Duprat, Reeves et al., no. 9,814, 16 June 1855

State v. Durker, no. 5,929, 15 March 1851

State v. Emily and Elisabeth Eubanks, f.w.c., no. 15,017, 6 March 1861

State v. Emily and Elisabeth Eubanks, f.w.c., no. 15,176, 7 November 1861

State v. Eubanks, f.w.c., no. 8,462, 18 April 1852, 21 February 1856

State v. Eubanks, f.w.c., no. 8,031, 11 November 1856

State v. Evans, f.w.c., no. 5,410, 22 November 1850

State v. Fannin alias Gallatin Mary, no. 13,682, 26 November 1856

State v. Fanning, no. 7,572, 19 May 1852

State v. Feenan, no.12,221, 15 May 1856

State v. Field, no.7,579, 29 April 1852

State v. Fields, f.m.c., no. 12,193, 17 June 1856

State v. Fink and Hayes, no. 5,930, 20 March 1851

State v. Florian, f.w.c., no. 1,301, 19 November 1847

State v. Fluhart, no. 2,904, 24 January 1849

State v. Freeman, no. 7,159, 19 January 1852

State v. Freeman, no. 14,020, 1 April 1856

State v. Gallagher and Snaffer, no. 15,113, 13 May 1861

State v. Gibson, f.w.c., no. 5,136, 29 June 1850

State v. Gibson, f.w.c., no. 8,562, 3 January 1853

State v. Gibson, f.w.c., no. 12,398, 10 June 1857

State v. Gibson, f.w.c., no. 14,634, 4 July 1860

State v. Giggons, f.w.c., no. 15,493, 25 October 1861

State v. Gobet, f.w.c., no. 2,612, 27 November 1850

State v. Godfrey and O'Neill, no. 12,844, 16 June 1857

State v. Golding, no. 12,810, 11 April 1857

State v. Golden alias Hoozier Mary, no. 33, 23 July 1846

State v. Green, no. 4,578, 6 January 1850

State v. Greene, no. 8,315, 3 November 1852

State v. Handly, no. 13,878, 12 November 1858

State v. Hanna, no. 7,507, 13 May 1852

State v. Harris, no. 7,574, 19 May 1852

State v. Harris, f.w.c., no. 148, 27 August 1848

State v. Hartigan alias McLigh alias Calleday, no. 9,131, 20 June 1849

State v. Helvring, no. 1,246, (date illegible) 1847

State v. Hernandez, f.w.c., no. 323, 6 March 1847

State v. Hickey, Dutch Kitty and McNaff, no. 14,218, 24 October 1859

State v. Hill, no.5,080, 29 May 1850

State v. Hines, no. 15,479, 18 October 1861

State v. Hollingshade, no. 9,237, 19 April 1854

State v. Holmes, no. 13,374, 28 January 1858

State v. Holmes, no. 14,159, 14 November 1859

State v. Hopkins, no. 4,550, 14 February 1850

State v. Horn, no. 8,046, 23 October 1852

State v. Hubbard, no. 34, 28 July 1846

State v. Hubbard, f.w.c., no. 9,856, 13 April 1855

State v. Hulsey, no. 8,542, 14 April 1853

State v. Jenkins, no. 2,547, 16 December 1846

State v. Jet, f.w.c., no. 6,172, 11 March 1851

State v. Johnson alias Layton, no. 12,826, 30 May 1857

State v. Jones, no. 340, 16 November 1846

State v. Jones, no. 8,441, 1 January 1853

State v. Jones, no. 9,661, 31 October 1854

State v. Jones and Lewis, no. 15,580, 18 December 1861

State v. Kane, no. 13,349, 15 January 1858

State v. Kearns, no. 9,874, 10 January 1855

State v. Keller, no. 7,199, 15 January 1852

State v. Kelly and Kearny, no. 9,119, 17 November 1853

State v. Kent, no. 8,825, 5 March 1853

State v. Kent, no. 12,631, 5 May 1857

State v. Kent, no. 10,535, 20 May 1857

State v. Knight, f.w.c., no. 14,826, 27 February 1861

State v. Lattimore and Johnson alias Cincinnati Mary, no. 8,630, 19 April 1853

State v. Leinahan, no. 14,302, 18 November 1859

State v. Lopez, no. 5,973, 1 March 1851

State v. Love, f.w.c., no. 2,567, 17 July 1848

State v. Love, f.w.c., no. 10,291, 13 May 1855

State v. Lowrie, no. 7,671, 3 May 1852

State v. Lucy, no. 8,391, 31 December 1852

State v. Marrah, no. 8,281, 20 January 1853

State v. Mayfield, no. 2,799, 11 November 1848

State v. Mayfield, no. 3,910, 20 May 1849

State v. Mayfield, no. 5,258, 23 December 1850

State v. Mayfield, no. 7,959, 31 October 1854

State v. Mayfield, nos. 9,431, 9,432, 9,433, 14 June 1854

State v. Mayfield, no. 9,759, 31 October 1854

State v. Mayfield, no. 9,946, 15 May 1855

State v. Mayfield and Kenner, no. 7,074, 2 February 1852

State v. McCann, no. 8,928, 27 January 1857

State v. McElroy, no. 9,323, 19 December 1853

State v. McGiff, Foley, and McDonald, no. 5,184, 26 June 1850

State v. McGlove, no. 9,948, 11 December 1856

State v. McGriffin, no. 8,247, 13 July 1852

State v. McLaughlin alias Doris, no. 4,697, 2 January 1850

State v. McKinney, no. 12,094, 4 April 1857

State v. McNabb, no. 14,321, 17 January 1860

State v. Miller, no. 9, 810, 1854 (missing record)

State v. Miller, no. 12,784, 4 May 1857

State v. Montgomery, no. 3,652, 7 May 1849

State v. Montgomery, no. 4,998, 22 May 1850

State v. Montgomery and Greene, no. 12,848, 18 March 1857

State v. Montreville, no. 8,955, 1 May 1853

State v. Moore alias Turner, no. 2,546, 14 November 1848

State v. Moran and McDonald, no. 3,177, 22 November 1848

State v. Mr. and Mrs. McGlove, no. 9,951, 24 March 1855

State v. Mr. and Mrs. Reims, no. 12,676, 26 June 1857

State v. Murphy, no. 6,108, 11 March 1851

State v. Murphy, no. 6,943, 25 October 1851

State v. Murphy, no. 9,274, 31 October 1856

State v. Murphy, no. 10,871, 7 February 1857

State v. Murphy and Rowan, no. 3,165, 22 November 1848

State v. Murray, no. 9,763, 30 October 1854

State v. Myers, no. 453, 30 November 1846

State v. Nolan, no. 9,764, 6 May 1854

State v. Nougan, no. 4,752, 23 March 1850

State v. O'Brien, no. 2,553, 13 June 1848

State v. O'Brien, no. 9,765, 13 May 1854 (missing record)

State v. O'Marah, no. 13,249, 9 December 1857

State v. Osnaburg, no. 7,771, 26 May 1852

State v. Palfrey, f.w.c., no. 8,464, 23 April 1853

State v. Parker, no. 6,505, 17 June 1851

State v. Parker, f.w.c., no. 13,610, 21 May 1858

State v. Parsons, f.w.c., no. 680, 19 May 1847

State v. Parsons, f.w.c., no. 1,284, 8 November 1847

State v. Patton, no. 8,444, 16 July 1856

State v. Pickett, no. 1,578, 26 November 1847

State v. Purdy, no. 12,651, 5 May 1857

State v. Quintera, no. 9,052, 18 July 1853

State v. Raymond, nos. 2,495, 2,868, 19 January 1849, 24 January 1849

State v. Reels alias Charleston Pet, no. 15,441, 25 October 1861

State v. Reid, no. 940, 27 May 1847

State v. Reid, no. 10,648, 24 October 1855

State v. Revel, no. 7,010, 26 August 1851

State v. Reynolds, f.w.c., no. 203, 24 November 1846

State v. Richardson, nos. 8,491, 8,504, 26 April 1853

State v. Ritchie, no. 3,583, 4 May 1849

State v. Ritchie, no. 6,107, 11 March 1851

State v. Roan alias Higham, no. 5,635, 9 March 1851

State v. Robinson, Riley, and Massit, no. 7,421, 13 May 1852

State v. Rose and Blunk, no. 552, 10 December 1846

State v. Royal, no. 7,571, 18 May 1852

State v. Royal, Jackson, and Wilson, no. 7,230, 19 December 1851

State v. Royal alias McMahon, no. 7,571, 19 May 1852

State v. Sanadet, no. 205, 9 September 1846

State v. Schneider, no. 14,737, 12 December 1860

State v. Scott, slave of Stewart, no. 10,830, 4 February 1856

State v. Seines, no. 2,444, 2 June 1848

State v. Seligman, no. 15,250, 10 November 1861

State v. Sloan, no. 1,311, 15 November 1847

State v. Smith, no. 1,936, 18 March 1848

State v. Smith, no. 15,229, 17 October 1861

State v. Smith alias Carrollton, no. 2,418, 27 June 1848

State v. Stacey and Gallagher, no. 12,666, 29 June 1857

State v. Stewart, no. 9,046, 6 June 1853

State v. Stewart, no. 9,351, 11 May 1854

State v. Stillman, no. 14,114, 22 June 1859

State v. Stillman and St. Clair, no. 13,394, 10 January 1858

State v. Stone, no. 5,111, 14 June 1850

State v. Stubblefield, no. 2,901, 14 December 1848

State v. Sullivan, no. 12,690, 21 February 1857

State v. Sweany alias Big Anna, no. 10,883, 20 September 1856

State v. Swift alias Fury, no. 13,778, 16 May 1859

State v. Tarride and Schnexnayder, no. 5,975, 8 April 1851

State v. Taylor, no. 84, 27 July 1846

State v. Taylor, no. 4,752, 6 February 1850

State v. Taylor, no. 9,762, 3 January 1855

State v. Thayer, f.w.c., no. 9,350, 10 May 1854

State v. Thompson, Brunel, and Doane, no. 13,612, 3 June 1858

State v. Thompson alias Robinson and Baer, no.13,539, 5 June 1858

State v. Venere, no. 9,231, 24 February 1854

State v. Viosca, no. 5,932, 30 January 1851

State v. Viosca, no. 5,931, 29 May 1851

State v. Vorygrumbler, no. 9,824, 19 March 1855

State v. Walsh alias Connolly alias Brian, no. 9,720, 27 November 1854

State v. Washington, f.w.c., no. 5,123, 15 June 1850

State v. West, no. 7,642, 25 April 1852

State v. Williams, no. 2,903, 20 December 1848

State v. Williams, no. 7,643, 15 April 1852

State v. Williams, no. 15,410, 16 November 1861

State v. Willey, no. 2,902, 29 November 1848

State v. Wilson, no. 583, 8 February 1847

State v. Wilson, no. 7,623, 16 October 1852

State v. Wilson, no. 9,172, 31 January 1854

State v. Wilson and Leblanc, no. 12,119, 15 May 1857

State v. Wood, no. 5,981, 14 February 1851

State v. Wright and Montgomery, no. 4,587, 26 January 1850

SECOND DISTRICT COURT OF NEW ORLEANS

City of New Orleans v. Castello, no. 11,925, 5 November 1857

THIRD DISTRICT COURT OF NEW ORLEANS

Desban v. Pickett, no. 12,088, 11 February 1858

State of Louisiana in rel. Yerger, Harper and Lambert, no. 14,185, 7 December 1859

FOURTH DISTRICT COURT OF NEW ORLEANS

Succession of Fluhart, no. 3,549, 5 April 1852

FIFTH DISTRICT COURT OF NEW ORLEANS

Arbuckle, f.w.c., v. Bouny and Talbot, no. 1,570, 11 October 1848

Arbuckle, f.w.c., v. Bouny and Talbot, no. 2,523, 4 June 1849, 22 July 1865

Valory v. City of New Orleans and Lewis, no. 10,788, 14 February 1856

FOURTH JUSTICE OF THE PEACE COURT

Municipality no. 1 v. Wilson, no. 8,478, 21 August 1850

SUPREME COURT OF LOUISIANA

Arbuckle, f.w.c., v. Bouny and Talbot, no. 1,380 (unreported) (1849)

Arbuckle, f.w.c., v. Bouny and Talbot, no. 1,632, 5 La. Ann. 699 (1850)

Carmelite, f.w.c., v. Lacaze, no. 2,506, 7 La. Ann. 629 (1852)

City of New Orleans v. Castello, no. 5,408, 14 La. Ann. 37 (1859)

Coulter v. Cresswell, no. 2,734, 7 La. Ann. 367 (1852)

Succession of Cresswell, no. 2,423, 8 La. Ann. 122 (1853)

Desban v. Pickett, no. 5,973, 16 La. Ann. 350 (1861)

Fluhart v. Golding, no. 1,930, 7 La. Ann. 233 (1852)

Lyman v. Townsend, no. 2,631, 24 La. Ann. 625 (1872)

Municipality no. 1 v. Wilson, no. 1,925, 5 La. Ann.747 (1850)

State v. Brunetto, no. 5,376, 13 La. Ann. 45 (1858)

State v. David, slave of Drake, no. 312 (unreported) (1862)

State v. Parker, no. 2,392 (unreported) (February 1852)

State v. Swift alias Fury, no. 6,318, 14 La. Ann. 827 (1859)

State v. Thompson alias Robinson and Baer, no. 5,799, 13 La. Ann. 515 (1858)

OFFICIAL DOCUMENTS

"An Act for the Punishment of Crimes and Misdemeanors." Act of 4 May 1805. *Orleans Territory Acts, 1805.*

"An Act Prescribing the Rules and Conduct to Be Observed with Respect to Negroes and Other Slaves of This Territory." Act of 7 June 1806. *Orleans Territory Acts, 1806 (Black Code).*

"An Act Relative to Crimes." Act of 14 March 1855. *Louisiana Acts, 1855.*

"An Act to Amend the Penal Laws of This State." Act of 12 March 1818. *Louisiana Acts, 1818.*

"An Act to Organize District Courts for the Parish and City of New Orleans." Act of 28 April 1853. *Louisiana Acts, 1853.*

"An Act to Prescribe Certain Formalities Respecting Free Persons of Color." Act of 31 March 1808. *Orleans Territory Acts, 1808.*

"An Act to Prevent Free Persons of Color from Entering This State and for Other Purposes." Act of 16 March 1830. *Louisiana Acts, 1830.*

"An Act to Punish the Crimes Therein Mentioned, and for Other Purposes." Act of 16 March 1830. *Louisiana Acts, 1830.*

"An Act to Regulate Inns and Other Houses of Entertainment." Act of 21 May 1806. *Louisiana Acts, 1806.*

"An Act to Restrict the Charge of the Judge in Every Criminal Case to an Opinion on the Law." Act of 29 April 1853. *Louisiana Acts, 1853.*

City of New Orleans, Tax Registers, 1855–56.

Civil Code of the State of Louisiana. New Orleans: J. C. De St. Romes, 1825.

Constitution of the State of Louisiana, 1852. New Orleans: E. LaSere, 1852.

Faqua, James O., ed. *Code of Practice in Civil Cases for the State of Louisiana with the Statutory Amendments from 1825 to 1866 Inclusive.* New Orleans: Bloomfield Steele, 1867.

Journal of the House of Representatives of the State of Louisiana, 1852. New Orleans: E. LaSere, 1852.

Kerr, Lewis. *An Exposition of the Criminal Laws of the Territory of Orleans.* 1806. Reprint, New Orleans: William W. Gaunt and Sons, 1986.

Leovy, Henry J. *The Laws and General Ordinances of the City of New Orleans.* New Orleans: E. C. Wharton, 1857.

Records of the First District Court of New Orleans. Reports of the Grand Jury, 1845, 1855, 1856.

NEWSPAPERS

Louisiana Courier, 1846–60
New Orleans Bee, 1846–62
New Orleans Commercial Bulletin, 1846–62
New Orleans Daily Crescent, 1848–62
New Orleans Daily Delta, 1849–62
New Orleans Daily Picayune, 1846–62
New Orleans Daily True Delta, 1849–62

JOURNAL ARTICLES

Lucas, Ann M. "Race, Class, Gender, and Deviation: The Criminalization of Prostitution." *Berkeley Women Law Journal* 10 (1995): 47–50.
Newman, Gerald L. "Anomalous Zones." *Stanford Law Review* 48 (1996): 1197–1234.
Tansey, Richard. "Prostitution and Politics in Antebellum New Orleans." *Southern Studies* 18 (Winter 1979): 449–79.

THESES AND DISSERTATIONS

Karachuk, Robert Feikema. "A Workman's Tools: The Law Library of Henry Bullard." Master's thesis, University of New Orleans, 1996.
Kmen, Henry. "Singing and Dancing in New Orleans: A Social History of the Birth and Growth of Balls and Opera, 1791–1841." Ph.D. diss., Tulane University, 1961.
Levy, Russell. "Of Bards and Bawds: New Orleans Sporting Life before and during the Storyville Era, 1897–1917." Ph.D. diss., Tulane University, 1967.
Mackay, Thomas. "Red Lights Out: A Legal History of Prostitution, Disorderly Houses, and Vice Districts, 1870–1917." Ph.D. diss., Rice University, 1984.

BOOKS AND ESSAYS

Allain, Mathé. *"Not Worth a Straw": French Colonial Policy and the Early Years of Louisiana.* Lafayette: Center for Louisiana Studies, University of Southwestern Louisiana, 1988.
Archbold, John Frederick. *Archbold's Summary of the Law Relating to Pleading and Evidence in Criminal Cases.* New York: Gould, Banks, 1846.
Asbury, Herbert. *The French Quarter: An Informal History of the New Orleans Underground.* New York: Alfred A. Knopf, 1936.

Baade, Hans W. "The Law of Slavery in Spanish Louisiana, 1769–1803." In *The Past as Prelude: New Orleans, 1718–1968,* edited by Hodding Carter, 43–86. New Orleans: Pelican Publishing Co., 1968.

Barber, E. Susan. "Depraved and Abandoned Women: Prostitution in Richmond, Virginia, across the Civil War." In *Neither Lady nor Slave: Working Women of the Old South,* edited by Susanna Delfino and Michele Gillespie, 155–73. Chapel Hill: University of North Carolina Press, 2002.

Bell, Caryn Cossé. *Revolution, Romanticism and the Afro-Creole Protest Tradition in Louisiana, 1718–1868.* Baton Rouge: Louisiana State University Press, 1997.

Best, Joel. *Controlling Vice: Regulating Brothel Prostitution in St. Paul, 1865–1883.* Columbus: Ohio State University Press, 1998.

Billings, Warren M., ed. *The Historic Rules of the Supreme Court of Louisiana, 1813–1879.* Lafayette: Center for Louisiana Studies, 1985.

Brooke, Bergen. *Storyville: A Hidden Mirror.* Wakefield, R.I.: Moyer Bell, 1994.

Burnham, John C. *Bad Habits: Drinking, Smoking, Taking Drugs, Gambling, Sexual Misbehavior, and Swearing in American History.* New York: New York University Press, 1993.

Cohen, Patricia Cline. *The Murder of Helen Jewett: The Life and Death of a Prostitute in Nineteenth-Century New York.* New York: Alfred A. Knopf, 1998.

Conrad, Glenn R., ed. *Dictionary of Louisiana Biography.* 2 vols. Lafayette: Center for Louisiana Studies, 1988.

DeLatte, Carolyn E. "Isaac Johnson." In *The Louisiana Governors: From Iberville to Edwards,* edited by Joseph G. Dawson III, 122–26. Baton Rouge: Louisiana State University Press, 1990.

Dudash, Tawnya. "Peepshow Feminism." In *Whores and Other Feminists,* edited by Jill Nagle, 99–118. New York: Routledge, 1997.

Everard, Wayne M. "Louisiana's 'Whig' Constitution Revisited: The Constitution of 1852." In *In Search of Fundamental Law: Louisiana's Constitutions, 1812–1974,* edited by Warren M. Billings and Edward F. Haas, 37–51. Lafayette: Center for Louisiana Studies, 1993.

Garber, Marjorie. *Vested Interests: Cross-Dressing and Cultural Anxiety.* New York: Routledge, 1992.

Gilfolye, Timothy J. *City of Eros: New York City, Prostitution, and the Commercialization of Sex.* New York: W. W. Norton and Co., 1992.

Greenleaf, Simon. *A Treatise on the Law of Evidence.* 2 vols. Boston: Little, Brown, 1842–46.

Hachard, Marie-Madeleine. *De Rouen à la Louisiane: Voyage d'un Ursuline en 1727.* Rouen, France: Publications de l'Université de Rouen, 1988.

Hill, Marilyn Wood. *Their Sisters' Keepers: Prostitution in New York City, 1830–1870.* Berkeley: University of California Press, 1993.

Hobson, Barbara Meil. *Uneasy Virtue: The Politics of Prostitution and the American Reform Tradition.* Chicago: University of Chicago Press, 1987.

Hodes, Martha. *White Women, Black Men: Illicit Sex in the Nineteenth-Century South.* New Haven: Yale University Press, 1997.

Holmes, Jack D. L. "Do It! Don't Do It! Spanish Laws on Sex and Marriage." In *Louisiana's Legal Heritage,* edited by Edward F. Haas, 19–42. Pensacola: Perdido Bay Press, 1983.

How New York City Transformed Sex in America. New York: Scala Publishers, 2002.

Johnson, Phil. "Good Time Town." In *The Past as Prelude: New Orleans, 1718–1968,* edited by Hodding Carter, 233–57. New Orleans: Pelican Publishing Co., 1968.

Latrobe, Benjamin H. *Impressions Respecting New Orleans: Diary and Sketches, 1818–1829.* Edited by Samuel Wilson. New York: Columbia University Press, 1951.

Lewis, Pierce F. *New Orleans: The Making of an Urban Landscape.* Sante Fe, N.M., and Charlottesville, Va.: Center for American Places in association with the University of Virginia Press, 2003.

Long, Alecia P. *The Great Southern Babylon: Sex, Race, and Respectability in New Orleans, 1865–1920.* Baton Rouge: Louisiana State University Press, 2004.

Longstreet, Stephen. *Sportin' House: A History of New Orleans Sinners and the Birth of Jazz.* Los Angeles: Sherbourne Press, 1965.

Lowry, Thomas P. *The Civil War Bawdy Houses of Washington, D.C.:* Fredericksburg, Va.: Sergeant Kirkland's, 1997.

———. *The Story the Soldiers Wouldn't Tell: Sex in the Civil War.* Mechanicsburg, Va.: Stackpole Books, 1994.

MacNally, Leonard. *MacNally's Rules of Evidence on the Pleas of the Crown.* Dublin: J. Cook, 1802.

Mitchell, Reid. *All on a Mardi Gras Day: Episodes in the History of New Orleans Carnival.* Cambridge: Harvard University Press, 1995.

New Orleans As It Is, by a Resident. Ithaca, N.Y.: De Witt C. Grove, 1849.

Niehaus, Earl F. *The Irish in New Orleans, 1800–1860.* 1965. Reprint, North Stratford, N.H.: Ayer Publishers, 1998.

Northup, Solomon. *Twelve Years a Slave.* Edited by Sue Eakin and Joseph Logsdon. 1863. Reprint, Baton Rouge: Louisiana State University Press, 1968.

Olmsted, Frederick Law. *The Cotton Kingdom: A Traveller's Observations on Cotton and Slavery in the American Slave States.* Edited by Arthur M. Schlesinger Sr. New York: Random House, 1984.

Pease, Jane H., and William H. Pease. *Ladies, Women and Wenches: Choice and Constraint in Antebellum Charleston and Boston.* Chapel Hill: University of North Carolina Press, 1990.

Potter, Gary. *The Antecedents of Southern Organized Crime.* At www. policestudies.eku .edu/POTTER/International/Southhistory.htm (accessed July 2004).

Reinders, Robert C. *End of an Era: New Orleans, 1850–1860.* New Orleans: Pelican Publishing Co., 1964.

Roberts, Nickie. *Whores in History: Prostitution in Western Society.* London: Harper-Collins, 1992.

Roscoe, Henry. *A Digest of the Law of Evidence in Criminal Cases.* London: Stevens, Sweeny and Maxwell, 1835.

Rose, Al. *Storyville, New Orleans: Being an Authentic, Illustrated Account of the Notorious Red-Light District.* Tuscaloosa: University of Alabama Press, 1979.

Rosen, Ruth. *The Lost Sisterhood: Prostitution in America, 1900–1918.* Baltimore: Johns Hopkins University Press, 1982.

Rousey, Dennis C. *Policing the Southern City: New Orleans, 1805–1889.* Baton Rouge: Louisiana State University Press, 1996.

Ryan, Mary R. *Women in Public: Between Banners and Ballots, 1825–1880.* Baltimore: Johns Hopkins University Press, 1990.

Sanger, William W., M.D. *The History of Prostitution: Its Extent, Causes and Effects throughout the World.* 1858. Reprint, New York: Medical Publishing Co., 1897.

Schafer, Judith Kelleher. *Becoming Free, Remaining Free: Manumission and Enslavement in New Orleans, 1846–1862.* Baton Rouge: Louisiana State University Press, 2003.

Stansell, Christine. *City of Women: Sex and Class in New York, 1789–1860.* Urbana: University of Illinois Press, 1987.

Sterkx, H. E. *The Free Negro in Antebellum Louisiana.* Cranberry, N.J.: Associated University Presses, 1972.

Tallant, Robert. *The Romantic New Orleanians.* New York: Dutton, 1950.

Upton, Dell, ed. *Madaline: Love and Survival in Antebellum New Orleans.* Athens: University of Georgia Press, 1996.

Way, Frederick, Jr., comp. *Way's Packet Directory, 1848–1983: Passenger Steamboats of the Mississippi River System since the Advent of Photography in Mid-Continent America.* Columbus: Ohio State University Press, 1983.

Winick, Charles, and Paul M. Kinsie. *The Lively Commerce: Prostitution in the United States.* Chicago: University of Chicago Press, 1971.

Wolfe, Mother St. Therese. *The Ursulines in New Orleans and Our Lady of Prompt Succor.* New York: P. J. Kennedy and Sons, 1925.

INDEX

Valory v. City of New Orleans and Lewis, 160*n*3
Venere, Julia, 102
Venere, State v., 174*n*37
Verbal abuse: insulting a white person, 26–27, 64, 71, 98–100; obscene language, 21, 30, 104, 163*n*8; between prostitutes, 98–100
Vice. *See* Ballrooms; Brothels; Drinking houses; Drunkenness; Prostitutes
Violence: by brothel keepers and brothel customers, 91–98, 108–25; brothel riots, 64–65, 66; brothels associated with, 6–7, 40, 44–45, 91–107; between free women of color and white men, 38; and larceny, 82–83, 85, 87; police connection with, on Gallatin Street, 127; between prostitutes, 100–107; by prostitutes, 60–69, 81, 83, 93, 95, 100–107, 183*n*18; prostitutes as victims of, 64–72, 76, 94–95, 97–98, 100–107. *See also* Assault; Killings; Suicide and suicide attempts
Viosca, Salvador, 54–55, 81, 138
Viosca, State v., 167*n*18, 183*n*22
Virago, 73, 169*n*43
Vivrant, Felicita, 127
Vogelsang, Marie Auguste, 50
Vorygrumbler, John, 58–59
Vorygrumbler, State v., 58–59, 167*n*24

Wall, Josephine, 131
Walsh alias Connolly alias Brian, State v., 170*n*5
Ward, Mrs., 149
Ware, Catherine, 24
Warlung, Eugene, 35
Warren, Mary Anne, 68
Washington, Brytania, 99–100
Washington, f.w.c., State v., 173*n*29
Waterman, M., 150
Watson, Dr., 4
Wearing, Catherine (English Kate), 103–4
Webster, Mary, 141
Welsh, Ann, 83

West, Mary, 41
West, State v., 171*n*16
Wheeler, Mary, 41
Whitaker, Mary, 105
Whitback, Benjamin, 81
White, Elizabeth, 76
White, Ellen, 72
White, Margaret, 84
White, Mathilda, 76
White men: assault of, by free man of color, 32; assault of free women of color by, 38; as brothel keepers, 42, 54–55; as brothel owners, 12, 18; cohabitation between black women and, 38, 39; sexual relations between black women and, 31–32, 38, 39; theft of, in brothel, 77–88; violence between free women of color and, 38. *See also* Brothel owners
White women: arrest of, as free woman of color, 100; assault against, 64–67, 71–72, 100–103; as brothel keeper, 41; insults against, by black women, 26–27, 71, 98–100; rape charges by, 46; sexual relations between black men and, 33–34, 36–40, 46. *See also* Prostitutes
Whitlow, John, 44, 65
Whitney, Charles, 52
Whorley, Martha, 150
Widowhood, 13, 24
Willey, State v., 182*n*17
Williams, Alice, 104
Williams, Amanda, 135
Williams, Caroline, 38
Williams, Catherine, 44, 62
Williams, Eliza, 30
Williams, Elizabeth, 64, 87
Williams, Kate, 76
Williams, Laura, 91
Williams, Mary, 80
Williams, Mary Ann, 21
Williams, Samuel, 130
Williams, State v., 171*n*16, 182*n*17
Williamson, Joseph, 84
Willis, Euphremia, 45–46